THE PENGUIN BOOK OF HELL

SCOTT G. BRUCE is a professor of history at Fordham University. He is the editor of *The Penguin Book of the Undead* and the author of three books about the abbey of Cluny: *Silence and Sign Language in Medieval Monasticism: The Cluniac Tradition, c. 900–1200* (2007); *Cluny and the Muslims of La Garde-Freinet: Hagiography and the Problem of Islam in Medieval Europe* (2015); and, with Christopher A. Jones, *The* Relatio metrica de duobus ducibus: *A Twelfth-Century Cluniac Poem on Prayer for the Dead* (2016). A coeditor of *The Medieval Review* and an active member of the Medieval Academy of America, he has lectured in Israel and throughout the United States, Canada, and Europe and has held visiting research appointments at Technische Universität Dresden, in Germany; the Universiteit Gent, in Belgium; and Emmanuel College, University of Cambridge, in the United Kingdom. He worked his way through college as a grave digger.

The Penguin Book of Hell

Edited by SCOTT G. BRUCE

PENGUIN BOOKS

PENGUIN BOOKS

An imprint of Penguin Random House LLC
375 Hudson Street
New York, New York 10014
penguinrandomhouse.com

Translations and renderings into modern English by Scott G. Bruce, unless otherwise indicated.

Grateful acknowledgment is made for permission to use the following copyrighted works:

"Tartarus, Prison of the Titans" from *Theogony* and *Works and Days* by Hesiod, translated by Dorothea Wender (Penguin Classics, 1973). (In a volume with *Elegies* by Theognis). Copyright © Dorothy Wender, 1973. Reproduced by permission of Penguin Books Ltd.

"Odysseus at Death's Door" from *The Odyssey* by Homer, translated by Robert Fagels. Translation copyright © 1996 by Robert Fagels. Used by permission of Viking, an imprint of Penguin Publishing Group, a division of Penguin Random House LLC.

"Socrates Ponders the Punishment of Souls" from *The Last Days of Socrates: Euhyphro, Apology, Crito, Phaedo* by Plato, translated by Christopher Rowe (Penguin Books, 2010). Translation copyright © Christopher Rowe, 2010. Reproduced by permission of Penguin Books Ltd.

"Into the Realm of Shadows" from *The Aeneid* by Virgil, translated by Robert Fagels. Translation copyright © 2006 by Robert Fagels. Used by permission of Viking, an imprint of Penguin Publishing Group, a division of Penguin Random House LLC.

"Dryhthelm Returns from the Dead" from *Ecclesiastical History of the English People* by Bede, translated by Scott G. Bruce. First published in *The Penguin Book of the Undead: Fifteen Hundred Years of Supernatural Encounters* by Scott G. Bruce. Translation copyright © 2016 by Scott G. Bruce. Used by permission of Penguin Classics, an imprint of Penguin Publishing Group, a division of Penguin Random House LLC.

"Warnings from Beyond the Grave" from *Dialogue on Miracles* by Caesarius, translated by Scott G. Bruce. First published in *The Penguin Book of the Undead: Fifteen Hundred Years of Supernatural Encounters* by Scott G. Bruce. Translation copyright © 2016 by Scott G. Bruce. Used by permission of Penguin Classics, an imprint of Penguin Publishing Group, a division of Penguin Random House LLC.

"The Hell of Treblinka" from *The Road: Short Fiction and Essays* by Vasily Grossman, translated by Robert Chandler and Elizabeth Chandler with Olga Mukovnikova. Copyright © by E. V. Korotkova-Grossman and F. B. Guber; translation © 2010 Robert Chandler. Used by permission of the Vasily Grossman estate c/o Robin Straus Agency, Inc., New York, acting in conjunction with Andrew Nurnberg Associates, Ltd., London. Any third party use of this material, outside of this publication, is prohibited. Interested parties must apply directly to Robin Straus Agency, Inc. for permission. Reproduced by permission of Quercus Editions Limited.

"Fire in the Sky" from "Testimony of Yoshitaka Kawamoto," *Voices of Hibashuka,* Hiroshima Peace Cultural Center and NHK. http://inicom.com/hibakusha/yoshitaka.html. (Used under a Creative Commons license).

"A Sentence Worse Than Death" by William Blake, originally published on Solitary Watch (www .solitarywatch.com) and in *Hell Is a Very Small Place: Voices from Solitary Confinement*, edited by Jean Casella, James Ridgeway, and Sarah Shourd (New York and London: The New Press, 2016). Copyright © 2013 by William Blake. Used with permission of Solitary Watch.

LIBRARY OF CONGRESS CATALOGING-IN-PUBLICATION DATA
Names: Bruce, Scott G. (Scott Gordon), 1967– editor.
Title: The Penguin book of hell / edited by Scott G Bruce.
Description: New York: Penguin Books, 2018. | Includes bibliographical
references and index.
Identifiers: LCCN 2018021796 (print) | LCCN 2018022760 (ebook) | ISBN
9781524705275 (ebook) | ISBN 9780143131625 (pbk.)
Subjects: LCSH: Future life. | Hell.
Classification: LCC BL545 (ebook) | LCC BL545 .P46 2018 (print) | DDC
202/.3—dc23
LC record available at https://lccn.loc.gov/2018021796

Printed in the United States of America
1   3   5   7   9   10   8   6   4   2

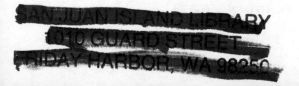

For Giles Constable,

lo mio maestro e 'l mio autore

who led me through dark places

"No sight so sad as that of a naughty child," he began, "especially a naughty little girl. Do you know where the wicked go after death?"

"They go to hell," was my ready and orthodox answer.

"And what is hell? Can you tell me that?"

"A pit full of fire."

"And should you like to fall into that pit, and to be burning for ever?"

"No, sir."

"What must you do to avoid it?"

I deliberated a moment; my answer, when it did come, was objectionable: "I must keep in good health, and not die."

—CHARLOTTE BRONTË, *JANE EYRE*

I descend from grace
in arms of undertow.
I will take my place
in the great below.

—TRENT REZNOR, "THE GREAT BELOW"

Contents

Hell of Our Own Making:
The Twentieth Century and Beyond

Introduction

Hell, the punitive afterlife of the Christian religion, is arguably the most powerful and persuasive construct of the human imagination in the Western tradition. A subterranean realm of eternal suffering, a prison for sinful souls governed by a fallen angel who surpassed all other creatures in wickedness, Hell has inspired fear and thereby controlled the behavior of countless human beings for more than two thousand years. Despite advances in scholarship that have called into question the authority of the Christian scriptures and scientific developments that have changed the way we think about the human race and our place in the cosmos, the idea of Hell has remained tenacious in Western thought. In modern discourse, "hell" serves as an all-pervasive metaphor for any kind of difficulty ("hard as hell") or extreme ("hot as hell"), but the word has lost none of its religious currency in our so-called age of reason. A 2014 survey by the Pew Research Center found that 58 percent of American adults still believe in the existence of a place "where people who have led bad lives and die without being sorry are eternally punished."

The tenacity of the belief in Hell in the modern world invites inquiry into its long history. Depictions of a punitive afterlife are as old as writing itself. Ancient Mesopotamians imagined a grim otherworld in "the house of dust," while ancient Egyptians trembled at the thought of the judgment of the death god Anubis, but these traditions did not exert as much influence on Western culture as the realms of shadow and gloom awaiting the dead as portrayed in the Hebrew scriptures (Sheol) and in Greek and Roman literature (Hades). The account of Aeneas's

descent into the underworld and the descriptions of its landscape and megafauna in *The Aeneid* of the Roman poet Virgil
(70–19 BCE) were especially formative; the poem would exert
an enormous influence on medieval intellectuals and poets, especially Dante Alighieri (1265–1321 CE). The earliest Christians thus inherited a rich tradition of thoughts and images
about the afterlife from their Jewish and pagan contempo-
raries, but they were not slavish imitators of other religions in
their thinking about the underworld. In the centuries between
the time of Christ and the triumph of the Church in the lifetime of Saint Augustine (354–430 CE), Christian thinkers
began to delineate the contours and function of a distinctly
Christian Hell, informed by ancient models yet particular
to their own understanding of original sin and God's inscru-
table mercy.

During the first millennium CE, early medieval authors in-
vented a punitive underworld with distinctive features and
dire inhabitants and articulated its details in popular stories
unauthorized by the Church, including the apostle Paul's
guided tour of Hell in the company of an angel and the tradition that Christ descended to the underworld during his three
days in the tomb in order to rescue the virtuous Jewish patriarchs from the prison of Hades, the so-called Harrowing of
Hell. They also composed vivid and fanciful visionary tours of
Hell, its inhabitants, and its torments written with didactic intent to help monastic readers avoid the sins that would bar
them from Heaven. The articulation of these beliefs as official
Church doctrine took almost a millennium to work out, but
by the High Middle Ages (c. 1000–1300 CE) theologians like
Thomas Aquinas were explaining with detached reason the
kinds of punishments that evil persons could expect in Hell
and the relationship between the blessed and the damned. At
the end of the Middle Ages, Dante Alighieri wedded medieval
popular beliefs about the punitive afterlife and the reasoned
deductions of scholastic thinkers about the workings of divine
punishment in his towering poem *The Divine Comedy*. His
poetic portrayal of Hell (*Inferno*) represented the apogee of
the punitive underworld in the medieval imagination.

Early modern thinkers challenged medieval understandings of Hell during the Protestant Reformation. In the sixteenth century, Protestant reformers agreed with their Catholic rivals that Hell was the destination of the wicked, but they were much more likely to couch the punitive afterlife in abstract terms of remorse and wounded conscience rather than in concrete terms of torment in Hell-fire familiar from the Catholic tradition. New scientific knowledge and social change in the nineteenth century brought the concept of Hell to the center of debate once again, as Victorian Christians cast doubt on the merciless perpetuity of infernal punishment, while defending their belief in the afterlife in the face of evolutionary theories forwarded by Darwin and other scientists. During this period, secular criticism of the very concept of Hell abounded. Surely, the idea of a punitive afterlife had no place in a world governed by science and reason?

Despite the erosion of traditional religious beliefs in the modern era, Hell has survived and prospered. While the belief in Hell as an actual place has declined in recent centuries, the idea of Hell has endured as a dominant metaphor and, frighteningly, as an inspiration for how to treat other people. From the world wars and the Holocaust to the plight of prisoners and detainees, the political calamities of the modern world have increased the currency of the concept of Hell as a metaphor for torment and suffering. Although many modern people have turned their backs on a literal understanding of Hell as a place of future punishment, they nonetheless draw inspiration from imaginative traditions about the punitive afterlife to cause suffering to others in this present life, to "give them hell." The modern technologies and rational ways of thinking that supposedly mark our progress over earlier generations now allow us to commit mass murder and replicate infernal landscapes at the touch of a button; in an ironic reversal, we have become the very demons our ancestors trembled to meet when death foreclosed on their lives.

In this book, the reader will discover the many forms that the torments of Hell have taken in the Western imagination, with sinful souls immersed in rivers of fire, gnawed away by giant worms, bound up in fiery chains, trembling in intense cold, and devoured whole by hellish monsters. The landscape of Hell is as diverse as its torments. In medieval visions, monks and knights traversed towering mountains, dark valleys, and fetid swamps filled with demons and mythological creatures. In modern accounts, Hell became a vast prison of red-hot iron and choking smoke with great gates built to withstand the seething tide of furious, tormented souls who crashed inexorably against them in their futile attempt to escape their suffering. The literature of Hell boasts famous villains, but most of the damned are ordinary people like you and me, each judged to be deserving of eternal punishment for their own private sins. Stories about Hell were almost always didactic and hortatory; they were written to teach the reader by evoking fear and thereby to persuade the sinner to seek absolution through confession or, better yet, to avoid sin altogether. This does not make them any easier to read. More frightening still, even as Hell has begun to lose its grip on the modern imagination as a place of eternal punishment, it has persisted as a dominant metaphor in Western society and has played a formative role in the ways that we treat one another. Despite all our recourse to reason and compassion, the power of Hell has not been undone.

SCOTT G. BRUCE

Suggestions for Further Reading

Almond, Philip C. *Heaven and Hell in Enlightenment England.* Cambridge: Cambridge University Press, 1994.

Bernstein, Alan E. *The Formation of Hell: Death and Retribution in the Ancient and Early Christian Worlds.* Ithaca, NY: Cornell University Press, 1993.

———. *Hell and Its Rivals: Death and Retribution Among Christians, Jews, and Muslims in the Early Middle Ages.* Ithaca, NY: Cornell University Press, 2017.

Casey, John. *After Lives: A Guide to Heaven, Hell, and Purgatory.* Oxford: Oxford University Press, 2009.

Ferguson, Robert A. *Inferno: An Anatomy of American Punishment.* Cambridge, MA: Harvard University Press, 2014.

Moreira, Isabel, and Margaret Toscano (eds.). *Hell and Its Afterlife: Historical and Contemporary Perspectives.* Burlington, VT: Ashgate, 2010.

Rowell, Geoffrey. *Hell and the Victorians: A Study of the Nineteenth-Century Theological Controversies Concerning Eternal Punishment and the Future Life.* Oxford: Oxford University Press, 1974.

Turner, Alice K. *The History of Hell.* New York: Harcourt Brace & Company, 1993.

Walker, D. P. *The Decline of Hell: Seventeenth-Century Discussions of Eternal Torment.* Chicago: The University of Chicago Press, 1964.

Wheeler, Michael. *Death and the Future Life in Victorian Literature and Theology.* Cambridge: Cambridge University Press, 1994.

Acknowledgments

This book is in many respects a companion volume to *The Penguin Book of the Undead* (Penguin Classics, 2016). Like that book, it owes its existence to the vision and generosity of my editor, John Siciliano. The support of a Faculty Fellowship from the Center for the Humanities and Arts at the University of Colorado at Boulder freed me from my teaching duties in the fall of 2017, thereby allowing me to devote all of my time to conducting the research and preparing the translations for this book. My thanks to the Fiend Club (Sean Babbs, Tom Bartovics, Sarah Luginbill, and Amanda Racine) for reading the manuscript and saving me from many damning errors. I am especially grateful to Anne E. Lester, who suffered along with me on this journey through the darkest channels of the human imagination.

The Penguin Book of Hell

REALMS FORBIDDEN TO THE LIVING: ANCIENT GREECE AND ROME

Under the pitiless skies of the ancient world, human beings held out hope that their mortal lives were not the sum of their entire existence, but the prospects for the afterlife were usually grim. In the early civilizations of Mesopotamia and Egypt, most people who survived to adulthood toiled as subsistence farmers, whose lives were ended at an early age by injury, illness, and childbirth. The threat of death haunted their every step. In Mesopotamian lore, individual souls were not singled out for punishment in the otherworld; the end of life brought the same bleak fate to everyone, irrespective of their station in life. Upon death, souls entered "the world of no return," where they resided below the ground as insubstantial shadows in a "house of dust." It is no surprise that their ancient myths betrayed an interest in the defeat of this loathsome kind of death. In the earliest surviving work of human literature, The Epic of Gilgamesh *(c. 2100 BCE), a Mesopotamian king undertook a perilous voyage to discover the secret of immortality to escape the fate of all mortals, only to learn that it was unattainable. Only the gods lived forever.*

For their part, the ancient Egyptians nurtured a less somber view of the afterlife than their Mesopotamian neighbors. By the time of the Middle Kingdom (2055–1650 BCE), they held the firm belief that the realm of the dead was open to all people. Unlike other ancient cultures, however, they believed that a person's experience in the next life was intimately bound with her conduct in this one. Egyptians who lived in accordance

with ma'at *(an ethical disposition characterized by kindness
and justice) could expect to enter the bountiful halls of Osiris.
Those whose consciences betrayed them when the death god
Anubis weighed their hearts against a feather (the symbol of
ma'at) faced a terrifying second death. Flame-faced spirits
waited to "hack them asunder" and cast them into pits of fire.*

Ancient Mesopotamian and Egyptian traditions about the afterlife did not carry the same weight in Western culture as the
stories told by the Greeks and later by the Romans. There was
no ethical judgment of ordinary souls in the Greek underworld. The spirits of human beings inhabited the grim abode
of Hades as listless shades, stripped of every remnant of their
former selves except for their sad memories of the lives they
once lived. When the hero Odysseus visited the House of
Death, an episode recounted in Homer's Odyssey, the ghost of
the mighty warrior Achilles warned him that the afterlife was
a pitiful state of existence: "No winning words about death to
me, shining Odysseus! By god, I'd rather slave on earth for another man—some dirt-poor tenant farmer who scrapes to
keep alive—than rule down here over all the breathless dead"
(The Odyssey 11.488–91).

As depicted by Homer and other ancient poets, the Greek underworld was a gloomy realm inhabited not only by the shades
of the departed, but also by mythological monsters, like the
three-headed dog Cerberus, who prevented the dead from escaping the kingdom of Hades. The deepest section of the underworld was called Tartarus. It served as a prison for the
rebellious Titans and as a place of torment for mythical figures like Tityos, Tantalus, and Sisyphus, who merited eternal
punishments for their affronts against the gods. A few centuries later, however, a democratization of the punitive afterlife
had occurred. Around 400 BCE, the philosopher Socrates and
his interlocutors could imagine a fate in which the souls of the
dead endured pain for the crimes committed while they were
alive. Later still, we find the Roman poet Virgil (70–19 BCE)
depicting the underworld as a place where ordinary people

could expect to suffer tortures for a litany of offenses. He sin-gled out those who sowed discord in their families, perpe-trated fraud, hoarded wealth, killed for adultery, committed treason, and broke oaths, "all of them, walled up here, wait to meet their doom" (The Aeneid 6.709–10). *The Aeneid of Vir-gil became the most formative and widely read source of an-cient pagan beliefs about the underworld, shaping all subsequent accounts of the punitive afterlife in the Christian era that fol-lowed.*

TARTARUS, PRISON
OF THE TITANS[1]

*One of the most ancient Greek poets was Hesiod, who flour-
ished in the decades around 700 BCE. Among his many surviving poems is the* Theogony *("The Birth of the Gods"),
which describes the origins of the cosmos and the genealogies
of the ancient Greek deities. Central to the poem is the story of
the Titanomachy, the struggle waged by Zeus and the Olympian gods against an older generation of divine beings—Zeus's
father, Kronos, and the Titans—for control of the universe.
After their defeat in a decade-long battle, the Titans were banished to a subterranean realm, "to misty Tartarus, as far beneath / the earth, as earth is far beneath the heavens." Zeus
stationed his allies, the hundred-handed giants Gyes, Kottos,
and Briareus, at the gates of Tartarus to ensure that the Titans
would never escape. Hesiod envisioned this dark realm primarily as a place of perpetual imprisonment, but he singled
out at least one of the Titans for everlasting punishment: Atlas,
the "son of Iapetos," who was condemned for all eternity to
hold up "broad heaven with his head and hands."*

According to the Theogony, *the vanquished Titans were not
the only inhabitants of Tartarus. The deep recesses of the
earth were also the abode of several Olympian gods, who by
their very nature felt most at home beyond the reach of the
sun's rays. Nyx, the personification of the night, dwelled there,
along with her children, the "dread gods" Sleep and his brother
Death, whom the other Olympians feared. Zeus's older sib-
ling Hades was the monarch of this lower world, where he
ruled with his fearsome bride Persephone. A monstrous dog,*

Cerberus, guarded their "echoing mansion," welcoming visitors with his wagging tail but devouring anyone who tried to leave. Earlier in the poem, Hesiod recounted that Cerberus was one of the fierce progeny of the serpentine Echidna and the giant Typhon, who together spawned many of the monsters of Greek antiquity. Unlike most ancient authors, however, the poet described Cerberus as an unspeakable, flesh-eating, "bronze-voiced" hound with no fewer than fifty heads.

The boundless sea roared terribly around,
The great earth rumbled, and broad heaven groaned,
Shaken; and tall Olympus was disturbed
Down to its roots, when the immortals charged.
The heavy quaking from their footsteps reached
Down to dark Tartarus, and piercing sounds
Of awful battle, and their mighty shafts.
They hurled their wounding missiles, and the voice
Of both sides, shouting, reached the starry sky,
And when they met, their ALALE! was great.[2]

Then Zeus no longer checked his rage, for now
His heart was filled with fury, and he showed
The full range of his strength. He came from heaven
And from Olympus, growing brighter as he came,
Continuously; from his mighty hand
The bolts kept flying, bringing thunder-claps
And lightning-flashes, while the holy flame
Rolled thickly all around. The fertile earth
Being burned, roared out, the voiceless forest cried
And crackled with the fire; the whole earth boiled
And ocean's streams, and the unfruitful sea.
The hot blast reached the earthborn Titans; flame
Unspeakable rose to the upper air;
The flashing brightness of the thunderbolt
And lightning blinded all, however strong;
The awful heat reached Chaos. To the ear
It sounded, to the eye it looked as though
Broad Heaven were coming down upon the Earth:

For such a noise of crashing might arise
If she were falling, hurled down by his fall.
Just such a mighty crash rose from the gods
Meeting in strife. The howling winds brought on
Dust storm and earthquake, and the shafts of Zeus,
Lightning and thunder and the blazing bolt,
And carried shouting and the battle-cry
Into the armies, and a dreadful noise
Of hideous battle sounded, and their deeds
Were mighty, but the tide of war was turned:
Until that moment, they had kept it up
Continually, in the long, hard fight.

Among those gods who made the fighting harsh
Foremost were Kottos and Briareus
And Gyes, who loved war insatiably.
With their strong hands, they hurled three hundred rocks
In quick succession; with their missiles, they
Overshadowed the Titans, put them down
In everlasting shade. Under the earth
Broad-pathed, they sent them, and they bound them up
In painful chains. Proud though the Titans were,
They were defeated by those hands, and sent
To misty Tartarus, as far beneath
The earth, as earth is far beneath the heavens.

An anvil made of bronze, falling from heaven,
Would fall nine nights and days, and on the tenth
Would reach the earth: and if the anvil fell
From earth, would fall again nine nights and days
And come to Tartarus upon the tenth.
A wall of bronze runs around Tartarus,
And round this runs a necklace, triple-thick,
Of purest Night, while up above there grow
The roots of earth and of the barren sea.
There, in the misty dark, the Titan gods
Are hidden, in a moldering place, lowest
And last of giant Earth, by the will of Zeus

Who drives the clouds, and they may never leave.
Poseidon set bronze gates upon the place,
And all around it runs a wall; there live
Gyes, Kottos, and Briareus
As faithful guards, for aegis-bearing Zeus.

And there, in order, are the ends and springs
Of gloomy earth and misty Tartarus,
And of the barren sea and starry heaven,
Murky and awful, loathed by the very gods.
There is the yawning mouth of hell, and if
A man should find himself inside the gates
He would not reach the bottom for a year;
Gust after savage gust would carry him
Now here, now there. Even the deathless gods
Find this an awesome mystery. Here, too,
Is found the fearsome home of dismal Night
Hidden in dark blue clouds. Before her house
The son of Iapetos, unshakeable,
Holds up broad heaven with his head and hands
Untiring, in the place where Night and Day
Approach and greet each other, as they cross
The great bronze threshold. When the one goes in
The other leaves; never are both at home,
But always one, outside, crosses the earth,
The other waits at home until her hour
For journeying arrives. The one brings light
All-seeing, to the earth, but deadly Night,
The other, hidden in dark clouds, brings Sleep,
Brother of Death, and carries him in her arms.
There live the children of dark Night, dread gods,
Sleep and his brother Death. The shining Sun
Has never looked upon them with his rays
Not going up to heaven, nor coming back.
The one of them is kind to men and goes
Peacefully over the earth and the sea's broad back;
The other's heart is iron; in his breast
Is pitiless bronze; if he should touch a man,

That man is his. And even to the gods
Who are immortal, Death is an enemy.

There, further on, the echoing mansion stands
Of mighty Hades, god of the lower world,
And feared Persephone. A monstrous dog
Stands pitiless guard in front, with evil ways:
He wags his tail and both his ears for all
Who enter, but he will not let them go.
Lying in wait he eats up anyone
He catches leaving by the gates of strong
Hades and greatly feared Persephone.

NETHERWORLD
MEGAFAUNA[1]

In the ancient imagination, the monstrous dog Cerberus guarded the gateway to the kingdom of the dead, the dominion of his masters Hades and Persephone. He was a warden of the shades rather than a tormentor, his presence a firm reminder of the perpetual boundary that separated the living from the deceased. Although he was frightful to behold, Cerberus was not particularly effective at keeping Greek heroes from entering the underworld. When Eurydice died from a snakebite, her heartbroken husband, the mythical singer Orpheus, descended to Hades to retrieve her. At the gates, he easily lulled Cerberus to sleep with his song and snuck past. Likewise, in a famous cycle of myths, the hero Heracles subdued the hound of Hades with the help of Theseus as the last of the twelve tasks imposed on him by King Eurystheus of Argos. Ancient authors and artists depicted the labors of Heracles in plays and on pottery for centuries, but the most detailed rendering of his struggle with Cerberus appeared in the first century CE in a Latin tragedy composed by Seneca the Younger (c. 4 BCE–65 CE) called The Madness of Heracles (Hercules furens). Narrated by Theseus, Seneca's play depicted the hero fighting the monstrous dog with nothing more than a club and no protection except for the pelt of the invulnerable Nemean Lion, a trophy from his first labor. The submission of Cerberus, depicted here in his traditional three-headed form, proved once and for all the unearthly strength of the unassailable Heracles.

After this, the palace of grasping Dis [Hades] comes into view. Here a savage Stygian dog [Cerberus] guards the kingdom and terrorizes the shades of the dead, shaking his three heads with a devastating bark. Serpents lick his gore-stained head, his mane bristles with vipers, and his twisted tail hisses like a long dragon. His wrath matches his form. When he senses footfalls, he raises his hairy mane with its writhing snakes and with a cocked ear he catches any sound made, for he is accustomed to perceive even the shades of the dead. When the son of Jupiter [Heracles] stood nearby, the dog sat hesitant in his cave and felt a touch of fear—then behold, he terrified those silent places with a great barking. The menacing serpents hissed from both of his shoulders. The booming of his horrifying bark from his three mouths terrified even the blessed shades [in Elysium]. Then Heracles released the grinning pelt [of the Nemean Lion] from his left arm and positioned the Cleonaean head to protect himself beneath its ample covering. Wielding a massive club in his conquering right hand, he swung now here, now there with an unrelenting assault, repeating his attacks. Subdued, the dog gave up his threats, lowered all his heads in exhaustion, and departed from his cave. Sitting on their thrones, each of its masters [Hades and Persephone] shuddered in fear and ordered Cerberus to be taken away. They also released me [Theseus] as a favor at Heracles' request.

Then, stroking the monster's heavy necks with his hand, Heracles bound him with a collar of adamant. Once the sleepless guardian of that kingdom of the shades, the dog forgot himself, lowered his ears as though tame, and suffered himself to be led, acknowledging his master, following with his muzzles restrained, while his snake-bearing tail beat both of his sides. Afterward, when they came to the shores of Taenarum and the strange brightness of an unknown light struck his eyes, though subdued, Cerberus recovered his spirit and shook his great chains in anger. The dog almost carried away his captor, dragging him back bent forward and forcing him to yield a step. Then Heracles looked even for my help and with our combined strength we both dragged the dog, mad with wrath and waging a futile war, and brought the beast to the surface. When Cerberus saw the brightness of the day and looked upon the clear expanse of the shining sky, night fell upon the dog as he cast his gaze to the ground, closed his eyes, and expelled the day unseen. He turned back his face and with each of his necks he sought the earth, then hid his heads beneath Heracles' shadow. But then, with joyous cries a great crowd arrived, bearing laurel wreathes on their brows and singing worthy praises of great Heracles.

ODYSSEUS AT DEATH'S DOOR[1]

Homer's epic poem The Odyssey *(c. 700 BCE) offers one of the earliest and most vivid glimpses of the punitive afterlife in the ancient imagination. It tells the story of the decade-long voyage of Odysseus, a Greek veteran of the Trojan War, back to his home on the island of Ithaca. Hindered on his return voyage by the sea god Poseidon, Odysseus takes the advice of the enchantress Circe to venture to the threshold of the underworld to consult with the ghost of Tiresias of Thebes, a famous seer, about how best to return to Ithaca. In Homer's story, the land of the dead is not deep beneath the earth but on a dark and distant shore: "the Ocean River's bounds, where Cimmerian people have their homes—their realm and city shrouded in mist and cloud." There Odysseus performs a necromantic ritual and speaks to the souls of the dead who answer his summons, including the shade of his own mother. The last to approach him is the ghost of Ajax, a hero of the Trojan War who fought alongside Odysseus but took his own life after the two quarreled over the possession of the god-forged armor of their fallen ally Achilles. As Ajax's shade recedes in resentful silence, Odysseus peers deeper into the darkness of Erebus to glimpse "men who died in the old days." Much to his horror, he beholds the endless torments of the Titans before fear forces his retreat back to his waiting ship.*

Now the rest of the ghosts, the dead and gone
came swarming up around me—deep in sorrow there,
each asking about the grief that touched him most.
Only the ghost of Great Ajax, son of Telamon,
kept his distance, blazing with anger at me still

for the victory I had won by the ships that time
I pressed my claim for the arms of Prince Achilles.
His queenly mother had set them up as prizes,
Pallas and captive Trojans served as judges.
Would to god I'd never won such trophies!
All for them the earth closed over Ajax,
that proud hero Ajax . . .

So I cried out but Ajax answered not a word.
He stalked off toward Erebus, into the dark
to join the other lost, departed dead.
Yet now, despite his anger,
he might have spoken to me, or I to him,
but the heart inside me stirred with some desire
to see the ghosts of others dead and gone.

And I saw Minos there, illustrious son of Zeus,
firmly enthroned, holding his golden scepter,
judging all the dead . . .
Some on their feet, some seated, all clustering
round the king of justice, pleading for his verdicts
reached in the House of Death with its all-embracing gates.

I next caught sight of Orion, that huge hunter,
rounding up on the fields of asphodel those wild beasts
the man in life cut down on the lonely mountain-slopes,
brandishing in his hands the bronze-studded club that time can
    never shatter.
                    I saw Tityus too,
son of the mighty goddess Earth—sprawling there
on the ground, spread over nine acres—two vultures
hunched on either side of him, digging into his liver,
beaking deep in the blood-sac, and he with his frantic hands
could never beat them off, for he had once dragged off
the famous consort of Zeus in all her glory,
Leto, threading her way toward Pytho's ridge,
over the lovely dancing-rings of Panopeus.

And I saw Tantalus too, bearing endless torture.
He stood erect in a pool as the water lapped his chin—
parched, he tried to drink, but he could not reach the surface,
no, time and again the old man stooped, craving a sip,
time and again the water vanished, swallowed down,
laying bare the caked black earth at his feet—
some spirit drank it dry. And over his head
leafy trees dangled their fruit from high aloft,
pomegranates and pears, and apples glowing red,
succulent figs and olives swelling sleek and dark,
but as soon as the old man would strain to clutch them
fast, a gust would toss them up to the lowering dark clouds.

And I saw Sisyphus too, bound to his own torture,
grappling his monstrous boulder with both arms working,
heaving, hands struggling, legs driving, he kept on
thrusting the rock uphill toward the brink, but just
as it teetered, set to topple over—
                                        time and again
the immense weight of the thing would wheel it back and
the ruthless boulder would bound and tumble down to the plain
    again—
so once again he would heave, would struggle to thrust it up,
sweat drenching his body, dust swirling above his head.

And next I caught a glimpse of powerful Heracles—
his ghost, I mean: the man himself delights
in the grand feasts of the deathless gods on high,
wed to Hebe, famed for her lithe, alluring ankles,
the daughter of mighty Zeus and Hera shod in gold.
Around him cries of the dead rang out like cries of birds,
scattering left and right in horror as on he came like night,
naked bow in his grip, an arrow grooved on the bowstring,
glaring round him fiercely, forever poised to shoot.
A terror too, that sword-belt sweeping across his chest,
a baldric of solid gold emblazoned with awesome work . . .

bears and ramping boars and lions with wild, fiery eyes,
and wars, routs and battles, massacres, butchered men.
May the craftsman who forged that masterpiece—
whose skills could conjure up a belt like that—
never forge another! Heracles knew me at once, at first glance,
and hailed me with a winging burst of pity:
"Royal son of Laertes, Odysseus famed for exploits,
luckless man, you too? Braving out a fate as harsh
as the fate I bore, alive in the light of day?
Son of Zeus that I was, my torments never ended,
forced to slave for a man not half the man I was:
he saddled me with the worst heartbreaking labors.
Why, he sent me down here once, to retrieve the hound
that guards the dead—no harder task for me, he thought—
but I dragged the great beast up from the underworld to earth
and Hermes and gleaming-eyed Athena blazed the way!"

    With that he turned and back he went to the House of Death
but I held fast in place, hoping that others might still come,
shades of famous heroes, men who died in the old days
and ghosts of an even older age I longed to see,
Theseus and Pirithous, the gods' own radiant sons.
But before I could, the dead came surging round me,
hordes of them, thousands raising unearthly cries,
and blanching terror gripped me—panicked now
that Queen Persephone might send up from Death
some monstrous head, some Gorgon's staring face!
I rushed back to my ship, commanded all hands
to take to the decks and cast off cables quickly.
They swung aboard at once, they sat to the oars in ranks
and a strong tide of the Ocean River swept her downstream,
sped by our rowing first, then by a fresh fair wind.

SOCRATES PONDERS THE PUNISHMENT OF SOULS[1]

The otherworldly punishment of mythic figures who had offended the gods was a commonplace in ancient Greek mythology and poetry, but the fate of ordinary souls was a subject worthy of philosophical speculation. On the final day of his life, the philosopher Socrates (c. 470–399 BCE) pondered the punishment of the soul in the company of friends. The goal of philosophy, he argued, was the cultivation of virtue, which prepared human beings for the separation of the body and soul that took place at the moment of death. Socrates believed that individuals weighed down by "the enormity of their errors" would be thrown into the subterranean prison of Tartarus with no hope of release. Perpetrators of lesser crimes received a lighter sentence. After a year in Tartarus, they would be freed to petition for mercy those whom they had injured in life. Meanwhile, virtuous individuals who purified themselves through philosophical inquiry would avoid the underworld altogether and ascend as beings of pure spirit to "that pure place of residence above." Socrates's parting message to his followers was clear: the pursuit of philosophy was the surest way to avoid punishment in the afterlife.

This, then, is the nature of the regions under the earth. Now when the dead come to the place to which each is conveyed by his divine guide, they first submit themselves to judgment, both those who have lived fine and pious lives and those who have not. Those judged to have lived a middling kind of life journey to the river Acheron, where they board the vessels available to them and use these to journey to the lake; there they reside and undergo purification, each as he deserves, paying penalties to absolve him from any crimes committed and receiving honors for any benefits bestowed. As for those judged incurable because of the enormity of their errors— whether they have repeatedly stolen large sums from temples, persistently killed people contrary to justice and the law, or committed other such crimes as there may be, the fate of these, fittingly, is to be cast into Tartarus and never to emerge again. Another category fated to be thrown into Tartarus consists of those judged to have committed errors that are curable but serious, for example, people who have committed an act of violence toward a father or a mother but live out the rest of their lives regretting it, or who have become killers under some other similar circumstances; but when these have been in Tartarus for a year, the surge of the great river disgorges them, the killers by way of Cocytus and the father- and mother-beaters by way of Pyriphlegethon, and as they are carried along beside the Acherusian lake they scream and call out, the first sort to those they killed, the second to those they assaulted; their calls are followed by supplication, as they beg their victims to permit their exit from their river to the lake, and to admit them there; if they succeed in persuading them, they get out, and cease from their suffering, but if not, then they are carried off again into Tartarus, and from there back again into the rivers, and that will go on happening to them until they manage to persuade those they have wronged; because that is the penalty imposed upon them by the judges. But those judged to have done exceptionally well toward living piously are the ones who are freed from these regions here, within the earth, and are released as if from prisons, moving to that pure place of residence above and dwelling on the surface of the earth. And from among these very people, those who have purified themselves sufficiently well by means of philosophy dwell entirely without bodies for a time thereafter, and come to reside in places still more beautiful than those, places that it is not easy to show you, and not in the time we presently have. But it is for the sake of the things we have described, Simmias, that one must do everything to ensure one's share of goodness and wisdom in one's life; fine is the prize, and the hope great.

INTO THE REALM OF SHADOWS[1]

No ancient author was more influential in his depiction of the punitive afterlife than the Roman poet Virgil (70–19 BCE). Modeling himself after Homer, Virgil composed an epic poem called The Aeneid *about the founding of Rome by a refugee from the Trojan War named Aeneas. Commissioned by the Roman emperor Augustus (63 BCE–14 CE), Virgil's* Aeneid *was an instant bestseller. Romans adopted the poem not only as a sublime statement of their national identity but also as a model of Latin eloquence. The influence of* The Aeneid *in the Western tradition is difficult to overstate. The poem became a mainstay of the Roman education system for centuries. Even after the fall of the Roman Empire and the end of ancient paganism, Christian monks learned* The Aeneid *by heart, imitated its style in their own poems, and interpreted its mythological content as allegories for Christian truth.*

In imitation of Homer's hero Odysseus, who sought the advice of Tiresias's ghost at the threshold of the House of Death, Virgil's hero Aeneas ventures into the realm of shadows to speak with the shade of his dead father. With the assistance of a priestess of Apollo known as the Sibyl, he obtains a golden branch from a tree in the forest near her cave as a gift for Hades' queen Persephone. With the priestess, Aeneas descends into the subterranean realm, where he meets the dreadful Charon, who ferried the souls of the dead across the River Styx; evades the three-headed Cerberus, the monstrous watchdog of Dis; and encounters the mournful shade of his former lover Queen Dido of Carthage, who committed suicide when Aeneas abandoned her to fulfill his destiny as Rome's founder. Virgil's harrowing depiction of the torments awaiting individuals who committed crimes like fraud, murder, incest, and sedition against the state inspired many medieval authors, including most famously Dante Alighieri (1265–1321 CE), who cast the shade of Virgil as his guide on his own journey through Hell and Purgatory in The Divine Comedy *(see pp. 139–65, below).*

The rite

performed, Aeneas hurries to carry out the Sibyl's orders.
There was a vast cave deep in the gaping, jagged rock,
shielded well by a dusky lake and shadowed grove.
Over it no bird on earth could make its way unscathed,
such poisonous vapors steamed up from its dark throat
to cloud the arching sky. Here, as her first step,
the priestess steadies four black-backed calves,
she tips wine on their brows, then plucks some tufts
from the crown between their horns and casts them
over the altar fire, first offerings, crying out
to Hecate, mighty Queen of Heaven and Hell.
Attendants run knives under throats and catch
warm blood in bowls. Aeneas himself, sword drawn,
slaughters a black-fleeced lamb to the Furies' mother,
Night, and to her great sister, Earth, and to you,
Proserpina, kills a barren heifer. Then to the king
of the river Styx, he raises altars into the dark night
and over their fires lays whole carcasses of bulls
and pours fat oil over their entrails flaming up.
Then suddenly, look, at the break of day, first light,
the earth groans underfoot and the wooded heights quake
and across the gloom the hounds seem to howl
at the goddess coming closer.
"Away, away!"
the Sibyl shrieks, "all you unhallowed ones—away
from this whole grove! But you launch out on your journey,

tear your sword from its sheath, Aeneas. Now for courage,
now the steady heart!" And the Sibyl says no more but
into the yawning cave she flings herself, possessed—
he follows her boldly, matching stride for stride.

                                      You gods
who govern the realm of ghosts, you voiceless shades and Chaos—
you, the River of Fire, you far-flung regions hushed in night—
lend me the right to tell what I have heard, lend your power
to reveal the world immersed in the misty depths of earth.

On they went, those dim travelers under the lonely night,
through gloom and the empty halls of Death's ghostly realm,
like those who walk through woods by a grudging moon's
deceptive light when Jove has plunged the sky in dark
and the black night drains all color from the world.
There in the entryway, the gorge of hell itself,
Grief and the pangs of Conscience make their beds,
and fatal pale Disease lives there, and bleak Old Age,
Dread and Hunger, seductress to crime, and grinding Poverty,
all, terrible shapes to see—and Death and deadly Struggle
and Sleep, twin brother of Death, and twisted, wicked Joys
and facing them at the threshold, War, rife with death,
and the Furies' iron chambers, and mad, raging Strife
whose blood-stained headbands knot her snaky locks.

There in the midst, a giant shadowy elm tree spreads
her ancient branching arms, home, they say, to swarms
of false dreams, one clinging tight under each leaf.
And a throng of monsters too—what brutal forms
are stabled at the gates—Centaurs, mongrel Scyllas,
part women, part beasts, and hundred-handed Briareus
and the savage Hydra of Lerna, that hissing horror,
the Chimaera armed with torches—Gorgons, Harpies,
and triple-bodied Geryon, his great ghost. And here,
instantly struck with terror, Aeneas grips his sword
and offers its naked edge against them as they come,
and if his experienced comrade had not warned him
they were mere disembodied creatures, flimsy

will-o'-the-wisps that flit like living forms,
he would have rushed them all,
slashed through empty phantoms with his blade.
                                        From there
the road leads down to the Acheron's Tartarean waves.
Here the enormous whirlpool gapes aswirl with filth,
seethes and spews out all its silt in the Wailing River.
Here the dreaded ferryman guards the flood,
grisly in his squalor—Charon . . .
his scraggly beard a tangled mat of white, his eyes
fixed in a fiery stare, and his grimy rags hang down
from his shoulders by a knot. But all on his own
he punts his craft with a pole and hoists sail
as he ferries dead souls in his rust-red skiff.
He's on in years, but a god's old age is hale and green.

   A huge throng of the dead came streaming toward the banks:
mothers and grown men and ghosts of great-souled heroes,
their bodies stripped of life, and boys and unwed girls
and sons laid on the pyre before their parents' eyes.
As thick as leaves in autumn woods at the first frost
that slip and float to earth, or dense as flocks of birds
that wing from the heaving sea to shore when winter's chill
drives them over the waves to landfalls drenched in sunlight.
There they stood, pleading to be the first ones ferried over,
reaching out their hands in longing toward the farther shore.
But the grim ferryman ushers aboard now these, now those,
others he thrusts away, back from the water's edge.
                                        Aeneas,
astonished, stirred by the tumult, calls out: "Tell me,
Sibyl, what does it mean, this thronging toward the river?
What do the dead souls want? What divides them all?
Some are turned away from the banks and others
scull the murky waters with their oars!"

   The aged priestess answered Aeneas briefly:
"Son of Anchises—born of the gods, no doubt—
what you see are Cocytus' pools and Styx's marsh,

Powers by which the gods swear oaths they dare not break.
And the great rout you see is helpless, still not buried.
That ferryman there is Charon. Those borne by the stream
have found their graves. And no spirits may be conveyed
across the horrendous banks and hoarse, roaring flood
until their bones are buried, and they rest in peace . . .
A hundred years they wander, hovering round these shores
till at last they may return and see once more the pools
they long to cross."
                Anchises' son came to a halt
and stood there, pondering long, while pity filled his heart,
their lot so hard, unjust.
                [· · ·]
So now they press on with their journey under way
and at last approach the river. But once the ferryman,
still out in the Styx's currents, spied them moving
across the silent grove and turning toward the bank,
he greets them first with a rough abrupt rebuke:
"Stop, whoever you are at our river's edge,
in full armor too! Why have you come? Speak up,
from right where you are, not one step more! This
is the realm of shadows, sleep, and drowsy night.
The law forbids me to carry living bodies across
in my Stygian boat. I'd little joy, believe me,
when Hercules came and I sailed the hero over,
or Theseus, Pirithous, sons of gods as they were
with their high and mighty power.
Hercules stole our watchdog—chained him, the poor
   trembling creature,
dragged him away from our king's very throne! The others
tried to snatch our queen from the bridal bed of Death!"

But Apollo's seer broke in and countered Charon:
"There's no such treachery here—just calm down—
no threat of force in our weapons. The huge guard
at the gates can howl for eternity from his cave,
terrifying the bloodless shades, Persephone keep
her chastity safe at home behind her uncle's doors.

Aeneas of Troy, famous for his devotion, feats of arms,
goes down to the deepest shades of hell to see his father.
But if this image of devotion cannot move you, here,
this bough"—showing the bough enfolded in her robes—
"You know it well."
                              At this, the heaving rage
subsides in his chest. The Sibyl says no more.
The ferryman, marveling at the awesome gift,
the fateful branch unseen so many years,
swerves his dusky craft and approaches shore.
The souls already crouched at the long thwarts—
he brusquely thrusts them out, clearing the gangways,
quickly taking massive Aeneas aboard the little skiff.
Under his weight the boat groans and her stitched seams
gape as she ships great pools of water pouring in.
At last, the river crossed, the ferryman lands
the seer and hero all unharmed in the marsh,
the repellent oozing slime and livid sedge.
                                                   These
are the realms that monstrous Cerberus rocks with howls
braying out of his three throats, his enormous bulk
squatting low in the cave that faced them there.
The Sibyl, seeing the serpents writhe around his neck,
tossed him a sop, slumberous with honey and drugged seed,
and he, frothing with hunger, three jaws spread wide,
snapped it up where the Sibyl tossed it—gone.
His tremendous back relaxed, he sags to earth
and sprawls over all his cave, his giant hulk limp.
The watchdog buried now in sleep, Aeneas seizes
the way in, quickly clear of the river's edge,
the point of no return.
                              At that moment, cries—
they could hear them now, a crescendo of wailing,
ghosts of infants weeping, robbed of their share
of this sweet life, at its very threshold too:
all, snatched from the breast on that black day
that swept them off and drowned them in bitter death.
Beside them were those condemned to die on a false charge.

But not without jury picked by lot, not without judge
are their places handed down. Not at all.
Minos the grand inquisitor stirs the urn,
he summons the silent jury of the dead,
he scans the lives of those accused, their charges.
The region next to them is held by those sad ghosts,
innocents all, who brought on death by their own hands;
despising the light, they threw their lives away.
How they would yearn, now in the world above
to endure grim want and long hard labor!
But Fate bars the way. The grisly swamp
and its loveless, lethal waters bind them fast,
Styx with its nine huge coils holds them captive.

   Close to the spot, extending toward the horizon—
the Sibyl points them out—are the Fields of Mourning,
that is the name they bear. Here wait those souls
consumed by the harsh, wasting sickness, cruel love,
concealed on lonely paths, shrouded by myrtle bowers.
Not even in death do their torments leave them, ever.
Here he glimpses Phaedra, Procris, and Eriphyle grieving,
baring the wounds her heartless son had dealt her.[2]
Evadne, Pasiphaë, and Laodamia walking side by side,
and another, a young man once, a woman now, Caeneus,
turned back by Fate to the form she bore at first.[3]

   And wandering there among them, wound still fresh,
Phoenician Dido drifted along the endless woods.
As the Trojan hero paused beside her, recognized her
through the shadows, a dim, misty figure—as one
when the month is young may see or seem to see
the new moon rising up through banks of clouds—
that moment Aeneas wept and approached the ghost
with tender words of love: "Tragic Dido,
so, was the story true that came my way?
I heard that you were dead . . .
you took the final measure with a sword.
Oh, dear god, was it I who caused your death?

I swear by the stars, by the Powers on high, whatever
faith one swears by here in the depths of earth,
I left your shores, my Queen, against my will. Yes,
the will of the gods, that drives me through the shadows now,
those moldering places so forlorn, this deep unfathomed night—
their decrees have forced me on. Nor did I ever dream
my leaving could have brought you so much grief.
Stay a moment. Don't withdraw from my sight.
Running away—from whom? This is the last word
that Fate allows me to say to you. The last."

    Aeneas, with such appeals, with welling tears,
tried to soothe her rage, her wild fiery glance.
But she, her eyes fixed on the ground, turned away,
her features no more moved by his pleas as he talked on
than if she were set in stony flint or Parian marble rock.
And at last she tears herself away, his enemy forever,
fleeing back to the shadowed forest where Sychaeus,
her husband long ago, answers all her anguish,
meets her love with love. But Aeneas, no less
struck by her unjust fate, escorts her from afar
with streaming tears and pities her as she passes.
                              [· · ·]
"Night comes on, Aeneas. We waste our time with tears.
This is the place where the road divides in two.
To the right it runs below the mighty walls of Death,
our path to Elysium, but the left-hand road torments
the wicked, leading down to Tartarus, path to doom."
                              [· · ·]
                                                        Aeneas
suddenly glances back and beneath a cliff to the left
he sees an enormous fortress ringed with triple walls
and raging around it all, a blazing flood of lava,
Tartarus' River of Fire, whirling thunderous boulders.
Before it rears a giant gate, its columns solid adamant,
so no power of man, not even the gods themselves,
can root it out in war. An iron tower looms on high
where Tisiphone, crouching with bloody shroud girt up,

never sleeping, keeps her watch at the entrance night and day.
Groans resound from the depths, the savage crack of the lash,
the grating creak of iron, the clank of dragging chains.
And Aeneas froze there, terrified, taking in the din:
"What are the crimes, what kinds? Tell me, Sibyl,
what punishments, why this scourging?
Why such wailing echoing in the air?"

    The seer rose to the moment: "Famous captain of Troy,
no pure soul may set foot on that wicked threshold.
But when Hecate put me in charge of Avernus' groves
she taught me all the punishments of the gods,
she led me through them all.
Here Cretan Rhadamanthus rules with an iron hand,
censuring men, exposing fraud, forcing confessions
when anyone up and above, reveling in his hidden crimes,
puts off his day of atonement till he dies, the fool,
too late. That very moment, vengeful Tisiphone, armed
with lashes, springs on the guilty, whips them till they quail,
with her left hand shaking all her twisting serpents,
summoning up her savage sisters, bands of Furies.
Then at last, screeching out on their grinding hinge
the infernal gates swing wide.
                        "Can you see that sentry
crouched at the entrance? What a specter guards the threshold!
Fiercer still, the monstrous Hydra, fifty black maws gaping,
holds its lair inside.
                      "Then the abyss, Tartarus itself
plunges headlong down through the darkness twice as far
as our gaze goes up to Olympus rising toward the skies.
Here the ancient line of the Earth, the Titans' spawn,
flung down by lightning, writhe in a deep pit.
There I saw the twin sons of Aloeus too, giant bodies
that clawed the soaring sky with their hands to tear it down
and thrust great Jove from his kingdom high above.

    "I saw Salmoneus too, who paid a brutal price
for aping the flames of Jove and Olympus' thunder.

Sped by his four-horse chariot, flaunting torches,
right through the Greek tribes and Elis city's heart
he rode in triumph, claiming as *his* the honors of the gods.
The madman, trying to match the storm and matchless lightning
just by stamping on bronze with prancing horn-hoofed steeds!
The almighty Father hurled his bolt through the thunderheads—
no torches for him, no smoky flicker of pitch-pines, no,
he spun him headlong down in a raging whirlwind.
                                                    "Tityus too:
you could see that son of Earth, the mother of us all,
his giant body splayed out over nine whole acres,
a hideous vulture with hooked beak gorging down
his immortal liver and innards ever ripe for torture.
Deep in his chest it nestles, ripping into its feast
and the fibers, grown afresh, get no relief from pain.

    "What need to tell of the Lapiths, Ixion, or Pirithous?
Above them a black rock—now, now slipping, teetering,
watch, forever about to fall. While the golden posts
of high festal couches gleam, and a banquet spreads
before their eyes with luxury fit for kings . . .
but reclining just beside them, the oldest Fury
holds back their hands from even touching the food,
surging up with her brandished torch and deafening screams.

    "Here those who hated their brothers, while alive,
or struck their fathers down
or embroiled clients in fraud, or brooded alone
over troves of gold they gained and never put aside
some share for their own kin—a great multitude, these—
then those killed for adultery, those who marched to the flag
of civil war and never shrank from breaking their pledge
to their lords and masters: all of them, walled up here,
wait to meet their doom.
                                    "Don't hunger to know their doom,
what form of torture or twist of Fortune drags them down.
Some trundle enormous boulders, others dangle, racked
to the breaking point on the spokes of rolling wheels.

Doomed Theseus sits on his seat and there he will sit forever.
Phlegyas, most in agony, sounds out his warning to all,
his piercing cries bear witness through the darkness:
'Learn to bow to justice. Never scorn the gods.
You all stand forewarned!'

   "Here's one who bartered his native land for gold,
he saddled her with a tyrant, set up laws for a bribe,
for a bribe he struck them down. This one forced himself
on his daughter's bed and sealed a forbidden marriage.
All dared an outrageous crime and what they dared, they did.

   "No, not if I had a hundred tongues and a hundred mouths
and a voice of iron too—I could never capture
all the crimes or run through all the torments,
doom by doom."

EARLY CHRISTIAN HELLSCAPES
(c. 100–500 CE)

The earliest Christian authors inherited from the Greeks and the Romans the notion that the souls of the dead lived in a realm either beneath the earth or on a distant shore (Hades), where particularly wicked individuals suffered eternal punishments (Tartarus), but the holy writings of the ancient Israelites exerted an equally powerful influence on Christian conceptions of the punitive afterlife. In contrast to Greek and Roman literature, the Hebrew scriptures offered no stories of heroes descending to the underworld; there was no Jewish Odysseus or Aeneas. Unlike other ancient religions, Judaism forbade commerce with the dead by means of necromancy, emphasized the living believer's relationship to God, and did not speculate at length about the fate of the soul after death. Nonetheless, the early Christians inherited two Hebrew words for the afterlife that shaped the way they formulated their idea of Hell: Sheol and Gehenna.

The word Sheol ("the underworld") appears many times in the Hebrew scriptures. Similar to the concept of Hades among the Greeks, Sheol was a place of darkness where souls abided in silence and forgetfulness. Hebrew prophets described it as a prison of sorts with gates and bars. Sheol was generally reserved for wicked and impious individuals, but it was not a place of otherworldly torture. To express their idea of the punitive afterlife, early Christians repurposed the Hebrew word Gehenna. The name derived from the Hebrew ge-hinnom ("valley of Hinnom"), a site on the southern side of the city of Jerusalem where the Israelites had once sacrificed their *children in fire to the Canaanite god Molech. For this idolatry, God sent the Babylonians to punish them and lead them into exile—the Babylonian captivity—for forty years (598–58 BCE). Upon their return, the Israelites treated the valley of Hinnom as an accursed place, where rebels against God would be punished: "And they shall go forth and look on the dead bodies of the men that have rebelled against me; for their worm shall not die, their fire shall not be quenched, and they shall be an abhorrence to all flesh" (Isaiah 66.24). The earliest Christians adopted the word* Gehenna *as the equivalent of Tartarus: the destination of the wicked who merited punishment after death for their sins. In the* Gospel of Mark, *Jesus warned his apostles directly: "If your eye causes you to sin, pluck it out; it is better for you to enter the kingdom of God with one eye than with two eyes to be thrown into Gehenna, where their worm does not die and the fire is not quenched" (Mark 9.46–47). Wedding the pagan notion of a punitive afterlife for those who offended the divine with the imagery of the fire and the worm from the Hebrew scriptures, early Christian authors imagined a host of otherworldly punishments that inspired theologians, artists, and poets throughout the European Middle Ages and beyond.*

THE FIRE AND THE WORM¹

Torment by fire was a recurrent motif in early Christian depictions of Hell. In the late first century, the author of the Book of Revelation foretold how the armies of Gog and Magog assembled against the saints would be consumed by fire from heaven, "and the devil who had deceived them would be thrown into a lake of fire and brimstone where the beast and the false prophet were, and they will be tormented day and night for ever and ever" (Revelation 20.10). No description of Hell's topography and the tortures practiced there was more popular in medieval Europe than the Apocalypse of Paul. *An anonymous work of the third century, this text purported to describe a vision of Heaven and Hell experienced by the apostle Paul, who spread the message of Christ to the Greeks and the Romans in the first century CE. Allegedly discovered alongside the apostle's shoes in a marble box hidden in the foundation of his house in Tarsus, the* Apocalypse of Paul *revealed for Christian readers a nightmarish landscape of molten rivers, where "angels of Tartarus" oversaw the punishment of men and women, each torture tailored for their specific sins. Singled out for suffering were church officials (bishops, deacons, etc.) who had failed to fulfill the duties of their office. While fire was the dominant form of punishment in Paul's vision, many sinners were also eaten alive by gnawing worms, abused by hellish angels, plunged into deep pits, and tormented by extreme cold. This apocryphal text was not accepted into the canon of Christian scriptures, but this did not prevent it from circulating widely throughout medieval Europe.*

When the angel had ceased speaking to me, he led me outside beyond the city through the trees and back from the places of the land of good things, and he set me at the river of milk and honey. And after that, he led me to the ocean that bears the foundation of heaven. The angel responded and said to me, "Do you know that you are departing this place?" And I said, "Yes, Lord." And he said to me, "Come and follow me, and I will show you the souls of the impious and the sinners, so that you may know what kind of place they have." And I went with the angel and he took me toward the setting of the sun and I saw the beginning of heaven built upon a great river of water, and I asked, "What is this river of water?" And the angel said to me, "This is the ocean that surrounds the entire earth." And when I was at the farthest reaches of the ocean, I looked and there was no light in that place, but only shadows and sadness and sorrow, and I sighed.

And I saw there a burning river of fire, and in it there was a crowd of men and women sunk up to their knees, and other men up to their navels, and indeed others up to their lips, and others up to their hair. And I asked the angel and said, "Lord, who are these people in the river of fire?" And the angel responded and said to me, "They are neither hot nor cold, for they have not been found in the reckoning of the just or the reckoning of the impious. For these people spent their lifetime on earth sometimes occupied in prayer, but sometimes occupied in sins and fornication until they died." And I asked and said, "Who are these ones, Lord, sunk up to their knees in the fire?" In response, he said to me, "These are the ones who, when they came forth from church, busied themselves in unsuitable conversations. But the ones who have been sunk up to the navel are those who, after they had received the body and blood of Christ, went and fornicated and did not stop in their sinning until they died. And the ones sunk up to the lips are those who slandered each other when they gathered in the church of God. And the ones sunk up to their eyebrows were those who conspired with one another, plotting evil against their neighbor."

And I saw to the north a place of various and diverse torments full of men and women, and the river of fire flowed upon them. I looked and I saw pits great in depth and in them were many souls together and the depth of the pit was about three thousand cubits and I saw the souls groaning and crying and saying, "Have mercy upon us, Lord" and yet, no one had mercy upon them.[2] And I asked the angel and said, "Who are they, Lord?" And in response, the angel said to me, "These are the ones who placed no hope in the Lord as a helper." And I asked and said, "Lord, if these souls remain like this, piled one upon the other for thirty or forty generations, unless they are cast deeper down, I do not believe that the pits will hold them all." And he said to me, "The abyss has no end, for beyond this follows what lies beneath it. And it is such that if someone hurled a stone with great strength and aimed it into a very deep pit and it took many hours for it to hit the bottom, this abyss is like that too. Indeed, when souls are cast in there, they barely reach the bottom after forty years have passed." Truly, when I heard this, I mourned and groaned for the human race. In response, the angel said to me, "Why do you mourn? Are you more merciful than God? Indeed, since God is good and he knows that there are punishments, he treats the human race with patience, allowing each person to do their own will during the time that he or she dwells upon the earth."

Yet I looked back at the river of fire and I saw there a man seized by the throat by angels of Tartarus, holding in their hands an iron implement with three hooks, with which they were piercing the entrails of this old man. And I asked the angel and said, "Lord, who is this old man who suffers such torments?" In response, the angel said to me, "The man whom you see was a presbyter, who did not fulfill his ministry well. When he was eating and drinking and fornicating, he was also offering Lord's sacrifice at his holy altar."

And I saw not far off another old man, whom four evil angels were leading, running with great haste, and they submerged him up to his knees in the river of fire and they struck him with stones and wounded his face like a storm and they did not allow him to say, "Have mercy on me." And I asked the angel, and he said to me, "This one whom you see was a bishop, and he did not fulfill his duties well. Indeed, he received a great title, but he did not enter into the holiness of the one who gave the name to him for his entire life, because he made no just judgment and he had no pity for widows and orphans. But now it is paid back to him according to his iniquity and his works."

And I saw another man sunk up to his knees in the river of fire. His hands were stretched out and covered in blood, and worms poured out of his mouth and nostrils, and he was moaning and lamenting. And crying out, he said, "Have mercy upon me, for I am suffering more than any of the others who are subject to this punishment!" And I asked, "Who is this, Lord?" And the angel said to me, "This one whom you see was a deacon, who ate the offerings and fornicated and did no right in the sight of God. For this reason, he suffers this torment forever more."

And I looked and saw at his side another man, whom they brought out in haste and they cast him into the river of fire, and he was sunk up to his knees. And an angel in charge of his torments arrived with a long flaming knife, with which he sliced the lips of this man and his tongue as well. And with sighs, I wept and asked, "Who is that man, Lord?" And he said to me, "That one whom you see was a lector and he read to the people, but he did not follow God's commandments, so now he suffers this particular torment."

And I saw another multitude of pits in the same place and in their midst a river filled with a crowd of men and women, and worms were devouring them. But I wept and with sighs I asked the angel and said, "Lord, who are these ones?" And he said to me, "These are people who demanded interest upon interest [on loans they had made] and placed their trust in their riches, holding out no hope in God, that he would be a helper to them."

And thereafter I looked and saw another exceedingly narrow place, and there was something like a wall and fire all around it. And I saw inside men and women gnawing on their own tongues, and I asked, "Who are these ones, Lord?" And he said to me, "These are people who diminished the word of God in church, paying no attention to it, but acting as though the Lord and his angels meant nothing. For this reason, they now likewise suffer this particular torment."

And I looked and saw another old man down in the pit and his appearance was like blood, and I asked and said, "Lord, what is this place?" And he said to me, "Into this pit flows every torment." And I saw men and women sunk up to their lips and I asked, "Who are these ones, Lord?" And he said to me, "These are sorcerers who provided magical deceptions to men and women and they could find no rest until they died."

And again I saw men and women with a very dark appearance in a pit of fire, and with sighs I cried and asked, "Who are these ones, Lord?" And he said to me, "These are fornicators and cheaters who had wives of their own and committed adultery; likewise, the women who already had husbands cheated in the same way. For this reason, they suffer these torments forever more."

And I saw there girls draped in black garments and four terrifying angels holding in their hands flaming chains, which they put on the necks of the girls and led them into the darkness. And again with tears I asked the angel, "Who are these ones, Lord?" And he said to me, "These are girls who had been virgins, but had lost their virginity without their parents' knowledge. For this reason they suffer these particular torments forever more."

And again, I saw there men and women whose hands and feet had been hacked off. They were naked in a place of ice and snow, and worms devoured them. Seeing them, I cried and asked, "Who are these ones, Lord?" And he said to me, "These are people who harmed orphans and widows and the poor and placed no hope in the Lord. For this reason, they suffer these particular torments forever more."

And I looked and saw others hanging over a channel of water, and their tongues were very dry, and many pieces of fruit were near at hand, but they were not allowed to consume them. And I asked, "Who are these ones, Lord?" And he said to me, "These are people who broke their fast before the proper time. For this reason, they suffer these particular torments forever more."

And I saw other men and women strung up by their eyebrows and hair and the river of fire dragged at them. And I said, "Who are these ones, Lord?" And he said to me, "These are people who did not commit themselves to their own husbands and wives but to adulterers. And for this reason, they suffer these particular torments forever more."

And I saw other men and women covered in dust and their appearance was like blood. And they were in a pit of pitch and sulfur and hastening away in the river of fire. And I asked, "Who are these ones, Lord?" And he said to me, "These are people who committed the wickedness of Sodom and Gomorrah, men upon men. Because of this, they suffer these torments forever more."

And I looked and saw men and women dressed in white clothes, having blind eyes and placed in a pit. And I asked, "Who are these ones, Lord?" And he said to me, "These are pagans who gave alms and yet did not recognize the Lord God. Because of this, they suffer these torments forever more."

And I looked and saw other men and women upon a flaming spit, and beasts were tearing at them, and they were not allowed to say, "Have mercy upon me, Lord." And I saw the angel of torments subjecting them to the worst torture and saying, "Recognize the son of God. For it was preached to you, but you did not listen when the holy scriptures were read to you. Because of this, the judgment of God is just. Your own evil actions have seized you and led you into these torments." But with sighs and tears, I asked, "Who are these men and women who are strangled in this fire and suffer these torments?" And he responded to me, "These are women who defiled the creation of God when they aborted infants from the womb, and those are the men who lay with them." Indeed, the infants of these women addressed the Lord God and the angels in charge of the torments, saying, "Protect us from our parents, for they have defiled the creation of God. They possessed the name of God but did not follow his commandments. They abandoned us to be eaten by dogs and trampled by pigs. Others they cast into the river." But these infants were delivered to the angels of Tartarus in charge of the torments, who led them to a spacious place of mercy. But their fathers and mothers were tortured in everlasting torment.

And after this, I saw men and women wrapped in clothing full of pitch and burning sulfur and there were dragons coiled around their necks and shoulders and feet, and angels with fiery horns grasped them and struck them and blocked up their nostrils, saying to them, "Why did you not know the time when it was right for you to repent and serve God and you did nothing?" And I asked, "Who are these ones, Lord?" And he said to me, "These are people who seemed to make a renunciation to the Lord (during baptism), wearing our habit, but the hindrances of the world made them miserable and unable to show love. They had no pity on widows and orphans, received no stranger or pilgrim, made no offering, and had no pity on their neighbor. Their prayer did not ascend pure to the Lord God even one day, but the many hindrances of the world held them back and they could not do right in the sight of God, and the angels surrounded them in the place of torments."

———

And with sighs, I wept and said, "Woe to humankind! Woe to sinners! Why were they born?" And in response, the angel said to me, "Why do you weep? Are you more merciful than the Lord God, who is blessed forever, who established the judgment and left everyone to choose good and evil by their own will and to do what they please?" Still I wept again very strongly and he said to me, "You weep, when you have not yet seen the torments that are greater still? Follow me and you will see torments seven times worse than these."

And he took me to the north and set me over a pit, and I found that it was sealed with seven seals. And the angel who was with me said to the angel in charge of that place, "Open the mouth of the pit, so that Paul, the most beloved of God, can look, because the power was given to him to see all of the torments of Hell." And the angel said to me, "Stand back, so that you can endure the stench of this place." Therefore, when the pit had been opened, immediately a harsh and very evil stench arose from it, which surpassed all of the torments. And I looked into the pit and I saw fiery heaps burning on every side, and there was anguish, and the mouth of the pit was so narrow that it fit only one person at a time. And the angel responded and said to me, "If anyone is thrown into this pit of the abyss and it is sealed over him, there will never be a memory of them in the sight of the Father and the Son and the Holy Spirit and the holy angels." And I said, "Who are these ones, Lord, who are thrown into the pit?" And he said to me, "They are people who did not confess that Christ had come in the flesh and that the Virgin Mary bore him and whoever says that the bread and the cup of the blessing of the Eucharist is not the body and blood of Christ."

And I looked farther north and I saw there the worm that does not sleep and in that place there was a gnashing of teeth. The worms had a length of one cubit and there were two heads on them. And I saw there men and women in the cold and gnashing their teeth. And I asked and said, "Lord, who are these ones in this place?" And he said to me, "These are the people who said that Christ did not rise from the dead and that his flesh did not rise again." And I asked and said, "Lord, is there no fire or heat in this place?" And he said to me, "In this place there is nothing except for cold and snow." And again, he said to me, "Indeed, if the sun rose upon them, they would feel no warmth because of the extreme cold of this place and the snow."

Hearing this, I extended my hands and wept and with sighs, I said once more, "It would be better for us if we had never been born because we are all sinners!"

THE RICH MAN AND
LAZARUS[1]

*The earliest Christians esteemed the Jewish patriarchs and
prophets as messengers who foretold the coming of Christ,
but theologians wrestled with the problem of the fate of these
righteous Jews after death. Would everyone who lived before
Christ's earthly ministry be damned to eternal torment simply
because of the bad timing of their birth? Augustine of Hippo
(354–430 CE) drew on the prophet Hosea 13.14 ("I will deliver them from the power of death. I will redeem them from
death. O death, I will be your death") to argue that Christ descended into the underworld after his death upon the cross to
rescue the Jewish patriarchs and prophets, who had expressed
their faith in him as a hidden mystery. On account of their
faith, they did not reside in Hell, but in a place adjacent to it
known as "the bosom of Abraham," where they awaited
Christ's birth in peace. Augustine and other theologians
found evidence for this inference in the parable of the rich
man and Lazarus (Luke 16.19–31). While the rich man was
unmistakably confined to Hell for his sins, Lazarus was in
close proximity to him, yet comforted in Abraham's bosom.
Later Christian tradition identified Lazarus's location not as
Paradise, but as a part of the underworld known as "the
Limbo of the Patriarchs."*

There was a rich man who dressed in purple and fine linen and
feasted every day in a splendid fashion. And there was a poor
man named Lazarus who lay at his gate covered in sores, longing to be fed by the scraps that fell from the rich man's table.

Moreover, the dogs came and licked his sores. Eventually, the poor man died and was carried by angels to the bosom of Abraham. The rich man died as well and was buried. While he was tormented in Hell, raising his eyes he could see Abraham far off and Lazarus resting in his bosom. And calling out, the rich man said, "Father Abraham, have mercy on me and send Lazarus to touch the tip of his finger in water to cool my tongue, for I am suffering in this flame." And Abraham said to him, "Son, remember how you received good things in your life and Lazarus received bad things, but now here he is comforted, while you in turn suffer. And besides there is a great chasm between us and you, so that those who wished to pass from here to you could not, nor could anyone cross from there to us." And the rich man said, "Then I beg you, Father, to send him to my father's house, for I have five brothers, so that he may warn them, lest they themselves wind up in this place of torments as well." But Abraham said to him, "They have Moses and the prophets; let them listen to them." And the rich man said, "No, Father Abraham, but if one from among the dead goes to them, they will repent." And Abraham said to him, "If they do not listen to Moses and the prophets, they will not be convinced if someone should rise from the dead."

DEATH'S DEFEAT: THE HARROWING OF HELL[1]

The legend of Christ's descent into Hell during the three days between his death on Good Friday and his resurrection from the tomb on Easter Sunday is one of the most popular stories in the Christian tradition, but like the Apocalypse of Paul, *it was never recognized as part of the authoritative canon of Christian scriptures. Attributed to a sympathetic Pharisee named Nicodemus, who visited with Jesus during his ministry (John 3.1–29) and later helped Joseph of Arimathea prepare his body for burial (John 19.38–42), the legend was most likely composed in Greek many centuries after the death of Christ. By the early Middle Ages, it had been translated into Latin and several other languages and circulated widely in western Europe as part of a story cycle known as the* Gospel of Nicodemus.

The Gospel of Nicodemus *recounted Christ's dramatic trial before Pontius Pilate and the machinations of the Jewish high priests Annas and Caiphas, who successfully sought the humiliation and execution of Jesus, whom they viewed as a rival to their religious authority. It concluded with the Harrowing of Hell, being an account of Christ's rescue of Adam and the Old Testament patriarchs and prophets from the underworld and the defeat of Satan and Death by his sacrifice on the cross. Much to the dismay of Annas and Caiphas, many people swore that they had seen Jesus alive after his crucifixion and had witnessed his ascension into Heaven. Moreover, when he freed the patriarchs and prophets from the underworld, Jesus also resurrected from their tombs many local individuals, including the twin sons of the high priest Simeon. The last section of the* Gospel of Nicodemus *reported the oath-bound testimony of these two brothers, who were rescued from Hell by Jesus and provided a firsthand account of their experience in the afterlife.*

Similar to Hades in Greek and Roman thought, the Gospel of Nicodemus *depicted the underworld as a holding pen for the dead, in this case only Adam and the righteous Jewish patriarchs and prophets, who foretold the coming of Christ and through their faith avoided punishment in the afterlife. This subterranean realm was under the dominion of Inferus, a personification of Hell, who ruled over a host of impious minions in a featureless kingdom protected by impenetrable gates of bronze. At the side of Inferus was the fallen angel Satan, "prince of perdition and duke of death." The relationship between these infernal allies deteriorated as Christ approached Hell, trampled its gates, and emptied the underworld of the righteous dead. At the end of the story, the patriarchs and prophets ascended to Heaven with Jesus, leaving Satan bound in solitary confinement as the last prisoner of Hell until the Day of Judgment.*

And rising up, Joseph of Arimathea said to Annas and Caiphas, "You are truly and well amazed because you have heard that Jesus was seen alive after being dead and has ascended into Heaven. Indeed, it is even more amazing because not only has he risen from the dead, but he has also restored to life from their tombs many others who have died, and they have been seen by many people in Jerusalem. And hear me now, for we all know blessed Simeon, the high priest, who held Jesus in his hands in the Temple when he was an infant. And Simeon himself had two sons, twin brothers, and we were all there when they were laid to rest and buried. Go, therefore, and see their tombs, for they are open because Simeon's sons have been raised from the dead and behold, they are now alive in the city of Arimathea. They can be heard crying out in their prayers, but otherwise they speak with no one; indeed, they are as silent as the dead. But come, let us go to them with all honor and decorum and let us bring them to Jerusalem. And under oath, perhaps they will tell us about the mystery of their resurrection from the dead."

Hearing this, everyone rejoiced. And setting out, Annas, Caiphas, Nicodemus, Joseph, and Gamaliel did not find the brothers in their tombs, but going to the city of Arimathea, they found them there praying on bent knees. And kissing them with all due veneration and fear of God, they led them to the synagogue in Jerusalem. And after the doors had been closed, lifting up the law of the Lord, they placed it in their hands, binding them by oath by the God of Adonai and the God of Israel, who spoke to our fathers through the law and the prophets, "If you believe that this is the one who restored you from the dead, tell us how you have been raised from the dead."

Hearing this oath, Karinus and Leucius trembled and groaned, troubled in their hearts. And looking up toward heaven together, they made a small sign of the cross with their fingers on their tongues and immediately they spoke as one, saying, "Give to each of us a roll of parchment and let us write down what we have seen and heard." And sitting down, each of them wrote in this way, saying,

"Jesus Christ, Lord God, the resurrection of the dead and life itself, allow us to declare your mysteries through your death of the cross, for we are sworn to you. For you have ordered your servants to reveal to no one the secrets of your divine majesty, which you wrought in Hell. When we were placed with all of our fathers in the depths in the blackness of the shadows, suddenly there appeared the golden glow of the sun and a regal, purple light shining upon us. At once, Adam, the father of all humankind, with all the patriarchs and prophets rejoiced, saying, 'That light is the author of everlasting light, who has promised to send his eternal light to us.' And Isaiah cried out and said, 'This is the light of the Father, the son of God, just as I foretold when I was alive on earth, "The land of Zabulon and the land of Neptalim across the river Jordan of the race of Galilee; a people who dwelled in darkness will see a great light and a light will shine upon those in the region of the shadow of death."[2] And now he has arrived and enlightened those of us who dwell in death.'"

And while we were all rejoicing in the light that shone upon us, our father Simeon came and rejoicing, he said to everyone, "Glorify the Lord Christ, Son of God, because I took him up in my hands as a newborn child in the Temple and, moved by the Holy Spirit, I said to him, confessing, 'Now my eyes have seen your salvation, which you have prepared in the sight of all people, a light for the revelation of the Gentiles and the glory of your people Israel.'"[3] Hearing these things, the entire multitude of saints rejoiced even more.

And after this there approached a man who looked like a little hermit and everyone asked, "Who are you?" Responding to them, he said, "I am John, the voice and prophet of the Most High, the herald before the face of his arrival to prepare his ways to give knowledge of salvation to his people for the forgiveness of sins. And seeing Jesus approach me, moved by the Holy Spirit, I said, confessing, 'Behold the Lamb of God, behold the one who takes away the sins of the world.'[4] And I baptized him in the river Jordan and I saw the Holy Spirit descending upon him in the form of a dove, and I heard a voice from heaven, saying, 'This is my beloved Son, in whom I am well pleased.'[5] And now I have come before his face and have come down to announce to you that the Son of God will visit us soon like the dawn from on high, coming to us who dwell in the darkness and the shadow of death."

And when the first-created man, our father Adam, had heard these things, that Jesus was baptized in the river Jordan, he called out to his son Seth and said, "Declare to your sons, the patriarchs and the prophets everything you heard from the archangel Michael when I sent out to the gates of Paradise to entreat God to send to you his angel, to give to you oil from the tree of mercy, so that you might anoint my body when I was sick." Then Seth, approaching the patriarchs and prophets, said, "When I was praying to the Lord at the gates of Paradise, behold, the angel of the Lord, Michael, appeared to me, saying, 'I have been sent to you by the Lord; I am appointed to preside over the human body. Indeed, I say to you, Seth, do not labor with tears in praying and entreating God for oil of the tree of mercy, so that you may anoint your father Adam to relieve his body's pain, because you cannot obtain it from Him by any means until the very last days, after five thousand and five hundred years have passed. Then Christ, the most beloved son of God, will come upon the earth; he will raise up the body of Adam and raise up with him the bodies of the dead and heal every sickness. And he himself will come to the river Jordan and be baptized. When he has come out of the water of the Jordan, then he will anoint everyone who believes in him with the oil of mercy and that oil of mercy will be for the generation of those borne from the water and the spirit into eternal life. Amen. Then coming down to earth, Christ, the most beloved son of God will lead your father Adam into paradise to the tree of mercy.'"

When all the patriarchs and prophets heard all these things from Seth, they rejoiced with great joy.

And while all of the saints were rejoicing, behold, Satan, the prince and captain of death, said to Inferus, "Prepare yourself to receive Jesus himself, who boasts that he is the Christ, the son of God, [when in fact] he is a man who fears death, saying, 'My soul is sorrowful, even unto death.'⁶ And he has opposed me in many ways, doing many evil things to me, and many whom I made blind, lame, bent, leprous, and tormented, he healed with a word, and those whom I brought to you dead, he has taken away from you alive."

Responding to Satan the prince, Inferus said, "How is this one so powerful when he is a man who fears death? For all of the powers of the earth have been made subject to my power, which you have brought down [to me] subject to your power. But if you are powerful, how is it that this man Jesus, who fears death, stands against your power? If he is so powerful in his human nature, truly I say to you that he is all-powerful in his divine nature and no one can resist his power. And if he says that he is afraid of death, he wished to ensnare you and woe it will be for you forever." Satan, the prince of Tartarus, said in response, "Why have you expressed doubt and fear to receive this Jesus, my adversary and yours? For I have tempted him, and I have stirred up my ancient people the Jews with jealousy and anger against him. I sharpened the spear for his suffering; I mixed the gall and vinegar to offer him a drink; I prepared the cross to crucify him and the nails to pierce him; and last of all I caused his death, so that I may lead him to you, subject to you and to me."

Responding, Inferus said, "You told me that this is the man who took away the dead from me. Indeed, there are many who have been kept here by me who, while they lived on earth, took the dead from me, not by their own powers, but by divine prayers; and their almighty God took them from me. Who then is this Jesus, who by his word took the dead from me without prayers? Perhaps he is the same person who raised Lazarus to life, whom I held as a dead man stinking and rotting for four days, whom I returned alive by the word of his power." Satan said to him in response, "That man is Jesus himself." Hearing this, Inferus said to him, "I order you by your powers and mine not to bring that man to me. For at that time, when I heard the power of his word, I trembled, terrified with fear, and all of my impious officials were likewise disturbed like me. And we were not able to detain Lazarus, but shaking himself like an eagle, he leaped up with all agility and swiftness and departed from us, and the very earth that had housed the dead body of Lazarus returned him alive. So now I know that that man, who can do these things, is God, strong in his power, mighty in his humanity, and the savior of humankind. And if you lead this man to me, he will set free everyone who is locked up here in the prison of their disbelief and bound with the unbreakable chains of their sins, and by the power of his divinity he will lead them to life everlasting."

And while Prince Satan and Inferus were talking about these matters to each other, there was a voice like thunder and an unearthly sound, "Lift up your gates, O princes, and rise up, everlasting gates, and the King of Glory will enter." Hearing these things, Inferus said to Prince Satan, "Depart from me! Go forth from my abode! If you are a mighty warrior, fight with the King of Glory. What have you to do with him?" And Inferus cast Satan out from his abode. And Inferus said to his impious officials, "Close the cruel bronze gates and set in place the iron bars and resist bravely so that we captors are not taken as captives."

Hearing these things, the whole multitude of saints rebuked Inferus, saying, "Open your gates so that the King of Glory may enter!" And David cried out, saying, "While I was alive on earth, did I not foretell to you, 'Let them confess to the Lord his mercy and his wonders to the sons of men, for he has crushed the bronze gates and broken the iron bars. He has taken them up from the path of their iniquity.'?"7 And likewise, after this Isaiah said to all of the saints, "While I was alive on earth, did I not foretell to you, 'Let the dead rise and let those in their tombs rise and let those on earth rejoice, because the dew that is salvation from the Lord is in them.?"8 And again I said, 'Death, where is your sting? Inferus, where is your victory?'"9

Hearing these things from Isaiah, all of the saints said to Inferus, "Open your gates! Now you will be defeated, weak and powerless." And there was a great voice like thunder, saying, "Lift up your gates, O princes, and rise up, everlasting gates, and the King of Glory will enter." Inferus, seeing that they cried these things twice, as though he did not understand, asked, "Who is this King of Glory?" Responding to Inferus, David said, "I recognize those words of acclamation because I foretold them through his spirit. And what I said previously I will now say to you, 'The Lord is strong and powerful. The Lord, mighty in battle, is himself the King of Glory. And the Lord himself has looked down from heaven upon the earth to hear the groaning of the prisoners and to free the sons of those appointed to die.'10 And now, most filthy and fetid Inferus, open your gates so that the King of Glory may enter!" While David was saying these things to Inferus, the King of Glory approached in the form of a man, the Lord of Majesty, and illuminated the eternal darkness, and broke the unbreakable chains. With the aid of his invincible power, he visited those of us residing in the darkness of our failures and in the shadow of the death of our sins.

Seeing these things, Inferus and Death and their impious officials with their cruel ministers were seized with fear in their own kingdoms once the brightness of such a great light had been discerned. When they saw Christ appear so suddenly in their midst, they cried out, saying, "We have been conquered by you. Who are you who has been directed by the Lord to cause us such confusion? Who are you who, with no taint of corruption, the irrefutable evidence of your majesty, condemns our power with rage? Who are you, at once so great and so small, so humble and so grand, soldier and emperor, an esteemed warrior in a servant's guise, and the King of Glory, dead yet alive, whom the cross carried off to death? You lay dead in the tomb, yet you have come down to us alive. And upon your death every creature trembled and all of the stars were shaken. And now you have your freedom among the dead and you confound our legions. Who are you who frees those captives who have been detained, bound by original sin, and summons them back to their former freedom? Who are you who imbues those blinded by the darkness of their sins with a divine light so splendid and dawn-bright?" Likewise, all of the legions of demons were seized with horror and creeping dread and cried out in one voice, saying "How is it, Jesus, that you are a man so strong and splendid in your majesty, so glorious without stain and pure beyond reproach? For that earthly world that has been subject to us until now, which sent us tributes for our use, has never sent such a dead man to us, never directed such gifts to Hell. Therefore, who are you who has entered our borders with such courage? Not only do you not cower before our torments, but you also attempt to free everyone from their chains. Perhaps you are that Jesus, concerning whom our prince Satan said that through your death on the cross he was going to receive the power of the entire world."

Then the King of Glory, the Lord, trampling Death with his majesty, seized Prince Satan, delivered him to the power of Inferus, and led Adam to his brightness.

Then Inferus, taking hold of Prince Satan, said to him with great indignation, "O prince of perdition and duke of death, Beelzebub, scorn of God's angels, spittle of the just, why did you want to do this? Why at the destruction of this man did you promise so many spoils of his death to us? Like a fool, you did not know what you were doing. Behold, now with the splendor of his divinity this Jesus puts to flight all of the shadows of death, and breaks the sturdy prison, and evicts the captives, releasing those who were bound. And everyone who used to groan under our torments now abuses us, and they topple our empires and overthrow our kingdoms with their prayers and the human race

fears us no longer. Furthermore, the dead who were never inso-
lent with us and the captives who had abandoned all joy now
threaten us boldly. O prince Satan, father of the evil, impious
and outcast, why did you want to do this? Among those who
from the beginning until the present had no hope of salvation
and life, now none of their usual moans is heard, nor do any of
their groans resound, and no hint of tears can be found on their
faces. O prince Satan, keeper of the keys of Hell, all of your
riches, which you had acquired through the forbidden tree and
the loss of paradise, you have now lost through the wood of the
cross and all of your joy has perished. When you crucified this
Christ, the King of Glory, you acted against your own interest
and mine. Now recognize how many eternal torments and infinite punishments you are going to suffer in my everlasting cus-
tody. O prince Satan, author of death and source of pride, you
should have first found a cause of sin in this Jesus. And when
you found no blame, why did you dare to crucify him unjustly
without a reason and why did you bring an innocent and just
man into our kingdom, and why have you lost the guilty, the impious, and the unjust of the entire world?"

And after Inferus had said these things to Prince Satan, then the
King of Glory said to Inferus, "Prince Satan will be under your
power forever in place of Adam and his sons, my righteous ones."

And holding out his hand, the Lord said, "Come to me, all of
my saints, who have my image and my likeness. You who have
been condemned by the tree and the devil and death, behold now
the devil and death condemned by the cross." Immediately, all
of the saints came together under the hand of God. Then, holding
the right hand of Adam, the Lord said to him, "Peace be with you
and all your sons, my righteous ones." Then Adam threw himself
at the knees of the Lord, offered up a tearful prayer, and pro-
claimed with a loud voice, "I will praise you, Lord, because you
have lifted me up, and you have not let my enemies triumph over
me. O Lord, my God, I have cried out to you and you have healed
me. Lord, you have brought forth my soul from Hell. You have
saved me from those falling down into the pit. Sing to the Lord,
O you his saints, and give praise to the memory of his holiness,
for there is wrath in his indignation and there is life in his good

will."[11] Likewise, all of the saints fell to their knees at the feet of the Lord and said in one voice, "You have come, O redeemer of the world; you have fulfilled with your deeds what you foretold through the law and your prophets. You have redeemed the living by your cross and you have come down to us by your death on the cross, to deliver us from Hell and death by your majesty. Lord, just as you have placed the banner of your glory in heaven and set up the sign of your redemption—your cross—on earth, place here in Hell, O Lord, a token of the victory of your cross, so that death may hold dominion no longer."

Then, holding out his hand, the Lord made the sign of the cross upon Adam and upon all of his saints, and holding Adam's right hand, he ascended from Hell and all of the saints followed the Lord. Then, holy David called out bravely, saying, "Sing to the Lord a new song because the Lord has made wonders. His right hand will make for him salvation and his arm is holy. The Lord has made known his salvation; he has revealed his justice in the sight of the Gentiles."[12] And the entire multitude of saints responded, saying, "This glory is to all of his saints. Amen. Alleluia."[13]

And after this, the prophet Habakkuk called out, saying, "You went forth for the salvation of your people to liberate your chosen ones."[14] And all of the saints responded, saying, "Blessed is he who comes in the name of the Lord; the Lord God has illuminated us. Amen. Alleluia." Likewise, after this, the prophet Micah also called out, saying, "What God is like you, O Lord, who takes away iniquities and removes sins? And now you hold back your wrath as a testimony because you are willingly merciful. And you have turned yourself away [from your wrath] and have had mercy on us and have forgiven all of our iniquities and all of our sins. And you have plunged all of our sins [into the depths] with the throng of death just as you promised to our fathers in the days of old." And all of the saints responded, saying, "This is our God forever and unto ages of ages and he will rule us forever more. Amen. Alleluia."[15] Thus, as all of the prophets uttered these sacred words with praises that they had already spoken in prophecy and as all of the saints called out "Amen, Alleluia," they followed the Lord out of Hell.

ON THE LIP OF THE ABYSS: THE EARLY MIDDLE AGES (c. 500–1000 CE)

Early medieval Christians inherited from pagan and Jewish traditions a firm understanding of Hell as a place where impious souls suffered after death, but they wrestled with the notion of where it was located. During the "dark ages" of European history (500–750 CE), monastic authors depicted the location and features of Hell in stories about visions of the afterlife. In these stories, the souls of ailing individuals made journeys to the otherworld to witness the horrors of Hell and the pleasures of Heaven, before returning to tell their tales to the living to encourage the cultivation of virtue and the avoidance of sin. The depiction of Hell in these stories was complicated by the fact that Christian thinkers like Pope Gregory the Great (c. 540–604 CE) and the Venerable Bede (672/73–735 CE) were also formulating the earliest ideas about Purgatory, a place between Heaven and Hell where the souls of the dead suffered in fire to purge them of their sins before they entered Heaven.

The introduction of the concept of Purgatory had a strong influence on depictions of Hell in the early Middle Ages. Whereas souls in Purgatory had every hope of entering Heaven once their painful cleansing by fire was complete, the wicked bound for Hell would never escape the punishments awaiting them there. Their suffering would last forever. As a result, early medieval visions of the afterlife written by Gregory the Great and the Venerable Bede focused on the transient torments of sinful souls preparing for entry into Heaven and brought the reader only to the lip of Hell's abyss without venturing any further, perhaps because the horrors awaiting unrepentant sinners were not as useful for encouraging the moral reform of individuals as the pains of Purgatory or perhaps because they were simply too terrible to contemplate. In contrast, the story of Saint Brendan's encounter with Judas Iscariot on the trackless ocean blended elements of pre-Christian Irish mythology, particularily the immram *tradition, in which heroes traveled by sea to the otherworld, and the ancient Homeric tradition, which located the entrance to Hades on a dark and distant shore.*

BEYOND THE BLACK RIVER [1]

In the sixth century, Pope Gregory the Great answered questions about the fate of the souls of ordinary Christians posed to him by a young disciple named Peter. His answers appeared in the final book of his four-volume Dialogues, *which Gregory completed in 594. In response to Peter's question about souls that seem to have been taken out of their bodies in error, Gregory told three anecdotes he had heard from reliable witnesses about individuals on the brink of death who had been given a glimpse of Hell before returning to their bodies. In some cases, these individuals learned from their experience and embraced a life of repentance in fear of what they had seen in the world to come. In other cases, however, the vision of Hell inspired no correction and served only as a dire foreshadowing of the torments awaiting the sinner.*

For a certain monk from Illyria, who once lived in Rome in the monastery with me, used to tell me that when he still lived in the wilderness, he knew a Spanish monk named Peter, who abided with him in a place of empty solitude called Evasa. He had learned from Peter that, before he had sought the wilderness, he had died due to a sickness of the body, but he was immediately restored to life and claimed that he had seen the punishments of Hell and an endless landscape of flames. He also said that he had seen powerful men of this world suspended in those flames.

As he was being carried to be plunged into Hell, Peter confessed that an angel in shining raiment suddenly appeared, who prevented him from being thrown into the fire. Indeed, it said to him, "Go back, and pay careful attention to how you live your life from now on." After this warning, his limbs warmed little by little as he awoke from the sleep of eternal death. He reported all of the things that had happened around him and devoted himself thereafter to so many vigils and fasts that his new way of life spoke of the torments of Hell that he had seen and feared, even though his tongue remained silent. Thus, the wonderous mercy of almighty God brought about his temporary demise so that he did not have to die forever.

But because the human heart is especially hard, a vision of the torments of Hell is not as useful to everyone. For a distinguished man named Steven, whom you know well, had told me himself that when he tarried in the city of Constantinople for some reason, he was overcome by a bodily illness and died. Since a doctor and an embalmer had been sought to open him up and embalm him, but had not been found on that day, his body lay unburied on the following night.

Led to the domains of Hell, Steven saw many things that he did not believe in when he had heard about them while he was alive. But when he was brought before the judge who presided there, he was turned away. As the judge said, "I did not order this Steven to be brought, but rather Steven the blacksmith." Our Steven was immediately sent back to his own body, and Steven the blacksmith, who lived near him, died that very same hour. Thus, it was shown that the words he had heard were true, as the blacksmith's death proved.

Our Steven died three years later during that epidemic that depopulated this city with such vehement destruction, during which, as you know, people saw with their own eyes arrows falling from heaven to strike particular individuals. At this time, a soldier was struck down in our city and brought near to death. As he lay at death's door, his soul was led from his body, but it quickly returned and he recounted everything that had happened to it.

For he said—as many reported at the time—that he saw a bridge. Under it flowed a black river veiled in mist that poured forth a cloud of intolerable stench. Across the bridge there were green and pleasant meadows adorned with scented flowers. In the meadows could be seen companies of people all clad in white. There was such an aroma of sweetness in that place that the fragrance pleased everyone who walked about and dwelt there.

There were dwellings of different sizes, full of light, including a magnificent house, which seemed to have been built of gold bricks, but whose house it was, he could not tell. Upon the banks of the river there were a few smaller dwellings. Some the vapors of drifting stench defiled; others the reek rising from the river barely touched at all.

Crossing the bridge was a trial. If the unjust tried to cross, they would slip into the black and fetid river, while those who were just and unburdened by sin could traverse it safely and easily to the pleasant meadows beyond.

The soldier confessed that he also saw Peter there, an overseer of the church, who had died four years before. He was thrust down in a filthy place, mired and bound with a great weight of iron. When the soldier asked why he suffered in this way, he said that he was told things that those of us who knew him in the church recalled, knowing what he had done. For Peter said, "I am suffering this torment because when I was ordered to punish someone, I obeyed and inflicted the blows more out of cruelty than out of obedience." No one who knew him had any doubts that this was true.

The soldier said that he saw a foreign presbyter approach the bridge and cross it with great confidence because he had lived with such integrity. On the same bridge, he swore that he recognized our Steven, whom I spoke about before. While he was crossing, his foot slipped and he fell with half of his body dangling from the bridge. Reeking creatures rose up from the river to pull him down by the hips, while the most handsome figures in white pulled him upward by the arms. While this struggle was taking place, as the good spirits tugged him upward and the evil ones dragged him down, the man who witnessed this returned to his body and did not learn any more about Steven's fate.

In this story, we learn something about the life of Steven

because in this man the evils of the flesh wrestled with the work of almsgiving. Indeed, as he was dragged down by the hips and pulled up by the arms, it is very clear that he had loved to give alms and yet had not completely forsaken the sins of the flesh that pulled him down. But which side won out in that trial of the hidden judge, neither we nor the one who saw him can say.

It is clear, however, that this Steven returned to his body after he saw the domains of Hell (as I described earlier) and did not completely correct his life. Several years later, he departed from his body, his soul the prize in a contest between life and death. Concerning this, we learn that when people experience visions of Hell, to some it is a help, but to others it serves as a testimony that those who witness evils that they can prevent will be punished all the more because they could not avoid the torments of Hell that they had already seen and known to be true.

BEHOLD, THE FIRE DRAWS NEAR ME[1]

The Venerable Bede, a monk of the abbey of Wearmouth-Jarrow in Northumbria, narrated two accounts of other-worldly journeys in his Ecclesiastical History of the English People *(completed 731). The first of these concerned a monk named Fursa. After falling into a trance due to an illness, this ascetic experienced a vision of Hell featuring a dark valley and four balls of fire that floated in the air, each one representing a particular sin. Although he was protected by angelic escorts, Fursa received burns from the scorching soul of a sinner he had known in life. Much to his surprise, upon his return to his own body, he discovered that he bore scars where the hellfire had touched him. These scars served not only as proof that his story was true but also as a painful reminder of the fate in store for sinners in the afterlife.*

Among these stories there is one, which we thought it would be useful to put in this history for the benefit of many. When Fursa had been lifted up on high, he was ordered by the angels who were carrying him to look upon the world. As he directed his eyes downward, he saw some kind of dark valley beneath him far below, and he saw four fires in the air very close to one another. And when he asked the angels what these fires were, he learned that these were the fires that would kindle and eventually consume the world: one is the fire of falsehood, when we do not fulfill what we promised in baptism to renounce Satan and all of his works; another is the fire of avarice, when we place our love of worldly riches before our love of the riches of heaven; the third is the fire of discord, when we do not fear to offend the souls of our neighbors even in superficial matters; and the fourth fire is irreverence, when we think it nothing to despoil and defraud those weaker than ourselves. Little by little, the fires merged together and became one immense conflagration. When the fires approached, Fursa said to the angel in fear, "Lord, behold the fire draws near me." But the angel replied, "What you did not kindle will not burn you.[2] Although this pyre seems great and frightening, it tests each person according to the merits of their works, and the sin of each person will burn in that flame. For just as someone's body burns due to illicit desire, thus the person freed from the body will burn due to the punishment owed for the sin."

Then Fursa saw one of the three angels, who had served as his guides in both of his visions, flying forward to divide the flames, and the other two flew around on either side of him to protect him from the threat of the fires. He also saw demons flying amid the flames to marshal the fury of hostilities against the just. There followed the accusations of evil spirits against him, the defences of good spirits on his behalf, and a fuller vision not only of the heavenly hosts but also of the holy men from his own nation.[3] Fursa learned from popular report that they had obtained high ranks of the priesthood in their day and from them he heard not a few things that were beneficial to himself or to anyone who wished to listen. When they had finished speaking and they returned to Heaven once more with the angelic spirits, the three angels, concerning whom we have spoken, remained with the blessed Fursa to take him back to his body. When they drew near to the great conflagration, the angel divided the flames, as before. But when Fursa came to the passage that the angel had opened amid the flames, evil spirits seized one of the souls that was roasting in the fire and hurled it directly at Fursa, striking his shoulder and jaw and burning him. Fursa recognized the man and recalled that he had received some of his clothing when he had died. The holy angel immediately grabbed the soul and cast it back into the fire. The malicious adversary taunted them, "Do not reject the one whom you once acknowledged, for just as you received the sinner's goods, so too you ought to share in his torments." The angel spoke against him, saying, "He did not receive it out of greed, but to save his soul." And just then, the fire died down. And turning to Fursa, the angel said, "What you kindled has burned you. For if you had not received the goods of this man, who died in his sins, his punishment would not have hurt you." And the angel then taught Fursa many things with saving words concerning what should be done for the salvation of those who repent at death's door.

After he had been restored to his body, for the rest of his life Fursa carried on his shoulder and jaw the scars of those burns that he had received in the spirit, visible for all to see. It is amazing that what the soul suffered in secret, the flesh displayed so openly. Fursa always took care, just as he used to do before, to model for everyone the work of virtues by his example and to preach it with his words. He talked about his visions only to those who asked him because of their desire to repent. There is an aged brother of our monastery who used to tell us that a very truthful and devout man had told him that he had seen Fursa himself in the kingdom of the East Angles and had heard the story of these visions from the saint's own mouth. He added that their conversation had taken place in a very harsh winter season in the grip of a hard frost. Although he was sitting in a thin garment while they spoke, Fursa was sweating as though in the heat of high summer, either because of the magnitude of the fear evoked by these memories or the enormity of his joy in their recollection.

DRYHTHELM RETURNS
FROM THE DEAD[1]

*The second otherworldly journey related by the Venerable
Bede concerned a monk named Dryhthelm, whose soul journeyed far from his body to witness a variety of torments that
the dead endured to prepare them for God's final judgment.
Dryhthelm's experience unmasked the ambiguous topography of the afterlife in early medieval thought. As the monk
watched souls being tortured in turn by scorching heat and
painful cold, he wondered if he was looking upon Hell, only
to be told by his angelic guide that he was not. Only later did
he venture farther on to a shadowy place infested with demons, where jets of flame filled with doomed souls spouted
over a dark pit. This was without doubt the entrance to Hell.
In the newly converted territories of the Anglo-Saxons,
Dryhthelm's vision of "the flame-spitting abyss" sounded a
dire warning. Only those believers who embraced the Christian faith with a true change of heart and a contempt for this
world would experience God's abiding presence in Heaven.
The rest could anticipate an eternity of excruciating torment
in the company of demons.*

Around that time, a remarkable miracle occurred in Britain
similar to those that happened long ago. For in order to arouse
the living from the death of the soul, a certain man who was
already dead returned to life and he recounted many things
worthy of remembering that he had seen. I think that it is
worth gathering some of them together briefly in this work.
There was a man, the father of a family in the region of

Northumbria called Cunningham, who was leading a religious life with the rest of his household. Laid low by a bodily illness and brought to death's door as it grew worse day by day, he died in the early hours of the evening. When the sun rose, however, he returned to life and immediately sat up. Everyone who had been sitting around his body in mourning was struck with a great fear and turned in flight. Only his wife remained, for she loved him very much, though she trembled with fright. He consoled her by saying, "Do not fear, for truly I have now risen from the death by which I was held and I have been permitted to live among humankind once more. Nevertheless, from this time forward I must conduct my life very differently than I had before." He immediately got up and went to the oratory in the village, where he prayed well into the day. Soon thereafter he divided everything that he possessed into three separate portions. He gave one portion to his wife and another to his sons, but the third he retained for his own good by giving it directly to the poor. Not long thereafter he abandoned the cares of this world by entering the monastery at Melrose, which is enclosed almost entirely by a bend in the river Tweed. Once he had received his tonsure, he entered his own secluded cell, which the abbot had provided for him. There until the day of his death he lived a life of great repentance of mind and body, so that even if his tongue was silent, his life would have revealed that this man had seen many things either dreadful or desired that have been concealed from other men.

He told us what he had seen with the following words: "A man with a luminous appearance and bright clothing was my guide. We went forth without speaking in what seemed to me to be the direction of the rising of the sun at the solstice. As we walked, we arrived at a valley that was very broad and deep and seemed to stretch on forever to our left. One side of the valley was very terrifying with raging flames; the other was equally intolerable owing to fierce hail and cold blasts of snow gusting and blowing away everything in sight. Both sides were teeming with the souls of men, which seemed to be thrown back and forth, as though by the onslaught of a storm. When those poor souls could no longer endure the intensity of the immense heat, they leaped into the midst of the deadly cold. And when they could find no respite there, they leaped back to the other side to burn in the midst of those unquenchable flames. Since a countless number of misshapen souls was subject to the torture of this alternating misery far and wide as far as I could see without any hope of respite, I began to think that perhaps this was Hell, for I had often heard stories about the agonizing torments there. My guide, who walked ahead of me, answered my thought: 'Do not believe this, for this is not the Hell you are thinking of.'

"But when he led me a little way further on, completely shaken by this terrifying scene, suddenly I noticed that the places before us began to grow gloomier and covered in darkness. As we entered this place, the shadows became so thick that I could see nothing else except for the outline and garment of my guide. As we progressed through the shadows in the lonely night, behold, suddenly there appeared before us thick masses of noisome flames spouting up into the air as though from a great pit before falling back into it again. When we arrived in this place, my guide suddenly disappeared and abandoned me alone in the midst of the shadows and this terrifying scene. As the masses of flames spouted to the heights and plunged to the depths of the pit over and over again, I saw that the tips of the rising flames were full of human souls, which like sparks ascending with smoke shot up to the heights and then, when the flames withdrew, fell back into the depths once again. Moreover, an incomparable stench poured forth with these flames and filled this entire realm of shadows. And after I had stood there for a long time, unsure what I should do or which way to turn or what fate awaited me, suddenly I heard behind me the sound of a great and most wretched wailing and at the same time raucous laughter as though some illiterate rabble was hurling insults at enemies they had captured. And as the noise became louder and finally reached me, I saw a crowd of evil spirits cheering and laughing as they dragged the souls of five people crying and wailing into the midst of the shadows. I could discern among these people one tonsured like a priest, a layman, and a woman. Dragging the souls with them, the evil spirits descended into the midst of the burning pit, and it happened that, as they went further down into the pit, I could not clearly distinguish the wailing of the people and the laughter of the demons, for the sound was confused in my ears. In the meantime, insubstantial spirits rose up out of that flame-spitting abyss and rushing forward, they surrounded me. With flaming eyes and flowing a putrid flame from their mouths and nostrils, they tormented me. They also threatened to grab me with the fiery tongs that they held in their hands, but although they terrified me, they never dared to touch me. Surrounded on every side by enemies and blinded by the shadows, I cast my eyes this way and that way to see if by chance the help that I needed might arrive from somewhere. Back on the road along which we had come there appeared something like the brightness of a star shining among the shadows, which grew little by little as it hastened quickly toward me. When the light approached, all of the vile spirits who were trying to seize me with their tongs scattered and fled.

"It was in fact my guide whose arrival put the spirits to flight. Presently he turned to the right and began to lead me in the direction of the rising sun in wintertime. Without delay he led me out of the shadows and into gentle breezes of serene light. As I followed him in the open light, I saw before us an enormous wall, the height and length of which seemed to have no end. I began to wonder why we were approaching the wall, for I could discern no door or window or stairway anywhere along it. But once we had reached the wall, we immediately found ourselves on top of it, I know not how. And behold there was an expansive and pleasant meadow, filled with such a fragrance of blooming flowers that sweetness of this wonderous smell quickly banished every trace of the stench of that dark furnace that still clung to me. Moreover, such a great light filled the entire place that the meadow seemed to be brighter than the day could ever be or even the rays of the sun at noontime. There were in this meadow countless groups of white-robed people and many parties of rejoicing companions. As

my guide led me among these companies of the glad inhabitants of that place, I began to think that this was perhaps the
kingdom of Heaven, concerning which I had often heard people speak about. He replied to my thought, saying, 'No, this is
not the kingdom of Heaven as you imagine it.'

"When we had moved on and left behind these dwellings of
the blessed spirits, I saw before us a much greater grace of
light than before, in which I could even hear the sweetest
sound of people singing, but the fragrance of such a marvel-
ous smell poured forth from that place that the smell which I
thought was incomparable a short time before paled in comparison to it, and the light of the flowering meadow seemed
very thin and weak. Just as I was hoping that we would enter
the sweetness of this place, suddenly my guide stopped. Without delay, he turned around and led me back by the way that
we had just come.

"When we returned once more to those happy dwellings of
the white-robed spirits, he asked me, 'Do you know what all
of these things are which you have seen?' And I responded,
'No.' And he said, 'That valley, which you saw, so frightful
with its fierce flames and harsh cold, that is the place where
souls are required to be tried and punished because they failed
to confess and make amends for the evil deeds that they committed for they waited to confess until the very moment of
death, and so they died. But even though they delayed confession and penance until their death, all of them will enter
Heaven on the day of judgment. Moreover, the benefits of repeated prayers by the living and alms and fasting and especially the celebration of masses may even release them from
this place before the day of judgment. Furthermore, that foul
pit that vomited flames, which you saw, is the very mouth of
Hell. Whoever falls into it will not be freed for all eternity.
That blooming meadow, in which you saw those very beautiful youths rejoicing and bright, that place receives the souls of
those who died having done good works, but they are not so
perfect that they merit arriving immediately in the kingdom of
Heaven. Nevertheless, on the day of judgment all of them will
enter into the sight of Christ and the joys of the heavenly

kingdom. For whoever is perfect in every word and deed and thought, as soon as they die, they will enter the heavenly kingdom, which is near to that place where you heard the sound of sweet singing accompanied by the pleasing fragrance and the brilliance of light. It is now time for you to return to your body and to dwell among the living once more. But if you apply yourself to paying attention to your actions with greater care and strive to behave and speak in the spirit of righteousness and honesty, then you will receive upon your death a place of dwelling among those rejoicing companies of blessed spirits you saw before. For when I abandoned you for a time, I did so in order to learn what would become of you when you die.' After he had told me these things, I returned to my body most displeased for I had delighted so much in the sweetness and beauty of the place I had seen and equally in the company of those whom I saw dwelling there. I did not dare to ask my guide any other questions, but meanwhile—I do not know how—I suddenly found myself back among the living."

The man of God did not speak about these and other things which he had seen to those who were inactive or careless with respect to their fates, but only to those who, terrified by the fear of torments or delighted by the hope of eternal joys, wanted to draw inspiration from his words for the fulfillment of their piety. For example, near his cell there lived a certain monk by the name of Haemgisl, a priest equal in his good work to his outstanding rank, who still lives as a hermit in Ireland and sustains the last age of his life with a diet of bread and cold water. Often coming to visit this man, Haemgisl learned from him through repeated questioning what kinds of things he experienced when he had departed from his body. Indeed, it was through Haemgisl's report that the few details that we composed above came to our attention. Moreover, he also related his visions to King Aldfrith, a very learned man in every way, who was well disposed to listen to him. At the king's insistence, he entered the monastery mentioned above and was crowned with a monastic tonsure. Whenever the king came to those parts, he went to the monastery very often to hear him speak about his visions. At the time, the community was governed by

Æthelwold, an abbot and priest reknowned for his simple and devout life, who now holds the seat of the bishop of the church of Lindisfarne with deeds worthy of that rank.

In that monastic community, the man received a more isolated dwelling place, where he could devote himself more freely to ceaseless prayers in the service of his Creator. And since his retreat was located on a river bank, he used to enter the water because of his great desire to punish his body and frequently immersed himself under the waves. In this way, he kept himself in the water for as long as he was able, reciting psalms or prayers, remaining still while the water of the river rose up to his loins and even to his neck. And when he left the water, he never bothered to take off his cold and wet garments until they had been warmed and dried by the heat of his own body. When in the winter months, while broken bits of ice floated around him, which he himself sometimes had to break in order to make a place for him to stand or immerse himself in the river, those who saw him would say: "Brother Dryhthelm"—for that was his name—"it is amazing that you have the strength to bear such bitter cold for any reason!" And he responded simply—befitting a man with a plain disposition and a humble nature—"I have seen colder." And when they said, "It is amazing that you wish to endure such a harsh way of life," he responded, "I have seen harder." Thus, until the day he died, with a tireless desire for heavenly joys he subdued his old body with daily fasting and he had a saving influence on many people both with his words and with his way of life.

THE ISLAND OF THE FIRE GIANTS[1]

In the eighth century, an anonymous monk composed an account of an epic sea voyage undertaken by a legendary Irish saint named Brendan, who set sail with sixteen of his brethren in search of the promised land of the saints. Monks of early medieval Ireland often undertook a voluntary exile from their homeland, a hardship that expressed their religious devotion. While these monks typically sought new homes in faraway places like Europe, The Voyage of Saint Brendan *depicted a holy man who ventured on uncharted seas, where he encountered strange islands and monstrous creatures. Toward the end of the voyage, Brendan's ship ventured close to the outskirts of Hell, where the saint and his companions had three fateful encounters: they discovered an island inhabited by hostile fire giants (reminiscent of the Cyclops in Homer's* Odyssey*), who hurled molten slag at their ship; they skirted an enormous mountain with a smoking summit, where demons carried off one of their crew; and they conversed with Judas Iscariot, who was given a rare reprieve from his torments on a storm-tossed crag in the open sea. Drawing upon ancient antecedents and the* immram *tradition of pre-Christian Irish mythology, these depictions of Hell upon the waves were unconventional for the time, but they enjoyed a wide currency among medieval readers.*

After eight days had passed, Brendan and his companions saw an island not far off. It was very rugged, rocky, and covered with slag, without any sign of trees or plants, but full of the forges of smiths. The venerable father said to his brethren, "Truly, brothers, I am distressed about this island. I do not want to go onto it or even to approach it, but the wind drives us toward it as though by the correct course." Then, as they approached even closer, until they were only a stone's throw away, they heard the sound of bellows blowing like thunder and the striking of hammers on iron and anvils. When he heard these sounds, the venerable father armed himself by making the sign of the cross on four parts of his body, saying, "Lord Jesus Christ, free us from this island."

Once the man of God had spoken, behold one of the inhabitants of the island appeared outside as though to do some work. He was very hairy, yet blackened and covered with flames. When he saw the servants of Christ passing close to the island, he withdrew into his forge. The man of God armed himself once more with the sign of the cross and said to the brethren, "Little brothers, raise the sails up high and row as fast as you can. Let us flee this island!" As soon as Brendan said this, behold the monster ran toward them from its lair as far as the shoreline, carrying tongs in its hands with a huge fiery mass of burning slag. He immediately hurled this mass toward the servants of Christ, but it did them no harm. Indeed, it missed them by the length of a stade or more.[2] Where it fell into the sea, the water began to boil as though the ruin of a fiery mountain had been there and smoke rose from the sea as though from a blazing furnace.

But by the time that they had sailed about a mile from the place where the slag mass had fallen, all of the creatures that lived on that island ran down to the shoreline, each carrying their own masses of slag. One after another, they threw these fiery projectiles into the sea after the servants of Christ. Then they returned to their forges and stoked them and it appeared as though that entire island was ablaze like one gigantic furnace. And the sea boiled like a cookpot full of meat, when a fire burns well beneath it. And for an entire day the brethren heard a great wailing from that island. Indeed, when they could see it no longer, the wailing of its inhabitants still reached their ears and a terrible stench assaulted their nostrils. Then the holy father encouraged his monks, saying, "O soldiers of Christ, take strength in your faith, which is not false, and in your spiritual weapons, because we are now on the threshold of Hell. For this reason, keep watch and act bravely."

On another day, they saw a tall mountain in the ocean not far off to the north. It looked as though it was wreathed in clouds, but it was in fact very smoky at the summit. And immediately the wind drove them on a very rapid course to the shore of this island until their ship came to rest not far from land. For the shore was, in fact, a cliff of such great height that they could barely see the top of it. It was black as coal and amazingly sheer like a wall.

One of the brethren, the last who remained of the three monks who had followed holy Brendan from his monastery, leaped out of the boat and began to wade to the foot of the cliff. He cried out, saying, "Woe to me, father, I am snatched from you and I do not have the power to return to you!" The brethren immediately turned the ship away from the land and cried out to the Lord, saying, "Have mercy on us, Lord, have mercy on us!" Then the venerable father with all of his companions saw how that unfortunate monk was carried off to torments by a multitude of demons and how he burned among them, and said, "Woe to you, brother, that you have earned in your life the bad fate that you deserved."

Once again, a fair wind carried them to the south. When they looked back at that island from far away, they saw that the mountain was clear of smoke. It spouted fire into the sky and then sucked the flames back inside, such that the entire mountain appeared to glow like a funeral pyre upon the sea.

After holy Brendan had sailed toward the south for seven days, there appeared to them upon the sea a shape like a man sitting on a rock. And a short distance in front of him was a sail about the size of a cloak, hanging between two iron prongs. And thus, he was buffeted by the waves like a ship when it is tossed by a storm. Some of the brethren contended that it was a bird; others thought that it was a boat. When the man of God heard them discussing such things among themselves, he said, "Stop your arguing and direct the course of the ship to that place."

When Brendan and his brethren approached, the waves remained still in their motion as though frozen. They found the man sitting upon a rough and craggy outcropping. When the waves crashed in from every side, they struck him up to the top of his head, and when they receded, they exposed the bare rock upon which this unfortunate person was sitting. Whenever the wind caught the cloth that hung before him, it lashed at his eyes and forehead.

Blessed Brendan began to ask this man who he was and for what crime he had been sent there and why he had deserved to suffer such a punishment. He responded, "I am the most unfortunate Judas, the worst of all merchants. I am in this place not due to my own merit, but thanks to the mercy of the unutterable Jesus Christ. This place is not reckoned as a punishment for me, but as an indulgence of the Redeemer because of the honor of the resurrection of the Lord." For it was the Lord's Day [Sunday] that day. "For it seems to me when I sit here that it is as though I was in a paradise of delights because of the fear of the torments that await me this evening. For I burn like a mass of molten lead both day and night in the bowels of the mountain that you saw. Leviathan dwells there with his minions. I was there when it swallowed your brother, and for this reason Hell rejoiced, sending forth huge gouts of flame, which it always does when it devours the souls of the impious. I have this refuge here every Sunday from evening until evening, and from Christmas Day until Epiphany and from Easter until Pentecost and on the Purification of the Virgin Mary and on the Feast of her Assumption. At all other times, I am tormented in the depth of Hell with Herod and Pilate and Annas and Caiphas. Therefore, I beg you through the Redeemer of the world to deign to intercede for me with the Lord Jesus Christ so that I have the power to remain here until dawn tomorrow, so that the demons will not torment me because of your coming and carry me off to my evil legacy, which I bought with blood money." Holy Brendan said to him, "Let the Lord's will be done. You will not feel the demons' sting until tomorrow."

Again, the man of God asked him, saying, "What is the purpose of this cloth?" Judas replied to him, "I gave this very cloth to a leper when I was the chamberlain of the Lord, but it was not mine to give, for it belonged to the Lord and his brethren, so I gain no relief from it; it is more of a hindrance to me. As for the iron tongs on which the cloth hangs, I gave those to the priests of the temple to hold up their cooking pots. The stone on which I sit, that I placed into a hole on the public road to protect the feet of pedestrians before I became a disciple of the Lord."

When the evening hour cast its shadows, behold an innumerable multitude of demons eclipsed the face of the sun, crying out and saying, "Depart from us, man of God, for we cannot approach our comrade until you move away from him, nor do we dare to have an audience with our prince until we return his friend to him. You have taken our morsel from us; do not defend him from us tonight." The man of God said to them, "I do not defend him; it is the Lord Jesus Christ who has allowed him to spend the night here until dawn." The demons responded, "How do you invoke the name of the Lord over this man, when he himself was the Lord's traitor?" The man of God explained, "I command you in the name of the Lord not to harm this man until the morning."

And so, when that night had passed, at the crack of dawn when the man of God was preparing to depart, behold an infinite number of demons covered the face of the abyss, crying out with harsh voices, saying, "O man of God, cursed be your coming and your going, for on this night our prince beat us with the worst possible blows, the reason being that we did not present to him this cursed captive." The man of God said to them, "Your curse does not pertain to us, but to you yourselves. For the one you call accursed is blessed, and the one you bless is accursed." The demons responded, "Unfortunate Judas will receive a double dose of torments over the next six days because you defended him last night." The venerable father said to them, "You have no power hereafter, nor does your prince, but the power of God endures." He added, "I command you and your prince in the name of the Lord Jesus Christ not to bear this man off to more torments than he suffered before." They responded, "Are you the lord of all, that we should obey your words?" The man of God said, "I am his servant and whatever I command in his name, I have authority concerning those affairs that he concedes to me." And so, the demons followed him until they could see Judas no longer. Then they turned around and lifted that most wretched soul among them with great speed and wailing. Afterward, holy Brendan and his followers sailed southward, glorifying God in all things.

INTO THE DEEPEST DARK: THE *VISION OF TUNDALE* (c. 1150)

The Visio Tnugdali *(Vision of Tundale) is without doubt the most graphic and horrifying tour of Hell composed before Dante's* Inferno *in the fourteenth century, but it remains little known among modern readers. Written in 1149 by an anonymous Irish monk residing in Regensburg (in modern Bavaria), this tableau of Hell differed from its late antique and early medieval predecessors in a number of important ways. First and foremost, the main character of the story, an Irish knight named Tundale, was a terrible sinner. Unlike the monks who populated earlier visions of the otherworld, Tundale, as he is conducted through Hell by his guardian angel, is also forced to submit to the cruel torments that he witnessed as a reminder to avoid sinful behavior when his soul was later reunited with his body. Second, the author depicted the topography of Hell with unprecedented attention to texture and detail. The infernal regions were a vast landscape of towering peaks, dark valleys, fetid swamps, and bottomless pits traversed by roads and bridges and inhabited by demons, monstrous creatures, and menacing characters, like the hellish innkeeper Phristinus. Likewise, the torments described in the text are especially lurid and visceral. Third, when Tundale plumbed the deepest pit of Hell, he glimpsed Satan himself, a monster of unrivaled size bound in eternal torment to a fiery grill. No other text from this period described the prince of Hell so vividly in the throes of agony, forever punished in the act of dispensing punishment to others. While scholars are quick to characterize the* Vision of Tundale *as a precursor to Dante's* Inferno, *it stands on its own as the most fully realized, and therefore the most terrifying, vision of Hell produced in medieval Europe. Its grisly imagery captured the popular imagination, spawning translations in numerous languages and inspiring nightmarish paintings of the afterlife by the Dutch master Hieronymus Bosch (c. 1450–1516) and his many imitators.*

1. WELCOME TO HELL[1]

ON THE DEPARTURE OF
TUNDALE'S SOUL.

Tundale said that when his soul departed from his body and he realized that it was dead, mindful of his faults, he began to grow frightened and had no idea what to do. Truly, he was afraid, but he did not know what he feared. He wanted to return to his body, but he was unable to enter it; he wanted to go further on, but he was frightened on every side. And so, this most wretched soul pondered his options, mindful of his faults, confessing in nothing except for the mercy of God. Then after hesitating for a little while and weeping and crying out, this trembling soul still did not know what to do. At last, he saw a great multitude of unclean spirits coming toward him, so many that they not only filled the entire house and courtyard, in which the dead man tarried, but also there was no place throughout the quarters and streets of the city that was not full of them. Moreover, as they surrounded that miserable soul, they were eager not to console him, but to bring him to the verge of tears, saying, "Let us sing the song of death owed to this poor soul, because he is the child of death and fuel for the fire that does not go out, a friend of the shadows, an enemy of the light." And they all turned to him, gnashing their teeth at him and with their claws they tore at their own horrid faces in their excessive rage, saying, "Behold, poor soul, the people whom you chose, with whom you will descend to burn in the depth of Hell. Nurturer of scandal, lover of discord, why are you not proud? Why do you not commit adultery? Why do you not fornicate? Where is your vanity and your empty delight? Where is your unrestrained laughter? Where is your bravery, that allowed you to insult so many? Why do you not wink now with your eyes, as you used to do? Will you not drag your foot, nor speak with your finger, nor contrive evil with your depraved heart?" Terrified by these and similar words, the wretched soul could do nothing other than cry, awaiting death delivered to him without delay by all of the unclean spirits in attendance. But the almighty, holy, and merciful Lord, dispensing all things well by his secret judgment, did not desire the death of this sinner and agreed to offer a remedy to him alone after his death; indeed, the Lord tempered his misery, as he wished.

ON THE ARRIVAL OF THE ANGEL SENT TO MEET TUNDALE'S SOUL.

For the Lord sent his angel to meet Tundale's soul. Watching him coming from a distance like the brightest star, Tundale held his gaze upon him without wavering and hoped that he would receive some counsel from him. Once the angel had approached him, he greeted Tundale, calling him by name, saying, "Hail, Tundale, what are you doing?" Seeing a handsome youth—for the angel had a beautiful countenance among the sons of humankind—and hearing himself called by his own name, with tears that poor man blurted out with joy in such a voice, "Oh, lord father, the sorrows of Hell surround me; the snares of death have seized me."[2] The angel said to him, "Why do you call me lord and father? You had me with you always and everywhere and you never judged me worthy of such a name." Tundale responded, "Lord, where have I ever seen you? Or where have I ever heard your very sweet voice?" The angel responded to him, "I have always followed you from the time of your birth, wherever you went, and you never wished to comply with my counsels." And pointing to one of the unclean spirits that had insulted Tundale with curses more so than the rest, the angel said, "Behold, you followed this one's counsels, and you neglected my will entirely. But because God always puts mercy before justice, his undeserved mercy will not be absent, even for you. Be very happy and untroubled, because you will suffer only a few of the many torments that you would have suffered if the mercy of our redeemer had not come down to you. Therefore, follow me and lock away in your memory everything that I show to you, because you have to return to your body again." Then that soul, terrified beyond measure, went with the angel, leaving behind the body over which he had been standing. Hearing this and realizing that they could not carry him off, the demons and other evil creatures, which had threatened his soul a few moments before, raised their voices to heaven, saying, "O how unjust and cruel is God, for he mortifies them as he wishes and revives them as he wishes, not as he promised: to render each one according to his own work and merit. He frees souls that should not be freed and damns those that should not be damned." And with these words, they rose up against each other and, in whatever way they could, they struck one another with blows and then, leaving behind an excessive stench, they retreated with great sadness and disdain. Moving forward, the angel said to Tundale's soul, "Follow me." He responded, "Oh, my lord, if I go any further, they will tear me away and drag me into the everlasting fires." The angel said to him, "Do not fear them, for there are more on our side than on theirs. If God is with us, who can stand against us? Indeed, two thousand fall on our left side and ten thousand on our right, so that nothing will approach you. Nevertheless, you will examine with your own eyes and witness the punishment of sinners. And you will suffer, just as I said, a few of the many torments that you deserve." And as soon as he finished speaking, they set out.

THE PUNISHMENT
FITS THE CRIME[1]

THE FIRST PUNISHMENT:
THE MURDERERS.

When they had proceeded together for a while with no light other than the splendor of the angel, at last they came to a very terrible valley of shadows covered by a dark shroud of death. It was very deep and filled with burning coals. It had an iron lid that seemed to be six cubits thick sitting atop of the brightly burning coals.[2] The stench of this place exceeded all of the tribulations that this soul had suffered up to this point. A multitude of very wretched souls fell upon the iron lid and there they were burned until they were reduced entirely to liquid, like fat rendered in a frying pan. Then, even worse, they were strained through the iron lid, like wax is strained through a cloth, and restored again to torment in the burning coals of the fire. When he saw these things, that soul was terrified and said to the angel, "Alas, my lord, I ask if you could please tell me what evil deed these souls have done to deserve such torments." The angel said to him, "These are murders, the killers of fathers and brothers. This is the first punishment of the perpetrators and their accomplices and after this they will be led to even greater torments, as you will see." "And will I suffer this, too?" Tundale asked. The angel replied, "Indeed, you deserve to, but you will not suffer now. It is true that you are not a killer of your father or mother or brother. You are a killer nonetheless, but there is no charge against you now. For the rest, take care, so that when you return to your body, you will not merit a punishment more grevious or greater than this." And he added, "Let us proceed, for we have a long way yet to go."

CONCERNING THE PUNISHMENT OF SPIES AND TRAITORS.

Then they came to a mountain of extraordinary size, a place of great horror and immense solitude. The mountain provided a very narrow path for those wishing to cross. For on one side of the path there was a putrid fire, sulfurous and dark, while on the other side there was icy snow and a horrible hail-ridden wind. On one side and the other, the mountain was ready to punish souls; it was full of torturers, so that no route appeared to be safe to those who wished to cross it. These torturers wielded fiery iron tongs and had very sharp tridents at the ready, with which they pierced any souls trying to cross and dragged them to torment. While those wretched souls suffered punishments enveloped in the flames, they were pierced by the tridents and thrown into the snow. Then they were thrown back once again from the pounding hail into the fiery flames. When he saw these things, Tundale was afraid and asked the angel, who walked ahead of him, "I ask, lord, since I can clearly see the ambushes prepared for my destruction, how can I take this route?" The angel answered, "Do not fear, but follow me or walk ahead of me." And then the angel went first and Tundale followed, as before.

CONCERNING THE VALLEY OF THE PROUD AND THEIR PUNISHMENT.

As they made their way cautiously out of fear, they came to a very deep valley, very putrid and covered in shadow. Tundale could not determine its depth, but he could hear the roar of a flaming river and the wailing of the multitude suffering in its depths. A fetid smoke rose up from the sulfur and from the bodies below, which exceeded all of the punishments that he had previously seen. A very long plank measuring a thousand feet long but only one foot wide extended over the valley from one mountain to another like a bridge. Only the saved could cross this bridge. Tundale saw many souls fall from it; no one except for a single priest was able to cross it unharmed. This priest was a pilgrim, who carried a palm branch and was dressed in a pilgrim's cloak; he bravely crossed first before all of the others. Then Tundale, spying the narrow path and recognizing the eternal ruin below, said to the angel, "Alas, poor me! Who will free me from the path of this death?" Looking upon him with a kind face, the angel responded, "Do not fear. You will be freed from this situation, but after this you will suffer another." And walking ahead, the angel held Tundale and led him across the bridge unharmed. And after they had crossed that narrow way, safe and relieved, Tundale said to the angel, "I pray, Lord, please show me, whose souls are these that I see tormented in this way?" The angel said to him, "This truly horrible place is the valley of the proud; the putrid and sulfurous mountain is the punishment of spies." And he added, "Let us go, until we arrive at other torments even worse than these."

CONCERNING THE GREEDY AND THEIR PUNISHMENT.

Then with the angel in the lead, they set out on a long and tortured and very difficult path. After they had labored much and made their way through the shadows, Tundale saw an incredibly large and intolerably horrible beast not far away from them. This monster exceeded every mountain that he had ever seen in the enormity of its size. Its eyes were truly like burning hills. Its mouth was gaping open so wide that it seemed to Tundale that it could hold nine thousand armed men. Moreover, in its mouth it had two parasites and these were very unnatural with twisted heads. One of them had its head up against the upper teeth of the beast and its feet down against the lower teeth; the other was just the opposite with its head down and its feet raised against the upper teeth. They stood like columns in its mouth, making its maw look as though it was divided into three gateways. A fire that never died belched out of its mouth, split into three parts through these three gateways and into this fire the souls of those sentenced to damnation were forced to enter. An indescribable stench billowed from this mouth. The crying and wailing of the multitude in its stomach echoed through the mouth; no wonder, since many thousands of men and women were suffering dire torments inside. In front of its mouth there was a host of unclean spirits forcing the souls to enter. But before they entered, these spirits attacked them with many lashes and blows. When Tundale had watched this horrible and fearful spectacle for a while, at once helpless because of his great terror and in fear of his own spirit, with a tearful voice he said to the angel, "Alas, alas, my lord, are these things that I see not clear to you, and why do you approach them?" The angel said in response, "We cannot complete our journey in any other way unless we stand in judgment personally before this torment. For no one except for the elect can avoid this torment. This beast is called Archeron, who devours all of the greedy. It is written in scripture concerning this monster: 'He will swallow the river and he will not wonder and he will trust that the river Jordan will flow into his mouth.'³ These figures, who have been placed between his teeth and in his mouth, are giants and in their own times they were faithful in their way, but their names are not known to you. Indeed, they are called Fergusius and Conallus."⁴ Tundale said to him, "Alas, lord, this disturbs me. You said that they were faithful in their way. Why does the Lord judge them worthy of such blows?" The angel replied, "All of these things that you have witnessed up to now are great kinds of punishments, but before you return you will be able to see even greater torments."

And after he had said these things, the angel went ahead of Tundale and stood before the beast and Tundale followed him unwillingly. Once they were standing together in front of the monster, the angel disappeared and poor Tundale was left alone. When they saw that Tundale had been abandoned, demons gathered around that wretched soul like rapid dogs and dragged

him with them, scourged, into the belly of the beast. Even
though Tundale was silent, in the color of his face and in the
change of his disposition, any person with an ounce of wisdom
who wished to know could recognize very easily how many
great torments he suffered there. And since we should try to be
brief, we cannot write down everything that we have heard. But
nonetheless, so that we do not seem to pass over this material in
silence, we wish to relate a few of the many torments he suffered
for the edification of our readers. For there Tundale suffered the
savagery of dogs, bears, lions, serpents, and innumerable other
unknown monstrous animals, the blows of demons, the heat of
fire, the severity of cold, the stench of sulfur, the darkness of the
eyes, the flow of burning tears, a wealth of tribulations, and the
gnashing of teeth. When Tundale had learned these and similar
things there, what else could this poor soul do, other than blame
himself for what had happened in the past and tear at his own
cheeks in his great sorrow and despair? As poor Tundale recognized his own guilt and feared that he would suffer the eternal
punishment that he deserved, he realized that he was outside of
the beast, though he did not know how he had been released.
And behold, after he lay there weak for a long time, he opened
his eyes and saw nearby that spirit of light who had gone with him
before. Then he rejoiced, though he was still greatly afflicted,
and he said to the angel, "O my one hope! O comfort granted to
me by God, though I am unworthy! O light of my eyes and staff
of my misery and calamity, what do you want poor me to for-
sake? How can a poor man like me pay back the Lord for all
that he gave me? If he had never done anything good for me except for sending you to meet me, what thanks can I give back to
you, O worthy one?" The angel said in response, "Just as you
said before, so you know it to be true: divine mercy is greater
than your iniquity. This one renders to each individual according to their work and merit, but he will judge each and every
one of us concerning our fate. Because of this, as I said before, it
is necessary for you to take care, so that you do not merit these
torments again, when your own strength returns." And after he
said this, the angel added, "Let us cross over to these punishments before us."

CONCERNING THE PUNISHMENT
OF THIEVES AND ROBBERS.

Tundale rose like a man who was ill and tried feebly to stay on course. He wanted nothing more than to follow the angel, but he was so greatly afflicted that he could not do so. The angel of the Lord comforted him with a touch and, setting out on the right course, he urged Tundale to complete his journey, as he had said before. After they had gone a long way, they saw a lake that was exceedingly full and tempestuous. Its billowing waves blocked out the sky. In it there was a vast multitude of terrible beasts. Their roars demanded nothing else except to devour souls. Spanning across the lake was a bridge that was very narrow and long. Its length was almost two miles, for this was the size of the lake. The width of the bridge was almost as wide as the palm of your hand. It was both longer and narrower than that bridge that we mentioned above. Indeed, its surface was pierced with very sharp iron nails, which punctured the feet of everyone who crossed it, so that no one's foot, if it touched the bridge just once, could avoid being wounded. All of the beasts gathered at the bridge to consume their food, namely, those very souls that could not cross. These were beasts of such enormous size that they could honestly be compared to great towers. Indeed, fire came out of their mouths, so that it seemed to onlookers that the lake boiled. On the bridge, Tundale saw one soul crying and accusing himself of many crimes. Indeed, he was burdened by a great weight of bundles of grain as he tried to cross the bridge. But while he suffered greatly when the iron nails punctured the souls of his feet, he was also terrified that he would fall into the burning lake, where he saw the gaping mouths of the beasts. Seeing the imminent danger, Tundale said to the angel, "Alas, lord, please, I wish to know why that soul is made to cross with such a great burden. Whose souls is this particular punishment for?" The angel said to him in response, "This punishment is especially appropriate for you and others like you who committed theft, whether it was great or small. But those who are guilty of lesser or great crimes do not suffer in

the same way, unless that lesser crime was, perhaps, a sacrilege." Then Tundale asked, "What do you call a sacrilege?"
The angel responded, "Whoever steals either a sacrament or
something from the sacristy, this is judged to be an act of sacrilege. Whoever is guilty under the cover of religion is judged
to be guilty of a major crime, unless they correct themselves
through penance." And to this, he added, "Let us hasten, for
we should cross this bridge." But Tundale said, "You will be
able to cross this bridge through divine power, but I do not
think that you will be able to take me with you." The angel
said, "I will not cross with you, but you will cross the bridge
by yourself, nor will you cross empty-handed, for you must
lead a wild cow alongside you and return it to me on the other
side of the bridge unharmed." Then Tundale wept bitterly and
said to the angel, "Woe is me! Why did God create me to suffer such things? And how can a poor soul like me cross this
bridge, when I am already in such danger? Unless divine mercy
intercedes, how can I stand at all?" The angel responded, "Re-
call to your memory that, when you were alive, you stole a
neighbor's cow." Tundale said, "Did I not return that cow you
just mentioned to its rightful owner?" The angel answered,
"You did return it, but only when you were unable to hide it,
and because of this you will not suffer the full punishment, for
to desire evil is a lesser offense than to act upon it, although
both are evil before the Lord." Once he had spoken these
words, the angel looked back at the soul and showed him the
wild cow. "Behold," he said, "the cow that you have to lead
across the bridge." When Tundale saw that he could not avoid
the punishment he owed, he took hold of the cow and by
whatever means he could, he urged it gradually to make its
way to the bridge. The roaring beasts came and awaited their
meal, which they saw upon the bridge. As Tundale began to
make his way, the cow refused to go with him. Why delay
with the story any longer? When Tundale stood, the cow fell,
and when the cow stood, Tundale fell. And so, back and forth,
they alternately kept their feet and stumbled until they came
to the middle of the bridge. When they arrived there, they saw
that the soul who carried the bundles was in their way. I do

not include this soul among those concerning whom it is said, "Coming, however, they came not with exultation carrying their burdens," but among those concerning whom scripture warns elsewhere, "Woe to you, who laugh now, because you will cry and weep."[5] For crying and weeping in this way, they hindered one another, but not like mercy and truth nor like justice and peace, which embraced one another. This soul, who had come with its burdens, asked Tundale not to take up so much of the bridge for himself. And for his part, Tundale entreated the other soul with whatever prayers he could not to block the way for him, which he had already completed in part with such great effort. But neither one of them was able to turn back, let alone look back. And thus these lamenting souls were at a standstill and they stained the bridge on which they were standing with the blood running from the soles of their feet. When they had stood for a long time and lamented there the guilt of their crimes, without knowing how, each knew that the other had somehow passed by. Moreover, when Tundale passed by, he saw his angel, whom he had left behind, and it addressed him with soothing words, "You are coming along well. Do not trouble yourself with the cow any longer, for you are duty bound to it no more." But when Tundale showed his feet to the angel and said that he was defeated and could go no further, the angel responded, "You should remember how quick your feet were in your rush to shed blood and for that reason you deserved sadness and unhappiness in your ways, if the mercy of the Almighty had not intervened for you." And when he said these things, the angel healed him with a touch and thus Tundale went on. Then when he asked, "Which way do we go?" the angel answered, "A terrifying torturer awaits our arrival. His name is Phristinus. There is no way for us to avoid his hospitality. His inn is always full of guests, but nevertheless this host loves to discover new visitors to punish."

CONCERNING THE PUNISHMENT OF THE GLUTTONS AND THE FORNICATORS.

When they had passed through dark and dry places, a house appeared before them, its doors open. This house that they saw was huge, as tall as a mountain in its great size, and it was round like an oven, where loaves are baked. Fire came out of it, which charred whatever souls it found within a thousand paces. But Tundale's soul, which had learned a similar torment from another experience, could not approach any closer. To the angel who led him, he said, "Poor me, what will I do? Behold we approach the gates of death and who will free me?" The angel responded, "You will be freed from this flame outside, but you have to enter that house from which it pours forth." And when they neared the house, they saw executioners with axes and knives and sticks and double-bladed instruments with pickaxes and bores and very sharp scythes, with spades and shovels and other equipment. With these tools, they could flay or decapitate or cleave or hack as they stood before the doors in the midst of the flames and under their hands the multitude of souls endured all of the torments we have already discussed. When Tundale's soul saw that this was much greater than all of the other penalties he had seen before, he said to the angel, "I pray, my lord, please free me from this punishment alone, and I will give myself over to all of the punishments that follow this one." The angel replied, "This punishment is greater than all of the others that you have previously seen. Neverthless, you will see all kinds of torments even greater than you were able to see or ponder before." He continued, "To administer this punishment, rabid dogs await your arrival inside." Trembling and weak with distress, with whatever prayers he could muster, Tundale asked to avoid this punishment. Nevertheless, he could not accomplish what he wished. When the demons saw that Tundale's soul was giving in, they surrounded him and reproached him with a great outcry. Then they tore him to pieces with their instruments of torture and dragged his mangled soul into the flames. What can I say concerning what happened inside this house of Phristinus?

For there was lamenting and sadness, pain and groaning and the gnashing of teeth. A tenacious fire was built outside, a vast conflagration inside. There was always an insatiable desire for food, and yet the excess of gluttony could not be sated. Their genitals were tortured with great wracking pains and corrupted with putrefaction that gushed with worms. These beasts burrowed not only into the genitals of laymen and laywomen, but also—even worse, which I cannot say without grave sorrow!—into the genitals of those abiding under the religious habit. No strength could suffice to endure these exhausting, ubiquitous tortures. No gender and no way of life was spared from these misfortunes. What I fear to relate, love compels me to say, that the monastic habit of men and women was present among those being tormented; and those whose profession seemed more holy were judged worthy of the harsher penalties. After Tundale's soul had endured these and similar unspeakable torments for a long time, he returned to himself and confessed that he was guilty and worthy of such punishments. But when it pleased the divine will, without knowing how, as we said, Tundale realized that his torments were over. Nevertheless, he sat in the darkness and in the shadow of death. After he had sat there for a little while, he saw a light, namely the spirit of life, who had previously served as his guide.

CONCERNING THE PUNISHMENT OF MONKS AND PRIESTS WHO FORNICATE AND THOSE WHO DEFILE THEMSELVES WITHOUT MODERATION IRRESPECTIVE OF THEIR STATION IN LIFE.

As the angel led the way, they saw a beast very different from all of the other beasts they had previously seen. It had two feet and two wings, a very long neck, and an iron beak. It even had iron claws and from its mouth it vomited a relentless flame. This beast sat in a swamp that was frozen over with ice, where it devoured any souls it could find. While they were in its stomach, these souls were reduced to nothing as their punishment. The beast then regurgitated them onto the surface of the frozen swamp, where their torments were renewed once again. All of the souls that descended into the swamp, men as well as women, were pregnant, and burdened in this way they awaited the time when they would give birth. The offspring that they had conceived stung their entrails like vipers, causing these wretched souls to thrash about in the fetid waves of a sea of death hardened over with ice. When the time came to deliver, they screamed, filling the depths with their cries as they gave birth to serpents. I repeat that not only the women, but also the men gave birth to them, not through those parts that nature made for this function, but through their arms and likewise through their chests, and the serpents came bursting out through all of their limbs. These newly born beasts had heads of burning iron and the sharpest beaks, with which they shredded the bodies from which they emerged. On their tails, they had many spines like twisted fishhooks, with which they pierced those souls that gave birth to them. These beasts sought to leave their hosts, but when they could not extract their tails, they turned their burning iron heads back into the bodies and did not stop consuming them until they were reduced to raw nerves and dry bones. And so, crying out together, the grating of the icy waves and the screaming of the suffering souls and the growling of the emerging beasts reached to the heavens, so much so that the demons, if there were any spark of pity in them, might be rightly moved to feel mercy born of sympathy. For upon all of their limbs and fingers you could see the heads of many beasts that gnawed them down to the very nerves and bones. These beasts had living tongues like vipers, which consumed the roof of the mouth and the windpipe all the way down to the lungs. Likewise, the genitals of the men and the women were like serpents, which eagerly mangled the lower parts of their stomachs and pulled out their guts. Then Tundale said, "Tell me, I ask, what evil deeds have these souls committed, for which this punishment has been prepared, for I believe that it is not comparable to any of the torments I have ever seen." The angel said, "As I told you earlier, because those who are considered to be holier are sentenced to harsher torments if they sin, it follows that they obtain a greater glory, if they do not earn this punishment through any kind of guilt." He continued, "For this is the punishment of the monks, the canons, the nuns, and all other members of ecclesiastical orders, who either through their tonsure or through their habit are known to have lied to God. For this reason, their members are consumed by diverse pains because they acted without constraint. Indeed, they sharpened their tongues like serpents and thus they suffer these flames. Also their genitals, which were not restrained from the forbidden pleasure of sexual intercourse, are either cast away or they produce savage beasts to increase their pain." And the angel added, "We have said enough about this. This punishment is particular to those who called themselves devout and were not; nonetheless, those who stained themselves with unbridled pleasure will also endure these torments. And for this reason, you will not escape this, because while you were in your body, you did not fear to defile yourself with immoderate behavior." After the angel said these things, demons assaulted Tundale, seized his soul, and gave him to the beast to be devoured. Once consumed, his soul suffered either inside the creature or in the fetid swamp, but we should not repeat what we have said earlier. After Tundale experienced the punishment of the birth of the vipers, a spirit of pity appeared and talking softly it consoled him, saying, "Come, my dearest friend, you do not have to suffer this anymore." And with a touch, the spirit healed him and enjoined him to follow him for the rest of the journey. Tundale did not know how far they went, for as we learned before, they had no light except for the brightness of the spirit of light. Indeed, they went through places that were terrible and more dire than what had come before. Their path was very narrow and it went down as though from the peak of the highest mountain into the depths, and the further he descended, the less Tundale hoped to return to life.

THE PUNISHMENT OF THOSE
WHO PILE SIN UPON SIN.

Then Tundale said, "Since we have seen so much evil thus far, so that I say what is worse could not be seen or even conceived, where again does this path lead from these so far into the depths?" The angel said in response, "That way leads to death." And Tundale said, "Since this path is so very narrow and difficult and we have seen no one on it besides ourselves, is this what the Gospel referred to when it said, 'Broad and wide is the way that leads to death and many enter through it'?"[6] The angel answered, "The evangelist did not speak about this road, but about the forbidden and shameless life of the world, for it leads through this to that." After they went on further and struggled a great deal, they came into a valley and saw there many foundries of smiths, in which they could hear a loud lamenting. Tundale said, "Do you hear what I hear, my lord?" The angel answered, "I hear it and I understand." And then Tundale asked, "Does this punishment have a name?" "This torturer is called Vulcanus," said the angel, "through whose ingenuity many souls are toppled and tormented by him when they fall." Tundale inquired, "My lord, do I deserve to suffer this punishment?" The angel replied, "You do." And after he said this, the angel walked ahead and Tundale followed in tears. As they approached, torturers rushed toward them with burning tongs and ignoring the angel, they seized the soul that followed him. Holding him tight, they threw him into a forge burning with fire and fanned the flames with bellows. Just as iron is weighed, so too the souls were weighed until the multitude that burned there was reduced to nothing. When they were liquefied in this way, so that nothing appeared to remain except for water, they were pierced with iron pitchforks and placed upon an anvil. There they were struck with hammers until twenty or thirty or a hundred souls were rendered into a single mass. Even so, what is worse, they did not die in this way, even though they longed for death and could not find it. The torturers spoke to each of them, saying, "Is that enough?" And others attending another forge answered, "Throw them to us and let us see if it is enough." When the demons threw them, others caught them with metal tongs before they struck the ground and, as before, dragged them through the flames. And thus, the wretched souls were tossed this way and that way, suffering and burning there until their skin and their flesh, their nerves and their bones were reduced to ash and a flickering flame. After Tundale's soul was tossed in these torments for a long time, his advocate appeared to him and in the usual way took him from the midst of the flame and asked, "How are you doing? Were the delights of the flesh so sweet to you that for them you would endure so many and such awful torments?" Tundale could not respond because after such suffering he did not have the strength to utter a word. When the angel of the Lord saw that he was so sorely afflicted, speaking softly, he consoled Tundale, saying, "Take heart, because the Lord is the one who leads you into the depths and back out again. Therefore, be brave because even though the punishments you have suffered are bad, there are greater punishments from which you will be freed if that is the will of our redeemer. For God does not long for the death of the sinner, but for his conversion and return to life." And after this, the angel said, "Everyone you saw above still awaits the judgment of God, but those who are in the depths below have already been judged, for you have not yet come to the very depths of Hell." And leading him in the usual way, he comforted Tundale and bid him to undertake the rest of the journey.

THE GREAT BELOW[1]

CONCERNING THEIR
DESCENT INTO HELL.

As they proceeded on in conversation with one another, behold a sudden horror and an unbearable cold and a stench never experienced before and shadows incomparable to those previously seen, tribulation and distress invaded Tundale's soul together, such that the entire foundation of the earth seemed to tremble, and Tundale was compelled to say to the angel who walked ahead of him, "Alas, my lord, what is making it so that I can barely stand on my own? I am so distressed that I barely have the will to speak." As he stood still waiting for the angel's response, for he could not move because of his great dread, his guide suddenly disappeared from sight. The poor soul saw that he was by far the lowliest of all the sinners he had seen before and, bereft of his light and solace, what else could he do, except to give up all hope of God's mercy? For, as Solomon said, there is no wisdom or knowledge in the depths, into which he hastened, and therefore he lacked counsel when God's help abandoned him.[2] While he tarried alone amid such great dangers, Tundale heard the shouts and wailing of an awesome multitude and also the sound of thunder so terrifying that our smallness could not comprehend it, nor could his tongue, as it is said, endeavor to express it.

CONCERNING THE DEEPEST
DEPTHS OF HELL.

As Tundale looked around to see whether he could discern the source of these terrors, he saw a four-sided hole like a cistern, which was in fact a well that emitted a putrid column of flame and smoke that stretched up to the heavens. In this column of flame there was a great number of souls and demons side by side, rising up like embers aglow with fire. When the smoke dissipated to nothing, the souls fell with the demons into the furnace, down into the deep. When Tundale witnessed this great spectacle, his soul wanted to retreat, but he could not lift his foot from the ground. Goaded by fear, he tried again and again and discerned that he could not accomplish what he desired to do. Filled with a great fury, he burned within and tearing his cheeks with his nails, he cried, "Woe to me! Why can I not die? And why did I, the most wretched of all, not wish to believe in the holy scriptures? What madness deceived me?" Overhearing his words, the demons ascending with the flame gathered around him with their instruments, with which they seized the miserable souls for torment. They surrounded him like swarming bees and burned like fire adorned with thorns and they spoke with one voice, saying, "O wretched soul, worthy of pains and tortures, from where have you come here? You are ignorant of the pains that you have not yet experienced; moreover, you will see the torment that fits your deeds, from which there is no escape, not even in death, but you will burn perpetually in agony, unable to die. You will see or find no consolation, no relief, and no light; you will have no hope of aid or mercy. For you have approached the gates of death and you will find yourself in the very depths of Hell without delay. Whoever led you here has deceived you; he would have freed you from our power, if he could, but you will not see him again. Grieve, poor soul, grieve, cry, shout and wail, for you will mourn with those who mourn, you will cry with those who cry, and you will burn forever with those who burn. There is no one who wants to free you from our power, and no one who can." The demons spoke to one another, saying, "Why should we delay any longer? Let us drag this soul away and show our cruelty to him. Let us give him to Lucifer to be devoured." And so, brandishing their weapons, they threatened him with everlasting death. These spirits were as black as coal, their eyes were like lanterns burning with fire, their teeth were whiter than snow, and they had tails like scorpions, very sharp iron nails, and wings like vultures. While they were tossing him about, for they had seized him without delay, and while they were singing the song of death to the grieving soul, the spirit of light appeared. Once those spirits of shadow had fled, the angel consoled Tundale with his accustomed words, saying, "Rejoice and be glad, child of light, because you will receive mercy rather than judgment. For you will see the punishments, but you will not suffer anymore."

CONCERNING THE PRINCE OF SHADOWS.

"Come, therefore," the angel said, "and I will show you the worst adversary of the human race." And proceeding on, he came to the gates of Hell and said to Tundale, "Come and see, but know this, that my light barely shines for those who are condemned here. You will be able to see them, but they will not be able to see you." Drawing near, Tundale looked upon the depths of Hell. The abundance and array of unspeakable torments that he saw there he could never reveal, even if he had one hundred heads and in each head one hundred tongues. But I think that it would not be useful to leave out a few of the things that he told us. For he saw the prince of shadows, the enemy of the human race, the devil, who surpassed in size all of the beasts that he had seen before. Tundale could not find anything to compare to the size of its body and we should not dare to presume anything that we did not learn from his lips, but we should not neglect the story that we heard from him. For the devil was the blackest black like a raven, with the shape of a human body from its feet to its head, except that it had many hands and a tail. This horrid monster had no fewer than one thousand hands and each of those hands was one hundred cubits in length and ten cubits in width.[3] Each of its hands had twenty fingers, which were one hundred palms long and ten palms wide.[4] Its nails were longer than the lances of soldiers and made of iron, and it had the same kind of nails on its feet. Moreover, it had a great, long beak and a tail that was long and very hard and ready to harm souls with its very sharp barbs. This horrifying spectacle lay inclined upon an iron grill, the burning coals placed beneath it fanned by the bellows of an unimaginable multitude of demons. Such a great crowd of souls and demons surrounded the Devil, too many for anyone to believe, because the world has produced so many souls since the beginning of time. The enemy of the human race was bound by every limb and through every joint of its limbs by immense, flaming chains of iron and copper. Moreover, when it moved in the coals and was charred all over, with great rage the burned beast thrashed from one side to the other and grasped with all of its hands for the multitude of souls. And when each hand was full, he squeezed them like a thirsty peasant pressing a bunch of grapes, so that no soul that was not already in pieces or lacking a head or feet or hands could possibly escape him unharmed. And then, as though breathing, he blew and scattered all of the souls into the different parts of Hell, and immediately the pit vomited its fetid flame, concerning which we have spoken before. And when the dire beast drew its breath, it sucked back all of the souls that it had scattered and devoured the ones that fell into its mouth with smoke and sulfur. But whoever fled from its hands, the Devil struck with its tail and in this way the wretched beast struck itself in its incessant lashings. Inflicting punishments on souls, it was tortured by its own torments. Witnessing this, Tundale asked the angel of the Lord, "My lord, does this monster have a name?" The angel said in response, "This beast before you is called Lucifer and he is the first of God's creatures to dwell in the delights of paradise. If he was freed, he would throw into confusion heaven and earth and everything, even into the depths of Hell all at once. Moreover, some of this multitude are angels of darkness and ministers of Satan; others are the sons of Adam, who did not merit mercy. For these are the ones who held out no hope of mercy from God nor did they believe in God and therefore with the prince of shadows they merit to suffer in this way without end, because in their words and deeds they did not wish to cleave to the Lord of Glory, who would have returned good to them forever." Tundale asked, "Have these souls already been judged or do they still wait for many others, who promised with words to live well, but denied it with their deeds?" The angel responded, "Those who deny Christ altogether or perform works of denial will endure such punishments, for they are adulterers, murderers, thieves, robbers, the proud, and those whose penance is not worthy of their crime. First, they will suffer those lesser punishments that you witnessed before and then they will be led to these torments, from which no one can escape once they have entered. Here also are prelates and leaders of the world, who desired to be foremost, not to be useful, but simply to be foremost. Those who did not reckon that their power to rule or to correct their subjects was given to them and conceded by God and indeed those who did not exercise the power entrusted to them, as they should have, will suffer without end. For this reason, scripture proclaims, 'The powerful suffer torments powerfully.'"⁵ Then Tundale said, "Since you say that power was given to them by God, why do they suffer because of it?" And the angel responded, "Power granted by God is not bad, but it is bad to use it badly." And Tundale asked, "Why does the almighty Lord not always grant power to the good, so that they can correct their subjects and rule over them, as they should?" The angel responded, "Sometimes power is granted to the good to drive out the sins of their subjects—although evil people do not deserve to have good leaders—and sometimes it is because of good leaders that the health of their souls are more secure." Then Tundale asked, "I wish to understand why this monster is called the prince of shadows, when it can defend no one and cannot even free itself?" And the angel responded, "He is called a prince not on account of his power, but on account of the primacy that he holds in the shadows. For although you have witnessed many punishments before these, they count for nothing when compared to this vast torment." And Tundale said, "This is undoubtedly true, for it disturbs me greatly to look upon that lake and it vexes me even more than everything I suffered before to endure this stench. I beg you, if it is possible, do not allow me to be dragged away from here quickly and tortured any more. For I see in this torment many relatives and companions and others known to me, whom I rejoiced to have with me as friends on earth, yet whose company here I very much abhor. Indeed, I know for certain that unless divine mercy comes to my aid, when my merits are weighed, I will suffer these torments no less than they do." And the angel said, "Come, O happy soul, turn toward your peace, for the Lord blesses you. Indeed, you will not suffer anymore nor will you see these punishments unless you earn them again. Up to this point you have seen the prison of the enemies of God; now you will see the glory of his friends."

TEACHING THE TORMENTS: THE HIGH MIDDLE AGES (c. 1000–1300)

In the High Middle Ages (c. 1000–1300), the fear of Hell escaped from the monasteries and found a rapt audience among ordinary Christians. Throughout the first millennium, tales about infernal torments taught cloistered individuals to cultivate virtue and thereby avoid punishment in the world to come, but after the year 1000 CE, elements of these stories began to spread to parish churches in towns and villages, carried on the tongues of monks and priests who ministered to laypeople in the countryside. Medieval Christians were preoccupied with Hell for different reasons. The doctrine of Purgatory—an intermediate place in the afterlife, where a cleansing fire burned away the impurities of souls bound eventually for Heaven—received its official definition at the First Council of Lyon (1245), but the formation of this doctrine in the preceding centuries had forced Christian thinkers to articulate how Purgatory differed from Hell with respect to its location, its duration, and the kinds of torments the wicked could expect to suffer there. In this same period, Christian authors also recognized the utility of stories about Hell in promoting an increased responsibility among ordinary Christians for their own salvation, especially in the wake of the Fourth Lateran Council (1215), which required all Christians to make confession at least once a year and to attend the Mass more frequently. While the doctrine of Purgatory embraced the hope that the souls of sinners would eventually find their way to Heaven, Hell was an efficient tool in medieval preaching because it provoked an unparalleled fear. As sermon after sermon made plain, there was no escape from the fiery, reeking pit that awaited the truly wicked. After centuries of cloistered seclusion, Hell was on the march in the High Middle Ages.

LESSONS IN HORROR[1]

In the early twelfth century, a Christian theologian and monk named Honorius of Autun (1080–1154) composed numerous treatises on aspects of the Christian faith, writing in a clear and unpretentious style of Latin that garnered him a wide audience. Among his most popular works was a handbook of Christian instruction intended to educate individuals who were about to receive baptism. He called this book Elucidarium, *because its contents "made clear" the important lessons about the truth of the Christian faith that it imparted to the reader. The* Elucidarium *had three parts: the first part treated the capacity of human beings to know God; the second part dealt with the problem of evil; and the third part contemplated the future life of the soul, that is, Paradise, Purgatory, and Hell. Honorius was a teacher who knew the limitations of his audience, who may have included not only young monks but also lay parishioners who lived in proximity to his abbey. Following the model of the* Dialogues *of Gregory the Great (see pp. 61–64), he presented the* Elucidarium *in the form of a dialogue between a teacher and a student and thereby distilled complicated theological teachings into a straightforward exchange. His lessons distinguished between an upper and lower Hell and articulated for the first time the nine terrible torments that sinners could expect to suffer in the world to come.*

STUDENT: What is Hell and where is it located?
TEACHER: There are two Hells, an upper one and a lower one. The upper Hell is located at the lowest part of this world; it is

full of punishments. For in this place excessive heat, great cold, hunger, and thirst abound, as well as a myriad of bodily afflictions, like lashings, and afflictions of the soul, like fear and shame. Concerning this, it is said, "Take my soul," that is, my life, "from prison," that is, from Hell.[2] The lower Hell is a place of the spirit, where the fire does not go out, concerning which it is said, "You have delivered my soul from the lower Hell."[3] It is said to be below the earth, for, just as the bodies of sinners are covered by the earth, thus the souls of sinners are buried under the earth in Hell, as it is said concerning the rich man, "He was buried in Hell."[4] In this lower Hell, there are nine kinds of torment.

STUDENT: What are those punishments?

TEACHER: The first torment is fire, which always burns, so that, even if the entire ocean flowed onto it, it would not be extinguished. The heat of it surpasses real fire like the heat of real fire surpasses painted flames. Hellfire burns, but it does not shed light. The second torment is unbearable cold, concerning which it is said, "If a mountain of fire was placed there, it would turn into ice."[5] Concerning these two torments, it is said, "Wailing and the gnashing of teeth," because the smoke from the fire coaxes tears from the eyes, while the cold causes the teeth to grind.[6] The third torment is undying worms, that is, serpents and dragons, terrifying to see and hear, which live in the flames like fish in water. The fourth torment is an unbearable stench. The fifth torment is cutting whips, like the hammers of those striking iron. The sixth torment is a thick darkness, as it is said, "a land of darkness, where chaos and an everlasting horror dwell."[7] The seventh torment is the shame of the sins that are revealed there to everyone and no one can conceal them. The eighth torment is the horrifying sight of demons and dragons, which the damned see by the glow of the flames, and the pitiful din of weeping and cursing. The ninth torment is fiery chains, by which individual limbs are bound.

PREACHING PAIN[1]

Although it drew on a long tradition of monastic visionary literature, Honorius of Autun's Elucidarium *achieved unexpected success as a tool for teaching the fear of Hell to laymen and -women. The impact of this catechetical handbook was rapid and widespread. In the later twelfth century, we can chart the influence of its litany of the nine torments of Hell in monastic sermons and scholastic treatises, but its reach extended beyond the cloister as well. The* Elucidarium *also inspired the author of a contemporary tract called* Treatise concerning the Principal Mysteries of our Religion *(*Tractatus de praecipuis mysteriis nostrae religionis)*, which concluded with a chapter on the nine torments that borrowed heavily from Honorius's work. This short text was a manual of Christian teaching composed for the use of parish priests, who were expected to memorize its contents and redeploy them as adornment for their sermons to their lay parishioners. In this way, the centuries-old tradition of monastic storytelling about the horrors of Hell began to trickle down to ordinary Christians. Transmitted in clear and simple language in sermons preached in towns and villages, the fear of infernal punishment slowly infiltrated the hearts and minds of western Europeans.*

Hell offers nine torments worthy of notice, as authoritative sources attest, setting aside the innumerable other torments that are in place to restrain evil: "Hammer and stench, with worms, fire and frost, visions of demons, darkness, shame, fiery chains."² In Hell there will be a fire that does not go out, cold without compare, undying worms, an intolerable stench, hammers striking repeatedly, a thick and palpable darkness; where chaos and an everlasting horror dwell, where all of the crimes of everyone are apparent to anyone; the faces of demons, which seem to spark like fire, compared to which nothing in the world is more frightening and terrifying; chains of fire restraining every limb; the heat there is so great, I say, that all of the rivers collected into one could not extinguish it. According to Matthew, "There will be wailing and the gnashing of teeth."³ For the smoke from the fire coaxes tears from the eyes; the cold causes the teeth to grind. If a mountain of fire was placed there, it would turn into ice. The wretched wander through, assigned to these miseries. One moment [they flee] from the heat to the cold, the next from the cold to the heat, seeking relief from these opposing pains with their contrasting qualities, no less tormented all the same. Because of this, Job said, "They will pass from the cold of the snows to the excessive heat."⁴

There are worms there that never die, serpents and dragons, repulsive to see and hear, which live in the flames like fish in water; they afflict the wretched, especially when they crawl on them and gnaw their limbs, waging war on their sins, attacking the genitals of the self-indulgent, the mouth and throat of the gluttonous, and likewise concerning the remaining parts of the body. Thus, according to the Wisdom of Solomon, "By which thing a man sins, by this also he is tortured."⁵ And according to Isaiah, "Their worm will not die and their fire will not be extinguished."⁶ The fire produces a heavy stench, which torments no less than the heat. According to Isaiah once more, "Instead of a sweet smell, there will be a stench."⁷ And the psalm, "Fire, sulfur, the wind of storms will be the measure of their cup."⁸ The wind of storms calls forth the exhalation of smoke and stench, which rises from the fire with vehemence in the likeness of storms. The wretched ones are struck repeatedly by hammering blows, by demons compelling them to confess their sins, for here in the world demons are the inciters of evil, but there they are the tormentors of the wicked. As

Solomon says, "Torments have been prepared for the mock-ers."[9] For the demons widen their mouths over the wretched ones, shouting with wild laughter, "Well done, well done! Our eyes have seen it"[10] because the sinners have neglected the nine orders of angels.

THREE TALES OF TORMENT[1]

By the thirteenth century, monastic authors told tales about the torments of Hell not only for their own benefit but also for the benefit of men and women of all stations in life. One of the most widely read storytellers in this period was the Cistercian author Caesarius of Heisterbach (c. 1180–1240), who included many anecdotes about Hell in his Dialogue on Miracles. *Presented as a conversation between a monastic teacher and his disciple, Caesarius's massive compendium of more than seven hundred tales provided vivid examples of the eternal consequences of evil behavior. He devoted the second book of his* Dialogue *to stories about conversion. There he included three anecdotes about unsavory individuals who converted to the monastic life after witnessing the torments of Hell. The first concerned a student who made an agreement with the Devil to obtain all worldly knowledge. The second involved a pact between two sorcerers who employed dark magic to speak with the dead. And the third implicated a necromancer, who journeyed to Hell to investigate the fate of a local ruler and returned shaken and repentant. In each case, the fear of eternal torment caused these individuals to join the Cistercian order as the surest way to avoid the fate of the wicked.*

CONCERNING THE CONVERSION OF AN ABBOT OF MORIMOND, WHO DIED AND CAME BACK TO LIFE.

Twenty-four years ago, there was an abbot of Morimond, who entered the Cistercian order out of necessity. What I am going to tell you about him I learned from the report of Lord Herman, the abbot of Marienstatt, who saw the same abbot, heard him speak, and examined the actions of this man attentively, as one who had died and come back to life.

When he was a young man, this abbot studied in Paris with other scholars. Since he had a stubborn intellect and a shoddy memory, so much so that he could barely understand or remember anything, everyone laughed at him and thought that he was an idiot. Because of this, he became upset and his heart was afflicted with many sorrows. It happened that he was sick one day and, behold, Satan appeared and said to him, "Do you wish to do me homage and I will give to you in return knowledge of all learning?" Hearing this, the young man was afraid and responded to the devil's suggestion, "Get behind me, Satan, for you will never be my lord nor will I ever be your man."[2] And when he did not give in, Satan opened the hand of this young man with force and placing a stone on it, he said, "As long as you keep this stone clenched in your hand, you will know everything." When the devil departed, the young man rose, went back to school, raised questions, and surpassed everyone in disputation. Everyone was amazed at the breadth of knowledge, the degree of eloquence, the unexpected change of this idiot. But he kept his secret safe and revealed to no one the source of his knowledge. Not long after, he fell badly ill and a priest was summoned to hear his confession. Among his other sins, the young man confessed how he had received the stone from the devil and with the stone, his unrivalled knowledge. The priest responded, "Throw this device of the devil away, poor boy, or you will never know the knowledge of God." Terrified, he cast away the stone he was holding in his hand and with the stone, his false knowledge. What more?

The young man died, and his body was placed in the church, where all of the scholars stood around his bier to sing the psalms according to Christian custom. But demons snatched his soul and carried it to a valley that was deep, awful, and pouring forth a sulfurous smoke. There they marshalled themselves on either side of the valley. The demons on one side hurled his poor soul as though playing a game of ball; the demons on the other side caught his soul in their hands as it flew through the air. Their claws were so very sharp that they far surpassed the sharpest needle and any point of steel. He was so tormented by these claws when they hurled him and caught him that, as he later said, no form of torture could be compared to this agony.

The Lord had mercy on him and sent—I know not how—a heavenly figure, a man inspiring great awe, who bore this message to the demons: "Listen, the Most High commands you to release this soul that has been deceived by you." At once, they released the soul and retreated, not daring to touch him anymore. The soul returned to his body, revived its dead limbs, and rose up alive, terrifying the scholars in attendance, who fled away. Climbing down from the bier, he explained that he was alive, and made plain more with his actions than his words what he had seen and what he had heard. For he immediately joined the Cistercian order and was very strict with himself, a harsh punisher of his own body, so that everyone who saw him understood that he had experienced the pains of Purgatory, or rather, of Hell itself.

NOVICE: Can you explain to me whether this place where he was tormented was within the bounds of Hell or of Purgatory?

MONK: If that valley belonged to Hell, then he made his confession without contrition. And this is clear enough from the fact that, by the testimony of the heavenly messenger, he endured that great punishment because he had consented to keep the Devil's stone.

CONCERNING A DEAD CLERIC
WHO HAD PRACTICED NECROMANCY
AND APPEARED TO A LIVING
COMPANION TO URGE HIM TO
ENTER THE CISTERCIAN ORDER.

As I learned by reading rather than direct report, there were two young men who studied necromancy together in Toledo. It happened that one of them became gravely ill. When he was about to die, his companion asked him to appear to him within twenty days and he promised to do so, if he was able. Then one day, while he was sitting in the church in the presence of an image of the blessed Virgin and reading the psalms for the soul of his friend, that wretched soul appeared, bearing witness to its torments with the most pitiful groans. When his friend had asked him where he was and how he fared, he responded, "Woe to me, for I am eternally damned because of the diabolical art that I learned, for it is the true death of the soul, as its name shows.[3] I advise you as my only friend to abandon this accursed knowledge and to make amends with God for your sins by adopting the religious life." When the living man asked him to show him the safest way to live, he replied again, "There is no safer path than the Cistercian order, and among every kind of person, fewer descend to Hell than members of this order." He related many other stories to him, which I have left out for the sake of brevity, the reason being that they have been written down in the book of the *Visions of Clairvaux*.[4] That young man immediately renounced necromancy and became a novice and eventually a monk of the Cistercian order.

NOVICE: I admit that the joy in my heart doubled at this story.

MONK: "For in the mouth of two or three witnesses stands every word."[5] Do you wish to hear about a third cleric who was converted in a very similar way?

NOVICE: Yes, very much so.

CONCERNING A CLERIC, WHO JOINED THE ORDER AFTER WITNESSING THE TORMENTS OF THE LANDGRAVE LUDWIG.

I learned what I am about to relate from a story often told to me by an old monk of ours named Conrad, who is now nearly one hundred years old. He was raised in Thuringia and trained in combat before his conversion [to the monastic life]. He knew a great deal about the deeds of the Landgrave Ludwig[6] . . . When this man passed away, he left behind his two sons as his heirs, namely, Ludwig III, who died on the first expedition to Jerusalem, which happened in the time of Emperor Frederick [Barbarossa, Holy Roman Emperor 1155–90], and Herman, who succeeded his father as landgrave and died only recently. Ludwig III was truly a reasonable and cultured man and, to tell the truth, less evil than many tyrants. He put forth a proclamation, in which he said, "If there is anyone who can tell me the truth with proven evidence about the soul of my father, he will receive from me a good homestead."

A poor knight heard this proclamation. He had as a brother a cleric who practiced necromancy for profit, to whom he pointed out the proclamation of the prince. The cleric responded, "Good brother, I used to summon the Devil at times through incantations; I learned from him whatever I wished, but for a long time now I have renounced all commerce with him and the skills that made it possible." When the knight insisted again and again, reminding him of their poverty and the promised reward, overcome by his requests at last, the cleric summoned the demon. When it appeared, it asked what he wanted. The cleric responded, "I regret that I have been out of touch with you for so long. Tell me, I pray, where the soul of my lord the Landgrave resides." The demon said, "If you will accompany me, I will show him to you." And the cleric answered, "I would like to see him, if I can do so without any danger to my life." The demon said, "I swear to you by the Most High and by his awful judgment that if you commit yourself to my care, I will lead you there unharmed and return you back here in the same condition." For his brother's sake, the cleric placed his soul in the demon's hands and climbed on its neck. In a short time, it placed him before the gates of Hell. Peering in, the cleric observed places too horrible to mention and all kinds of different punishments, and a demon, terrifying to behold, crouching over a covered pit. When he saw these things, the cleric trembled all over. That demon called out to the demon who was carrying him, "Who is that on your shoulders? Bring him over here." To whom it responded, "He is a friend of ours, and I have sworn to him by your great powers not to hurt him, but to show him the soul of his lord the Landgrave, and to return him safe and sound so that he can proclaim to everyone your great power."

Immediately that demon removed the fiery lid, on which he was crouching. Putting a bronze trumpet into the pit, the demon blew so hard that it seemed to the cleric that the entire world resounded with the sound. After what seemed to him like a very long hour, while the pit belched forth sulfurous flames, the Landgrave rose amid the drifting sparks and thrust forth his head as far as his neck, so that he could see the cleric, and said, "Behold, here I am, the wretched Landgrave, once your lord, and would that I was never born." The cleric replied, "I have been sent by your son to report back to him about your current state. If you can in any way be helped, please tell me." The Landgrave responded, "You can see clearly my current state, but know this, that if my sons can restore certain possessions of particular churches, which I usurped unjustly and left for them as their inheritance"—he told the cleric the names of the possessions and churches—"they will confer a great benefit on my soul." The cleric said, "Lord, they will not believe me." He replied, "I will share with you a sign that no one knows except for me and my sons." Once the sign had been imparted and the Landgrave was once more submerged in the pit, the cleric was returned by the demon. He did not lose his life, but he returned pale and weak, a shadow of his former self.

The cleric brought the Landgrave's message to his sons and showed them the sign, but it profited the Landgrave very little, for they had no desire to restore the possessions to their rightful owners. Nevertheless, the current Landgrave Ludwig III said to the cleric, "I recognize the sign and I do not doubt that you have seen my father, so I do not refuse to grant to you the promised reward." The cleric replied, "Lord, let your homestead remain in your hands; I will think now about what is best for my soul." Leaving everything behind, he became a monk of the Cistercian order, enduring every earthly labor if only to avoid eternal damnation. Behold, you have three examples of people who converted [to the monastic life] out of fear or the sight of hellish punishments!

WARNINGS FROM BEYOND THE GRAVE[1]

The twelfth and final book of Caesarius's Dialogue *narrated stories about the punishment and glory of the dead: "As the eleventh hour draws to sunset, so does the twelfth hour bring it to a close. Now it is fitting that we should in the twelfth book treat the rewards of the dead, because when the day is ended, the laborers in the vineyard receive their pay." More often than not, the dead received punishment as their "reward." At the request of the novice, the master began with tales of the torments of the wicked and singled out tyrants, oppressors, usurers, adulterers, the proud, and anyone who had offended God and not repented. As these stories made plain, no human being, however lofty or holy their station in this world, can escape the judgment of God in the world to come.*

CONCERNING THE PUNISHMENT OF LUDWIG THE LANDGRAVE.

Ludwig the Landgrave was a terrible tyrant, concerning whom I spoke about above in the thirty-fourth chapter of Book One.[2] When he was about to die, he gave this order to his friends: "As soon as I die, dress me in the cowl of the Cistercian order and be very careful that you do not do this to me while I am still alive." His friends obeyed; he died and was dressed in a cowl. When a knight saw him like this, he said to his companions with irony, "Truly, this does not look like my lord in all of his power. When he was a knight, he had no equal in combat;

now that he has been made a monk, he has become a model of discipline to everyone. See how carefully he guards his silence. He does not say a single word."

But when the Landgrave's soul had been taken from its body, it was presented to the captain of the demons, as it was very clearly revealed to someone. As that inhabitant of Hell sat over the pit and held a cup in his hand, he saluted the Landgrave with words of this kind, "Let our beloved friend be welcome! Show him our banquet halls, our storehouses, our cellars, and then bring him back."

After that wretched soul had been led to places of punishments, in which there was nothing but crying, wailing, and the gnashing of teeth, and brought back, the captain of the demons said this to the Landgrave, one prince to another, "Drink, friend, from my cup." Even though he was loath to do so, when he was forced to drink it, sulfurous flames burst forth from his eyes, his ears, and his nostrils. After this, the demon said, "Now you can inspect my pit, which has no bottom." Removing the cover, he threw the Landgrave in and withdrew. Behold, this is the very pit in which the cleric saw him, as I related in a previous chapter.[3]

CONCERNING THE PUNISHMENT OF A PRIEST, WHOSE OWN PARISHIONERS DROVE HIS SOUL INTO THE PIT.

There was in a certain village a very wretched priest, idling in excess and revelries and neglecting altogether the souls committed to his care. When he passed away, the parishioners who had died under his watch began to crowd around him in the infernal regions with stones in their hands, saying, "We were in your care and you neglected us. And when we sinned, you did not correct us with your word or your example. You have been the cause of our damnation!" After they harried him by throwing stones, he fell into the pit and was never seen again. These events concerning his fate were revealed to a devout woman.

CONCERNING THE DEAD KNIGHT WHO AT NIGHT HUNG SERPENTS AND TOADS AT THE DOOR OF HIS SON IN PLACE OF FISH.

When he died, a certain knight bequeathed to his son goods he had obtained by usury. One night he came knocking forcefully at the door. When a boy came running and asked why he was knocking there, he answered, "Let me in. I am the lord of this property" and gave his name. Looking through the opening and recognizing him, the boy responded, "My lord is most assuredly dead; I will not let you in." When the dead man went on knocking and received no answer, at length he said, "Take these fish, which I eat, for my son. Look, I am hanging them on the door." When they went out in the morning, they found a multitude of toads and snakes in a tangled mass. Truly this is the food served in hell, which is cooked in a sulfurous fire.

NOVICE: What is your opinion about those people who live a bad life and nevertheless give many alms to the poor?

MONK: It does not benefit them for eternal life.

CONCERNING THE BAVARIAN, WHO APPEARED TO HIS WIFE AFTER DEATH AND SAID THAT ALMSGIVING HAD NOT HELPED HIM.

Not many years have elapsed since the death of a very wealthy official of the duke of Bavaria. One night the castle in which his wife was sleeping trembled so much that it seemed as though there was an earthquake. And behold the door of the chamber in which she was lying opened and her husband entered, accompanied by a giant figure, blacker than black, which pushed him by the shoulders. When she saw and recognized her husband, she called him to her and made him sit upon a seat at her bedside. She felt no fear, but as she was only wearing a nightgown, she draped a part of the bed covering over her shoulders, the reason being that it was cold. She asked her husband about his condition and he responded with sadness, "I am consigned to eternal punishments." Hearing this, his wife grew very frightened and asked, "What are you saying? Did you not give alms in abundance? Your door was open to every pilgrim. Do these good deeds provide no benefit to you at all?" He responded, "They provide no advantage at all for eternal life, the reason being that I did them out of empty glory rather than out of love." When she wanted to ask him about other things, he answered abruptly, "I was allowed to appear to you, but I can linger here no longer. Behold my hellish handler stands waiting for me outside. Indeed, if the leaves of every tree were turned into tongues, they still could not describe my torments." After this, he was summoned and driven away; the entire castle trembled as before at his departure and his lamenting cries echoed for a long time. This vision was and remains especially renowned in Bavaria, as our monk Gerard (formerly canon of Ratison) was witness. He related this story to us. See how in all of these stories the scripture is fulfilled which says, "The mighty will be mightily tormented."[4]

NOVICE: This example and others like it should be preached to the mighty.

MONK: Because the lives of the priests themselves are for the most part bad and wayward, they flatter the mighty instead of pricking them.

CONCERNING THE NUN WHO CARRIED AROUND THE BURNING INFANT SHE HAD KILLED.

A nun from a certain convent near to us, which I do not wish to name, became pregnant. To prevent her disgrace from being revealed, she killed the child inside of her. Afterward, she became very seriously ill due to an excess of shame. Although she confessed all of her other sins, she remained silent about her disgrace and the murder of her child and thus expired.

A relative of hers labored on behalf of her soul. The dead woman appeared to her clearly while she was at prayer. She carried in her hands a burning child, saying, "I conceived and was pregnant with this baby, but I killed it while it lived inside me. I carry it around ceaselessly in my torments and its fire burns and devours me. If, while I was dying, I had made my confession concerning this, my greatest sin, I would have found grace." From this, it is gathered that sins which are not detected in this life through confession are revealed in the future through the difficulty of punishment.

CONCERNING THE PUNISHMENT OF RUDINGER AND HIS DRINK.

In the diocese of Cologne not far from the city of Cologne, there was a certain knight by the name of Rudinger. He was so entirely given over to wine that he would attend celebrations in different country estates for the sole purpose of drinking good wine. When he became ill and was about to die, his daughter asked him to appear to her within thirty days. Responding "I will do this if I can," he died. Indeed, after his death he appeared to his daughter in a vision, "Behold I am here just as you asked." And in his hand, he was carrying a small clay cup, which is commonly called a *cruselinum*, with which he was accustomed to drink in taverns. His daughter asked him, "Father, what is in that cup?" He responded, "My drink is made from pitch and sulfur. I am always drinking from it and I cannot empty it." Then he disappeared. And immediately the girl understood, as much from his previous life as from this punishment, that there was little or no hope in his salvation. For in the here and now wine goes down easily, but in the end, it will bite you like a snake.

THE ABOMINABLE FANCY[1]

Stories about the horrors of Hell circulated from the confines of the cloister to the pews of parish churches in the twelfth and thirteenth centuries, but during this period the nature of the damned and their relationship to the blessed in Heaven became a matter of theological speculation that occupied the most brilliant Christian minds of the later Middle Ages. Chief among them was Thomas Aquinas (1225–74), a Dominican friar of Italian origin, whose sprawling Summa Theologica *(The Sum of Theology) has become the most widely read compendium of theological teaching in the Western Christian tradition. Treating topics as diverse as the existence of God, the purpose of human life, and the necessity of Christ's incarnation, Aquinas approached each subject in the same way. After presenting a supposition and then giving several objections to it, he proceeded to support the supposition and to counter the objections he had offered. Aquinas supported his arguments with proof texts from the Christian scriptures but also with reference to the works of ancient philosophers like Aristotle and Plato. Toward the end of the* Summa Theologica, *Aquinas applied his reasoning to the relationship between the blessed in Heaven and the damned in Hell. How do the saints feel about the damned? Do they witness their infernal torments from Heaven? Do they rejoice in the suffering inflicted in Hell? He concluded that the blessed must find happiness in the eternal torments of the wicked because these punishments were an expression of divine justice and the blessed loved every manifestation of God's power. Moreover, Aquinas argued that the saints found joy in the suffering of the damned because it heightened their awareness of their own state of blessedness. In the late nineteenth century, the Anglican cleric Frederic William Farrar derided this notion as "an abominable fancy," but in the unrelenting logic of medieval Christian theology, the idea that the blessed found enjoyment in the horrific tortures inflicted on the damned became a cornerstone of Christian doctrine.*

ARTICLE 1. WHETHER THE BLESSED WHO ARE IN HEAVEN WILL SEE THE PUNISHMENTS OF THE DAMNED.

THE FIRST OBJECTION: It would seem that the blessed in heaven will not see the punishments of the damned. For the damned are more distant from the blessed than wayfarers.[2] But the blessed do not see the deeds of wayfarers, as a gloss on Isaiah 63.16 ("Abraham did not know us") says: "The dead, even the saints, do not know what the living are doing, even their own children."[3] Much less, therefore, do they see the suffering of the damned.

THE SECOND OBJECTION: Furthermore, the perfection of vision depends on the perfection of the visible object, as the Philosopher says, that "the most perfect operation of the sense of sight is when the sense is most disposed with reference to the most beautiful of the objects under its sight."[4] Therefore, on the one hand, any deformity in the visible object reflects the imperfection of the sight. But there will be no imperfection in the blessed. Therefore, they will not see the sufferings of the damned, in which there is extreme deformity.

ON THE CONTRARY, it is written in Isaiah, "They shall go out and see the carcasses of the men who have transgressed against me."[5] And a gloss says, "The elect will go out by understanding or seeing clearly, so that they may be urged all the more to praise God."

I ANSWER THAT nothing should be denied to the blessed that belongs to the perfection of their blessedness. Now everything is known all the more for being compared with its contrary, because when contraries are placed beside one another, they become more conspicuous. And, therefore, in order that the happiness of the saints may be more delightful to them and that they may render greater thanks to God for it, they are allowed to see perfectly the sufferings of the damned.

REPLY TO OBJECTION 1. This gloss speaks of what the departed saints are able to do by nature, for it is not necessary that they should know by natural knowledge all that happens to the living. But the saints in heaven know distinctly all that happens both to wayfarers and to the damned. For this reason, Gregory says that Job's words, "Whether his children come to honor or dishonor, he shall not understand," do not apply to the souls of the saints, because, since they possess the glory of God within them, we cannot believe that events outside of heaven are unknown to them.[6]

REPLY TO OBJECTION 2. Although the beauty of the thing seen helps to bring about the perfection of vision, there may be deformity of the thing seen without imperfection of vision, because the images of things by which the soul knows contraries are not themselves contrary. For this reason, God, who has the most perfect knowledge, sees all things, beautiful and deformed.

ARTICLE 2. WHETHER THE BLESSED PITY THE MISERIES OF THE DAMNED.

OBJECTION 1. It would seem that the blessed pity the miseries of the damned. For pity proceeds from charity, and charity will be most perfect in the blessed. Therefore, they will most certainly pity the miseries of the damned.

OBJECTION 2. Furthermore, the blessed will never be as removed from pity as God. Yet, in a sense, God has sympathy for our afflictions and for this reason He is said to be merciful. And likewise, so do the angels. Therefore, the blessed pity the miseries of the damned.

ON THE CONTRARY, whoever pities another person is a participant in their misery. But the blessed cannot participate in any misery. Therefore, they do not pity the miseries of the damned.

I ANSWER THAT, mercy or compassion may exist in a person in two ways: first, by way of passion; second, by way of choice. In the blessed, there will be no passion in them, except as a result of the choice of reason. Hence, compassion and mercy will not be in them, except by the choice of reason. Now, mercy or compassion result from the reason's choice, namely, when a person wishes another person's evil to be dispelled. It follows that in those things which, in accordance with reason, we do not wish to be dispelled, we have no such compassion. But as long as sinners are in the world, they are in such a state that, without prejudice to the divine justice, they can be rescued from a state of unhappiness and sin to a state of happiness. Consequently, it is possible to have compassion for them both by the choice of will—in this sense, God, the angels, and the blessed are said to pity them by desiring their salvation—and by passion, as they are pitied by good people who are wayfarers. But in their future state, it will be impossible for them to be rescued from their unhappiness, and consequently, it will not be possible to pity their miseries according to reason. Therefore, the blessed in glory will have no pity on the damned.

REPLY TO OBJECTION 1. Charity is the principle of pity, when it is possible for us out of charity to desire the end of a person's unhappiness. But the saints cannot desire this for the damned, because it would be contrary to divine justice. As a result, the argument is not convincing.

REPLY TO OBJECTION 2. God is said to be merciful, insofar as He helps those who it is appropriate to be released from their miseries in accordance with the order of wisdom and justice, but He does not show pity toward the damned, except perhaps in punishing them less than they deserve.

ARTICLE 3. WHETHER THE BLESSED REJOICE IN THE PUNISHMENT OF THE WICKED.

OBJECTION 1: It would seem that the blessed do not rejoice in the punishment of the wicked. For rejoicing in another's evil pertains to hatred. But there will be no hatred in the blessed. Therefore, they will not rejoice in the miseries of the damned.

OBJECTION 2: Furthermore, the blessed in heaven will conform to God in the highest degree. Now, God does not rejoice in our punishments. Therefore, neither will the blessed rejoice in the punishments of the damned.

OBJECTION 3: Furthermore, whatever is worthy of blame in a wayfarer has no place whatsoever in a comprehensor.[7] Now, it is very reprehensible in a wayfarer to take pleasure in the pain of others and most praiseworthy to grieve for them. Therefore, the blessed in no way rejoice in the punishment of the damned.

ON THE CONTRARY, it is written that "the just shall rejoice when he shall see the revenge."[8] Furthermore, it is written that "they shall satiate the sight of all flesh."[9] Here "satiate" denotes a refreshment of the mind. Therefore, the blessed will rejoice in the punishment of the wicked.

I ANSWER THAT a thing may be a matter of rejoicing in two ways. First, directly, when one rejoices in a thing as such, and in this way the saints will not rejoice in the punishment of the wicked. Second, indirectly, by reason namely of something pertaining to it, and in this way the saints will rejoice in the punishment of the wicked by considering the order of divine justice and their own deliverance, which will fill them with joy. And thus, divine justice and their own deliverance will be the direct cause of the joy of the blessed, while the punishment of the damned will cause it indirectly.

REPLY TO OBJECTION 1: To rejoice in another's evil as such belongs to hatred, but not to rejoice in another's evil by reason of something pertaining to it. Thus, a person sometimes rejoices in his own evil, as when we rejoice in our own afflictions as helping us to merit life, "My brethren, count it as joy when you shall fall into diverse temptations."[10]

REPLY TO OBJECTION 2: Although God does not rejoice in punishments as such, He rejoices in them insofar as they are ordained by His justice.

REPLY TO OBJECTION 3: It is not praiseworthy in a wayfarer to rejoice in another's afflictions as such, yet it is praiseworthy if he rejoices in them when they pertain to something else. It is not, however, the same with a wayfarer as with a comprehensor, because in a wayfarer the passions often prevent the judgment of reason, and yet sometimes such passions are praiseworthy and indicative of the mind's good disposition, as in the case of shame, pity, and repentance for evil, whereas in a comprehensor there can be no passion except for that which follows the judgment of reason.

ABANDON ALL HOPE: DANTE'S *INFERNO* (c. 1320)

The Divine Comedy (Divina Commedia) by Dante Alighieri (c. 1265–1321) is a masterpiece of Western literature and unrivaled in its depiction of the horrors of Hell. Written during the last decade of Dante's life, this long Italian poem told the story of the author's journey to the three domains of the dead, beginning with his descent to the place of eternal torment (the Inferno). Escorted through Hell by the shade of the Roman poet Virgil, whose depiction of Hades in The Aeneid did much to inspire the first part of The Divine Comedy (see pp. 22–32), Dante painted a vivid tableau of the hideous fates awaiting the wicked in a vast subterranean realm where divine justice doled out punishment to sinners according to the nature of their transgressions. In the poem, Hell has the organization and efficiency of a bureaucratic state: every impious soul has its appropriate place and every place apportioned a particular punishment keyed to a specific sin. More so than any previous author, Dante had a clear and logical understanding of the geography of the afterlife. He depicted Hell as a deep funnel with circular tiers. He and Virgil descended tier by tier from the gates of Hell, past the limbo of the virtuous pagans, and down through each circle, where those guilty of lust, gluttony, greed, wrath, heresy, violence, fraud, and treachery suffered for all eternity. At the bottom of Hell was Cocytus, a vast, frozen lake. Trapped in the ice of this lake was the gigantic, three-faced Satan, who beat his six massive, batlike wings in vain to escape his imprisonment. Satan's face was stained with tears and his chin *dripped with the gore of history's three worst traitors, whose souls he chewed endlessly and without pity in his monstrous mouths: Brutus and Cassius, who assassinated Julius Caesar in 44 BCE; and Judas Iscariot, who betrayed Jesus Christ himself.*

THROUGH THE
GATES OF HELL[1]

"Through me is the way into the woeful city
   Through me is the way to eternal pain
   Through me is the way among the lost people.

Justice inspired my exalted maker:
   The divine power, the supreme wisdom,
   And the primal love made me.

Before me nothing was created,
   Except eternal beings, and I endure eternally.
   Abandon all hope, you who enter."

These words in dark color I saw
   Written upon the summit of the gate.
   I said, "Their meaning is difficult for me, master."

And he replied to me, as one who understood,
   "Here you must abandon all your doubts.
   All cowardice must be laid to rest.

We have now come to the place, where I told you,
   You will see the woeful people
   Who have lost the good obtained by intellect."

And then he put his hand on mine and
   With a smile that comforted me
   He led me in among secret things.

There sighs and groans and plaintive wailing
    Resounded through the starless air,
    Which caused me to well up with tears.

Diverse tongues, horrible dialects,
    Words of agony, accents of anger
    And voices high and hoarse, and the sound of hands,

Made up a tumult that goes whirling on
    Forever in that air forever black,
    Just like the sand, when the whirlwind blows.

My head with horror bound, I said,
    "Master, what is this that I hear?
    Who is this, so overcome by pain?"

He said to me, "This miserable condition
    Afflicts the melancholy souls of those
    Who lived without infamy or praise.

They are commingled with that noisome choir
    Of angels, who were neither rebels nor
    Faithful to God, but only for themselves.

The heavens expelled them, for they were not beautiful;
    Nor did the depths of Hell receive them,
    In this way depriving the damned of their glory."

And I, "Master, what is so grievous to them
    That makes them lament so loudly?"
    He answered, "I will tell you very briefly.

They have no hope of death;
    And this blind life of theirs is so debased
    That they envy every other fate.

The world allows them to have no glory;
   Mercy and justice both despise them.
   Let us not speak of them, but look and then pass by."

And looking again, I saw a banner,
   Which whirled around and ran on so rapidly
   That it seemed like it would never stop;

And running after it there came so long a train
   Of people, that I never would have believed
   That Death could have ever unmade so many.

When I recognized some among them,
   I looked and I saw the shade of a man
   Who made, though cowardice, a great denial.

Immediately I understood and was certain
   That this group comprised those worthless wretches
   Hateful to God and to their own enemies.

These wretches, who were never truly alive,
   Were naked and stung repeatedly
   By the wasps and hornets that swarmed around them.

The insects caused their faces to pour with blood,
   Which mingled with their tears, to be consumed
   By the disgusting worms at their feet.

And when I looked farther on, I saw other people
   Arrayed along the bank of a great river.
   I said, "Master, Allow me

To know who these people are, and what makes them
   Appear so ready to cross over, as far as I can
   Discern from here in this weak light."

And he said to me, "These things shall all be revealed
    To you, as soon as our footsteps lead us
    To the dismal shores of Acheron."

Then, with my eyes ashamed and cast downward,
    Fearing that my words might irritate him,
    I refrained from speech until we reached the river.

And lo! in a boat there approached
    An old man with hair of gray,
    Crying, "Woe to you, you depraved souls!

Do not hope to look upon the sky ever again;
    I come to lead you to the other shore,
    To the eternal shades of fire and frost.

And you, standing over there, living soul,
    Depart from these people, who are dead!"
    But when he saw that I did not withdraw,

He said, "By other ways, by other ports will you
    come to the shore for passage, not here;
    A lighter vessel must carry you."

And to him my guide said, "Do not torment yourself, Charon;
    It is so willed there, where all is possible
    That is willed; and so, ask no further."

At that, the fleecy cheeks of the ferryman fell quiet,
    Who sailed the dark fen, his eyeballs
    Encircled by wheels of flame.

But all those souls who were weary and naked,
    Their complexions changed and they gnashed their teeth
    As soon as they heard those cruel words.

They blasphemed against God and their own kin,
   The human race, the place, the time, the seed
   From which they sprung, the day that they were born.

Then they all drew back together,
   bitterly weeping, to the accursed shore
   that waits for all who have no fear of God.

That demon Charon, with eyes like hot coals,
   Beckons to them, collects them all together,
   Beats with his oar whoever lags behind.

As in the autumn, when the leaves fall,
   First one and then another, until the branch
   Has surrendered all its spoils to the earth.

Likewise, the evil seed of Adam
   Throw themselves one by one from the riverside
   At a signal, like a bird comes to its call.

So, they depart across the dark waves,
   And before they land upon the other side,
   Once again, on this side, a new group has assembled.

"My son," my polite master said to me,
   "All those who perish in the wrath of God
   Meet here together from every land;

And they are eager to cross over the river
   Because divine justice spurs them on,
   So that their fear is turned into desire.

A good soul never passes this way;
   And so, if Charon complains about you,
   You may well now know what that means."

When he finished speaking, all of that dark country
   Trembled so violently, that my recollection
   Of that terror bathes me in sweat even now.

The land of tears gave forth a blast of wind,
   And a bright red light flashed,
   Which overcame all of my senses,

And like a man whom sleep has seized, I fell.

THE FILTHY FEN[1]

"Let us now descend into greater misery;
    Already each star that was ascending when I set out
    Sinks, and it is forbidden for us to loiter."

We crossed the circle to the other bank,
    Near to a spring that boiled and spilled out
    Along a sluice that ran out of it.

The water was far darker than indigo;
    And in the company of the murky waves,
    We travelled downward by a winding path.

Into a marsh, which is called the Styx,
    This sad brook makes its way down
    To the foot of those malign, gray shores.

And I paused, intent upon looking,
    And saw people caked with mud in that lagoon,
    All of them naked and fierce.

They struck one another not only with their hands,
    But their heads and bodies and feet,
    Tearing each other to pieces with their teeth.

My good master said, "Son, you now look upon
    The souls of those whom anger has overthrown;
    And also, I would like you to know for sure

Beneath the water are souls whose sighs
   Make the water bubble on the surface
   As you can see at every turn.

Trapped in the mire, they croak, 'Sullen we were
   In the sweet air, which the sun gladdens,
   Bearing within ourselves mournful fumes;

Now we are gloomy in this black ooze.'
   They gurgle this refrain in their throats,
   For they cannot utter it with unbroken words."

Thus, we went circling around the filthy fen
   A great arc between the dry bank and the swamp,
   With our eyes on those who gorged the mire;

Until we came at last to the foot of a tower.[2]

THE BOILING BLOOD[1]

The place where we hoped to descend the bank
    Was steep, and moreover, it was so precipitous,
    that it was difficult to look upon.

That ruined escarpment looked like the flank of the Adige
    On this side of Trent, after it was struck
    By an earthquake or a landslide.

For from the mountain's top, from which it slid down
    Onto the plain below, the cliff is shattered in such a way
    To provide a path downward to someone up above.

Likewise was our descent into that ravine
    And on the lip of the broken chasm
    The infamy of Crete lay stretched out,

Who was conceived in the womb of a false heifer;
    And when he saw us, he gnawed himself,
    Like someone whom anger racks within.[2]

My wise guide shouted toward him, "Do you suppose
    That the King of Athens has arrived,
    Who in the world above brought death to you?[3]

Go away, beast, for this one does not come
    Instructed by your sister, but in order
    To witness your punishments."

Just like a bull who breaks loose at the moment
   When he has received the killing blow,
   Who cannot walk, but staggers here and there,

The Minotaur, I saw, behaved like that;
   And watchful Virgil cried, "Run to the passage;
   Let us descend while he is overcome by rage."

Thus, we picked our way downward over the scree
   Of stone, which often shifted beneath my feet
   From the unaccustomed weight upon them.

I went on, deep in thought, and Virgil said, "You are thinking
   Perhaps about this ruin, which is guarded
   By that monster's anger, which we just evaded.

Now you should know that the other time
   I descended this way to the deepest parts of Hell,
   This precipice had not yet fallen down.

But truly, if I understand correctly, a little
   Before the arrival of the one who carried off from Dis
   The great prize of its highest circle,

Upon all sides, the deep and loathsome valley
   Trembled so much that I thought the Universe
   Was thrilled with love, by which (there are those who think)

The world sometimes turns into chaos;
   And at that moment, this ancient crag
   Both here and elsewhere was rent asunder.[4]

But fix your eyes below; for the river of blood
   Draws near, within which boils whoever did injury
   To others by violence."

O blind passion, O insane wrath
    That spurs us onward in our short life,
    And then stews us in torment for all eternity!

I saw a great ditch bent like a bow
    That encompassed the entire plain
    Exactly as my guide had described.

And between this and the foot of the embankment
    Centaurs were running in a line, armed with arrows,
    As they used to hunt in the world.

Seeing us descend, each one stood still
    And from the squadron, three detached themselves,
    Taking aim at us with their bows and arrows.

And from a distance, one of them shouted, "To what torment
    Do you come, you descending down the hillside?
    Tell us from there; if not, I will draw the bow."

My master said, "We will make our answer
    to Chiron, standing next to you there;
    that will of yours was always too hasty."

Then Virgil said to me, "This one is Nessus,
    Who perished for the lovely Deianeira,
    But then he avenged himself with his own blood.

And in the middle, eyes fixed upon his chest,
    Is the great Chiron, who raised Achilles;
    That other one is Pholus, who was so wrathful.[5]

Thousands and thousands of centaurs run around the ditch
    Shooting with arrows whatever soul emerges
    Out of the blood more than his crimes allows."

We approached these swift monsters;
 Chiron took an arrow and with the notch
 Backward upon his jaws he combed his beard.

After he had uncovered his great mouth,
 He said to his companions, "Have you noticed
 That the one behind moves whatever he touches?

The feet of dead men do not behave in this way."
 And my guide, who was now at his breast,
 Where the centaur's two natures are joined together,

Replied, "Indeed he lives, and thus it falls to me alone
 To show him the dark valley;
 Necessity, not pleasure, compels us.

Someone who paused from singing Halleluja
 Committed this new duty to me;
 He was no thief; and I am no furtive spirit.

But by that power at whose command I am making
 My way along this forlorn road,
 Loan us one of your entourage to accompany us,

And to show us where we can find the ford,
 And who can carry this one on his back;
 For he is not a spirit that can walk in the air."

Chiron turned to the right
 And said to Nessus, "Turn around and guide them,
 And tell any other band you meet to leave them alone."

With our faithful escort we moved on
 Along the shore of that bubbling blood,
 In which the boiled uttered their loud laments.

I saw people submerged up to their eyebrows,
    And the great centaur said, "These are tyrants,
    Who dealt in bloodshed and pillaging.

Here they lament their pitiless sins; here
    Is Alexander and fierce Dionysius
    Who caused such grievous years in Sicily.[6]

That forehead there with the black hair
    Is Azzolin; and the other, the blond one,
    Is Obizzo d'Este, who, in truth,

Was murdered by his stepson in the world above."[7]
    Then I turned to the poet and he said,
    "Now let him go first, and I will follow next."

A little farther on, the centaur stopped
    Above some people, who came out of that boiling stream
    As far down as their throats.

He pointed out a shade by himself to the side,
    Saying, "He stabbed in the bosom of God
    The heart that is still honored on the Thames."[8]

Then I saw people, who lifted their heads
    And also their chests out of the river
    And I recognized many of them.

Thus ever more and more that blood
    Grew shallower, until it covered the feet alone
    And there across the moat lay our passage.

"Even as you see on this side
    The boiling streams that slowly recede,"
    The centaur said, "I want you to know

That further on its bed declines more and more
    Until it reunites itself at a point
    Where tyrants groan in agony.

Down there, divine justice stings that Attila,
    Who was a scourge on the whole world,
    And Pyrrhus, and Sextus, and forever more it milks

The tears, which with the boiling it unseals,
    From Rinier da Corneto and Rinier the Mad,
    Who caused such strife upon the public roads."[9]

Then he turned back and crossed the ford once more.

THE FOREST OF THE SUICIDES[1]

Nessus had not yet reached the other side
   When we found ourselves within a forest
   That was not marked by any path whatsoever.

The foliage was not green, but dark in color.
   The branches were not smooth, but gnarled and tangled.
   There were no apple trees, but only thorns with poison.

Those savage beasts that hold in hatred
   The cultivated land between Cécina and Corneto
   Does not boast such dense and tangled thickets as their lairs.

There do the hideous Harpies make their nests,
   Who chased the Trojans from the Strophades
   With sad announcements of their impending doom;[2]

They have broad wings, and necks and faces like humans,
   And feet with claws, and their great bellies sport feathers.
   They make laments upon these strange trees.

And the good master said, "Before you go any farther,
   Know that you are within the second circle,"
   And he continued thus, "and shall be until

You come out upon the horrible sand;
   Therefore, have a good look around, and you will see
   Things that will lend weight to my words."

I heard on all sides the sound of lamentations,
    And I could see no one who uttered them,
    So, utterly bewildered, I stood still.

I think he thought that perhaps I might think
    That these voices issued from those tree trunks,
    From people who concealed themselves from us;

Therefore, the Master said, "If you break off
    Some little sprig from any of these trees,
    You will realize the error of your thoughts."

So I stretched forth my hand a little,
    And plucked a sprig from a great thorn bush;
    And the trunk cried, "Why do you injure me?"

After it grew dark with the flow of blood,
    It cried out again, "Why do you mangle me?
    Have you no spirit of pity at all?

We were once men, now transformed into trees;
    Indeed, your hand should be more pitiful,
    Even if we had been the souls of serpents."

Just like a green branch that is on fire
    Burns at one end, and from the other end drips
    and hisses with the wind that is escaping;

So from that splinter issued forth together
    Both words and blood; at this point, I let the stick
    Fall, and stood immobile, like a man struck with terror.

"If he had been able to believe,"
    My wise teacher answered, "O you wounded soul,
    What he had previously seen only in my verses,

He would not have stretched forth his hand upon you;
 But your fate is so unbelievable that
 I made him do something that I regret.

But tell him who you were, so that as a way
 To make amends, he can refresh your fame
 Up in the world, to which he can return."

And the tree trunk said: "Your sweet words are so alluring that
 I cannot remain silent; and do not be displeased
 That I am tempted to talk for a while.

I am the one who had in hand both keys
 Of Federigo's heart, and turned them to and fro
 So softly in unlocking and in locking,

That I kept most men from his secrets;
 I kept faith, that glorious office,
 So well, that I lost my sleep and my pulse.[3]

The harlot, who never turns aside
 Her painted eyes from Caesar's dwellings,
 —She is the doom of all and the vice of court life—

Inflamed against me all the other minds
 And they, inflamed, did so inflame Augustus
 So that my glad honors turned to dismal mournings.[4]

My spirit, disdainful in its taste,
 Thinking by dying to escape disdain,
 Made me unjust against myself, the just.

By the strange roots of this tree
 Do I swear to you that I never broke faith
 With my lord, who was so worthy of honor;

And to the world, if one of you returns,
    Let him comfort my memory, which is lying
    Prone from the blow that envy dealt to it."

The poet paused and then said to me, "Since he is silent,
    Do not waste the opportunity, but speak
    And question him, if you wish to learn more."

And I to him, "Can you inquire once again
    About what you think I wish to hear,
    For I cannot. Such pity is in my heart!"

Therefore, Virgil spoke again, "So that the man may
    Do for you freely what your word implores,
    Imprisoned spirit, once again please

Tell us in what way the soul is bound
    Within these knots of wood; and tell us, if you can,
    If anyone is ever freed from this state."

Then the tree trunk exhaled with force,
    And the wind became these words,
    "In haste shall I reply to you.

When the maddened soul abandons
    The body from which it tore itself away,
    Minos consigns it to the seventh abyss.

It falls into the forest, and no place
    Is chosen for it; but where Fortune hurls it,
    There like a grain of spelt it germinates.

It sprouts a sapling that becomes a forest tree;
    The harpies, feeding upon its leaves,
    Cause it pain, and a window for that pain.

Like others, we shall return for our spoils on Judgment Day;
    But none of us may clothe ourselves in our bodies again,
    For it is not right to have what one has cast off.

We will drag them back here, and along the dismal
    Forest our bodies shall be hung,
    Each on the thorn of the shade that harmed it."

We were still listening to the tree trunk,
    Thinking that it might want to tell us more,
    When we were surprised by a sudden crash,

In the same way that someone hears
    The boar and chase approaching toward his stand,
    Who hears the crashing of beasts and branches;

And look there upon our left-hand side, those two
    Naked and scratched, fleeing so furiously,
    That they broke every branch in their way.

The one in the lead called out, "Now help, Death, help!"
    And the other, who lagged further behind,
    Was shouting, "Lano, those legs of yours

Were not so quick at joustings of the Toppo!"[5]
    And then, perhaps because he was out of breath,
    He took shelter behind a bush.

Behind them, the forest was full of black dogs,
    Ravenous and as swift of foot
    As greyhounds, who are released from their chains

They set their teeth on the one crouched down
    And tore him piece by piece,
    And thereafter carried off his suffering limbs.

Thereafter, my guide took me by the hand
    And led me to that bush, that to no avail
    Was weeping from its bloody lacerations.

"O Jacopo da Santo Andrea!" it said,
    "What use was it for you to make me your shield?
    Am I to blame for your nefarious life?"

When my master came and stood near the bush,
    and asked, "Who were you, who through your many wounds
    Spits out your sad words with blood?"

And he said to us, "O souls, who have come here
    To look upon the shameful massacre
    That has torn my leaves away from me,

Gather them up beneath the dismal bush;
    I was from that city which changed its first patron
    From Mars to the Baptist. Therefore, for this offence

He will forever bring it sadness with the art of war.
    And were there not near the bridge over the Arno
    Some glimpses of him still remaining,

Those citizens, who afterward rebuilt it
    Upon the ashes left by Attila
    Would then have labored all in vain.

As for me, I hung myself in my own house."[6]

TRAPPED UNDER ICE[1]

"The battle standards of the king of Hell advance
      Toward us; therefore, look ahead there,"
      My master said, "and see if you can see it."

As when a heavy fog settles, or when
      Our hemisphere darkens into night,
      And there appears in the distance a windmill

I thought that I could make out a building like that
      And because of the wind, I took shelter behind
      My guide, because there was nowhere else to hide.

I was by now (I write this verse in fear)
      Where all the shades were completely trapped in ice,
      Their shapes glimmered through like straws in a glass.

Some were lying prone; others stood erect,
      This one with his head raised, and that one with her legs aloft;
      Another bent like a bow, touching face to feet.

When we had proceeded forward a little ways
      It pleased my master to show to me
      The creature who had once appeared so fair.

Standing before me, he made me stop,
      Saying, "Behold Dis, and behold the place
      Where you must arm yourself with fortitude."

How frozen I became at that moment and powerless,
 —Reader, do not ask, for I cannot write it,
 Because all language would be insufficient—

I did not die, and yet I did not remain alive;
 Just think for a moment, if you have any sense,
 What I became, deprived of life and death.

The emperor of this kingdom of gloom
 Came up out of the ice at the mid-point of his chest;
 And I compare better with a giant

Than do the giants with those arms of his;
 Consider now how large his whole body must be
 In proportion to those colossal arms.

If he was once as fair, as he is now foul,
 And lifted up his brow against his Maker
 Then all tribulation must indeed proceed from him.

O, what a marvel it appeared to me,
 When I saw three faces on his head!
 The one in front was a brilliant red;

There were two others that joined with this one
 Above the middle part of either shoulder,
 And they merged together at the crest of his hair;

The one on the right blended yellow and white;
 The left had the same dark color as those people
 Who come from where the Nile finds its source.

Underneath each face sprouted two mighty wings,
 All six proportioned for a bird of great size;
 I never saw sails of the sea so large.

They had no feathers, but they looked like the wings
   Of a bat; and he was flapping them
   So that three winds proceeded forth from him.

Cocytus was frozen over by them.
   With six eyes he wept, and down his three chins
   Trickled his tear drops and his drool mingled with blood.

In each of his mouths, his teeth were chewing
   A sinner, like flax pulled through a heckling comb.
   He tormented three of them in this way.

To the soul in front, the biting was nothing compared
   To the clawing it received, which sometimes stripped
   The spine completely of all the skin that remained.

"That soul up there in the greatest pain,"
   The master said, "is Judas Iscariot;
   With his head inside, he jerks his dangling legs in the air.[2]

Of the other two, whose heads face downward,
   The one who hangs from the black mouth is Brutus;
   See how he writhes there, and speaks no word.

And the other, who seems so stalwart, is Cassius.
   But the night ascends again, and it is time
   For us to depart, for we have seen enough."[3]

As he desired, I clasped him around the neck,
   And he weighed the best time and place to make our move,
   And when the wings were opened far apart,

He grabbed hold of the Devil's shaggy sides;
   From tuft to tuft we descended downward then
   Between the thick hair and the frozen crust.

When we reached the point where his thigh-bone turns
 Where his haunch was thickest,
 My guide, with effort and panting breath,

Turned his head around to where his legs had been,
 And clutched the hair, like one about to climb,
 So that I was under the impression that we were returning to Hell.

"Hold on tight, for by stairs like these,"
 My master said, panting with fatigue,
 "We need to take our leave from so much evil."

Then through a fissure in the rock he came forth,
 And down upon its lip, he seated me;
 Then he took a wary step toward me.

I lifted up my eyes and thought to see
 Lucifer in the same way we had left him
 But I saw instead his legs, held upward there.

And if I then became confused,
 Let slow-witted people think how they failed to see
 What point it was beyond which I had passed.

"Get up on your feet," my master said;
 "The way is long, and the road difficult,
 And now the sun returns to the morning."

It was not a palace corridor
 There where we stood, but a natural cave,
 With an uneven floor and scarcely any light . . .

My guide and I now entered that hidden road,
 To return once more to the shining world;
 And without care that we had no rest

We mounted up, he going first and I behind,
   Until through a round aperture I saw
   The beautiful things that the skies above us bear;

Now we came forth to look upon the stars.

A HEARTBREAKING CONSORT OF WOES: EARLY MODERN AFTERLIVES (c. 1500–1700)

In 1517, Martin Luther's public protest against the sale of indulgences by the Catholic Church heralded the full-blown critique and rejection of centuries-old Christian traditions known as the Protestant Reformation. Luther's actions had a profound impact on early modern thinking about the afterlife. By the early sixteenth century, Christian doctrine taught that there were at least five destinations for the souls of the dead: Heaven; Hell; Purgatory; the Limbo of Infants, for unbaptized children who died before they could commit personal sins but were nonetheless stained by original sin and thus ineligible to enter Heaven; and the Limbo of the Patriarchs, for those righteous Jewish patriarchs who could not enter Heaven until the resurrection of Jesus Christ (after the Harrowing of Hell, it stood empty; see pp. 47–56). The Protestants reduced the afterlife from five places to two: Heaven and Hell. They denied the existence of Purgatory and the Limbos because there was no direct proof in the Christian scriptures for their existence.

Despite these fundamental differences in their beliefs about the afterlife, Protestant thinkers found common ground with their Catholic opponents on the topic of Hell. Both camps agreed that Hell and its torments were real. Both groups concurred about the function of Hell as a punishment for sinners and allowed that divine justice matched the severity of this punishment with the sin in question. Protestant theologians in mainland Europe and their Anglican counterparts in England were far less likely, however, to follow Catholics in their certainty *that Hell was an actual, physical place underground. In 1714, the Anglican Tobias Swinden went so far as to publish a book called* An Enquiry into the Nature and Place of Hell, *in which he argued that the sun was the prison of evil souls, because it had the mass to hold the unnumbered damned and the great heat necessary to punish them. While Catholic thinkers ruminated on the cruel varieties of corporeal tortures awaiting the wicked, Protestant theologians tended to emphasize the sinner's banishment from God and wounded conscience as the worst aspects of Hell.*

THE SHARP PANGS OF A
WOUNDED CONSCIENCE[1]

*Preaching before King William and Queen Anne in the early
1700s, the Anglican William Dawes (1671–1724), bishop of
Chester and later archbishop of York, argued that Hell was an
essential deterrent to bad behavior that allowed human society to function. Moreover, it had always been so. Every ancient society from the Israelites to the Muslims believed in
infernal punishment of one kind or another. "We shall be hard
put to it," he wrote, "to give any one instance of a Man who
has been so far able to shake off his Notions and Fears of Hell,
that they should never after . . . haunt and perplex him." Typical of Anglican theologians, Dawes's sermon on "Hell-
torments" emphasized the absence of God and the "lashes of
their own guilty minds" as the principal suffering awaiting
sinners in Hell. The undying worm of Christian scriptures is
no longer a creature that gnaws painfully on the soul but a
metaphor for the sinner's eternal remorse. While Dawes did
not neglect medieval traditions about Hell—the diabolical
company awaiting the sinner, the pain of the fires, and the
eternal duration of the torments that vexed the souls of the
wicked—he demoted them to emphasize the interior Hell of
the wounded conscience.*

Now our Reason and Scripture make the greatness of Hell-
torments to consist in these particulars.

First, In the Wicked's being banished from the enjoyment of
God, and all that *fullness of Joy*, and those *Rivers of Pleasure*,
which are *in his presence* and *at his right hand*, *for evermore*,

and in all the miseries naturally consequent upon such their banishment.

Secondly, In the lashes of their own guilty Minds, and of all those vexatious Lusts and Passions, which they shall carry with them into another World, and which will be mightily heighten'd and inflam'd there.

Thirdly, In the loathsomeness and uncomfortableness of the place of Hell, and the troublesome Conversion of the Devil and wicked Spirits, which they shall be there confin'd to.

Fourthly, In the pains occasion'd by the Fire of Hell, or whatever is meant under that name.

And Lastly, In the uninterrupted continuance, and eternal duration, of every one of these.

First, in the Wicked's being banish'd from the enjoyment of God, and all that *fullness of Joy*, and *those rivers of pleasure, which are in his presence*, and *at his right hand for evermore:* and in all the miseries naturally consequent upon such their banishment. For so runs the former part of that dreadful Sentence, which shall be pronounc'd against the wicked at the Day of Judgment, *Depart from me, ye cursed*. Not that the wicked shall depart from God, as never to see or remember Him anymore, and to lose all knowledge of Him and Heaven for ever. No, this, as sad a punishment as it is, would be but a very light one in comparison of that, which they shall then be doom'd to. They shall see God, or, which is the same thing, have a most quick and lively notion of Him, but without hopes of ever being reconciled to Him. They shall see Heaven, or at least have always a fresh remembrance of that glorious sight, which they had of it at the general Judgment, but still, as the Rich Man in the Gospel did Paradise, with an impassible gulf betwixt it and them.[2]

But, oh my Soul! How canst thou ever sufficiently conceive of the dreadfulness of such a departure from God, as this is? How canst thou even in any tolerable measure, know what thou shalt lose, in losing that Infinite Abyss of Happiness? How canst thou bear the Thoughts of existing, so much as one moment, when thou shalt be frown'd upon by him, in whose favor alone, is life, that is, every thing which makes Life desirable? Oh! How wilt thou be able to endure thyself, when thy Father, thy most tender and compassinate Father, thy Savior, thy most loving and relenting Savior, the Holy Angels and just Men made perfect, those best natur'd of Created beings, when the *God of all comfort and giver of every good gift*, when he, who once lov'd thee so well, as to *lay down his life for thee*, when they, who have made it their constant business to minister to thee, and have rejoic'd without measure, when they have seen the least hopes of thy becoming happy; in one word, when all those beings who are good and continually delight in doing good, and from whom alone all good must come, shall not endure thee, shall detest and abhor thee, shall spurn thee from the presence, shall *laugh at thy calamity, and mock when thy fear cometh?* Good God! How will it vex and fret our Souls to reflect upon those bright and glorious Mansions of happiness, from which we shall then be banish'd? How will the Contemplation even of Heaven itself torment us, when it shall serve only to create in us strong and eager desires and longings after it, which must never be satisfi'd, and to remind us of a loss, which is as Infinite as God himself? But, above all, how will it gall and wound our Souls, how will it make us all rage and fury against ourselves, to consider that we have lost all this through our own fault; and that, when we had it all within our reach and in our power, we were contented (foolish Creatures that we were!) for mere gugaws and trifles, mere shadows and appearances of happiness, to part with it? Certainly, were there no other punishment for the wicked in Hell than this, they would have great reason to say of it, as *Cain* did of his, *it is greater than we can bear.*

But *secondly*, There will likewise be the lashes of their own guilty minds, and of all those vexatious Lusts and Passions, which they shall carry with them into another World, and which will be mightily heighten'd and inflam'd there. By the worm of the wicked, which shall never die, so often mentioned in Scripture as what is to be part of their Punishment in Hell, we are doubtless to understand the remorse of their own guilty minds or Consciences, which shall, as it were, gnaw and prey upon them, and give them much greater pain and torment than a worm preying upon their living flesh would do. Their Consciences, I say, which will there be continually and most sensibly reproaching them, not only with the loss of Heaven (though this will be reproach enough), but with all that baseness, ingratitude, unreasonableness, folly, and sinfulness toward God, which they shall have been guilty of in their past lives. And with all that shame, anguish, horror, inconceivable and endless Misery, which they shall thereby have brought upon their own Heads. And, as we are sure, from the nature of the thing itself, that, when the wicked shall no longer be cloth'd with such bodies of flesh, as they now are, which mightily obstruct and press down the Soul in her operations, but shall put on spiritual bodies, bodies in which their Souls may freely and uncontrollably exert their utmost powers, their apprehensions and resentments of things most necessarily become vastly more quick and vigorous, and consequently their sense of their own folly, guilt, and misery, and their remorse, anguish, and trouble for them, exceedingly more keen and poignant than they had ever been in this World. So have we all the reason that can be to believe that the Divine Vengeance will both add new stings to these, their own inbred Tormentors, and (as I have before proved to you, it sometimes does with the wounded spirits of Sinners, even in this World) whet and sharpen, in a supernatural manner, the points of their old ones. So that, whereas in this World their Consciences did only chastise them with whips, they shall there chastise them with Scorpions.

Besides this, some Divines have been of the opinion that wicked Men shall carry their appetites and lustings after sensual pleasures into Hell along with them, and there, to their unspeakable Torment, continually burn with the most raging and vehement desires and longings after these things, which yet at the same time they shall be infallibly assur'd, it shall never in the least be in their power to enjoy. But, this seeming not very agreeable to the notion of those spiritual Bodies which the wicked shall be clothed within a future State, I shall not insist upon it, but only suppose what I think very probable that

the wicked shall retain in *Hell* a *remembrance* of those pleasures which they once enjoyed in this World, in their Bodies of
flesh, and that this remembrance shall be extremely grateful
and pleasing to them, and put them upon wishing most ear-
nestly that they were again to be clothed in such Bodies, again
to act over the same pleasures, which having long accustom'd
themselves to, the full bent and inclination of their Souls has
been long wholly set toward them, and has made them utterly
incapable of relishing or delighting in any other. And, if there
shall be any such eager longings and hankerings after bodies
of flesh and the pleasures belonging to them, these join'd with
an utter despair of ever obtaining what they so much long for,
must needs be an unsupportable Torment to the damn'd.

But, be this as it will, it is certain both from Reason and Scripture that the wicked shall be subject to all those peevish and
uneasy Passions in Hell, which are purely Spiritual, as *Pride,
Envy, Malice, Anger, Hatred, Fear, Self-Revenge*, &c., and moreover shall have all these in a much higher degree there, much more
troublesome and vexatious to them than they were in this World.
All these we find ascrib'd to the Devil and his Angels, spiritual Beings, in Scripture. And indeed, it is inconceivable to Reason how
wicked souls can exist without them, and these being purely spiritual Passions, or Passions of the mind consider'd abstractedly
from the body, must needs grow and increase, as we become more
and more spirituraliz'd. Besides, that the objects of these vexatious
passions will be infinitely enlarg'd to the Damn'd in Hell, and that
they will there meet with the most provoking occasions of raising
and inflaming their passions to the utmost, and yet at the same
time with the most tormenting balks and disappointments to
them, that can possibly be imagin'd. Did the envious Man grow
big and swell with Envy here at the sight of the earthly prosperity
of his Brethren? He will even burst with it there at the Contemplation of the happiness of the Saints in Heaven. Did the Malicious
Man hate and malign those, who never did him much hurt here?
Oh, how will he rage and flame out with hatred and ill-will
against those malicious Beings, his Companions in Hell, who
shall continually be doing him all the mischief that they are able
there? Did not the proud man know how to brook any, even the

smallest, disappointments here? Alas! He shall meet with nothing else but disappointments, and those too of the highest kind, there. There, I say, where he shall be sure of having every such thing as he would not, and no one such thing as he would. Was the angry Man apt to be soon put into a passion here, by little Crosses and Vexations? He will there be continually heated, fired, nay, even made and kept red-hot, by a constant series of great ones. To say all at once, the fears of the wicked shall be there heightened into despair, their displeasure against themselves into the utmost indignation, and the most exasperated Rage, fretfulness and bitterness of Soul, the most unmix'd Sorrow, irksomeness and self abhorrency, the keenest Anger and Revenge, shall be the *portion of their Cup*. So that, indeed, the wicked Men seem to carry complete Misery into Hell along with them, while they carry such appetites as, though never so eager and craving, cannot in the least there be satisfied, such passions as, though never so vexatious and intolerable, cannot in the least be pacifi'd and allay'd there. And yet this Misery will still be enhanc'd.

Thirdly, By the loathsomeness and uncomfortableness of the place of Hell and the troublesome conversation of the Devil and wicked spirits, which the damn'd shall be there confin'd to . . . As to the company of Hell, we know that this is wholly made up of Devils and wicked Men. And these being all most malicious and ill-natur'd beings, and besides such, as, we shall then be sensible, have been highly instrumental in drawing us into this *place of Torments*, and moreover, some of them such, as are to be our *very Tormentors*, the bare sight of them must needs be extremely odious and uneasy to the wicked. And nothing can be expected from such company, but continual jangling, hatred, anger, snarling, and biting at one another, nothing but the most terrible Fears and jealousies of, the most malicious and spiteful bickerings against, each other. And good God! If it be thought so very irksome a thing here, to be oblig'd to spend only a few hours in Company that is disagreeable, how shall we ever be able to bear the thoughts of taking our dwelling among that Hellish Crew, who study nothing else, day and night, than how they may be best able to provoke and exasperate each other to the highest degree possible.

Besides the Damn'd must needs be very ghastly and doleful

Spectacles to each other and their perpetual *weeping, wailing, sighing, howling,* and loud *outcries,* occasion'd by their Torments, must needs be very dreadful and effecting. So far will it be, in this case, from being any comfort to us to have Companions in our Misery, that this very thing will be a great addition to our Torments. Oh! how sadly shall we read our own Miseries, in the melancholy countenances of every one of our Companions? How terrible and killing must the sound of those groans and complaints needs be, which are, as it were, but the faint echoes of our own? What a hideous, what a heartbreaking consort of woes must that be, which comes from an innumerable company of poor unhappy Wretches, laboring under the sharp pangs of a wounded Conscience, and a Mind gall'd and fretted by all the most vexatious Passions, and yet farther, burning and scorching in the flames of Hell fire, which is the *fourth* thing, which I propos'd to speak to.

And here I must freely confess that I cannot see any manner of reason, why we should suppose that the fire of Hell will not be a real and material, but only a metaphorical and figurative, fire . . . Certainly nothing, if it were purposely study'd and design'd, could serve more effectually to satisfy our Minds in this point than the Parable of the rich Man in the Gospel, who is there represented as burning in a material Fire in Hell and begging for water to cool his Tongue, an expression properly belonging only to a material Fire.[3]

If it is said that the Torments of Hell are sometimes expressed in Scripture by other things than that of fire, and that therefore fire is to be understood not properly but figuratively, I answer that there are other Torments of Hell, besides those of fire, and that these are they which are express'd by those other things, as that of a guilty Conscience in particular, which is represented in the Text from which these Men fetch this Argument by a *worm that dieth not,* but which is there plainly represented as a thing different from the fire of Hell: *Where the worm dieth not, and the fire is not quench'd.*[4]

―――――

Fifthly, The uninterrupted continuance and eternal duration of them. For so the Scripture tells us that *the smoke of the torment* of the wicked *ascendeth up for ever and ever* and that *they have no rest day nor Night*, and again that they shall *be tormented day and night for ever and ever.*[5] And what a dreadful addition will this be to the Torments of the Damn'd that they shall be without intermission and without end? Will not the very thoughts of this give a keener edge to all their sufferings and be a kind of new Hell to them? But I shall say no more of this here, because I design to treat particularly of the Eternity of Hell-Torments in my following Discourses, and under that shall have occasion to say something of the uninterrupted continuance of them.

INTO THAT ETERNAL
FURNACE[1]

For their part, Catholics did not abandon their millennium-old traditions about the torments of Hell. During the sixteenth century, the Catholic Church staged the "Counter-Reformation" to combat Protestant claims about Christian doctrine and to assert that scripture and tradition were equally authoritative in determining religious truth about the afterlife. Moreover, a new monastic order—the Society of Jesus, whose members were called Jesuits—spread the Catholic message about the dangers of Hell through their missionary activities around the globe from Canada to China to Brazil. The Jesuits practiced guided meditation on the passion and death of Christ as a way to cultivate compassion. As novices, they learned techniques of imaginative visualization that allowed them to self-identify with Christ's suffering. They applied these same techniques in their contemplation of the terrors of Hell. The Spiritual Exercises *of their founder, Ignatius Loyola (1491–1556), instructed Jesuits to imagine Hell with all of their five senses: "See in imagination the vast fires, and the souls enclosed, as it were, in bodies of fire . . . hear the wailing, the howling cries, and blasphemies against Christ our Lord and against His saints . . . smell the smoke, the sulfur, the filth and corruption. . . ." These techniques were on full display in a treatise called* Hell Opened to Christians to Caution Them from Entering into It *(1693), written by the Italian Jesuit Giovanni Pietro Pinamonti (1632–1703). With a startling vividness that recalled Christian visionary literature like the* Apocalypse of Paul *and the* Vision of Tundale, *Pinamonti evoked for the attentive reader a sensory experience of unending torment in Hell that stood in marked contrast to the emphasis on the wounded conscience and re-morse of the soul favored by contemporary Protestant and An-glican theologians.*

THE FIRST CONSIDERATION FOR SUNDAY: THE PRISON OF HELL

I. Its Straitness

Consider that the first injustice a soul does to God is the abusing of the liberty granted her by breaking his commandments, and in effect, declaring not to be willing to serve him, "You said, I will not serve."[2] To punish, therefore, so great a boldness, God has framed a prison in the lowest region of the universe, a very suitable place, as the farthest of all from heaven. Here, though the place itself is wide enough, the damned will not even have that relief, which either a poor prisoner has in walking between four walls, or the sick man in turning himself in bed, because here they shall be bound up like a faggot, [bundle of wood] and heaped upon one another like unfortunate victims; and this by reason of the great numbers of the damned, to whom this great pit will become narrow and strait; as also because the fire itself will be to them like chains and fetters, "He shall rain snares on sinners: fire and brimstone, and the spirit of storms will be part of their cup."[3] Besides, God will not concur with anything that can give them any manner of relief: making no more account of them, than if they had never been in the world; and, therefore, "forgotten by his mercy."[4] Those miserable wretches will not only be straitened, but also be immoveable; and therefore, "if a blessed saint," says St. Anselm, in his *Book of Similitudes*, "will be strong enough, should there be occasion, to move the whole earth, the damned will be so weak, as not to be able even to remove from the eye a worm that is gnawing it."[5] The walls of this prison are more than four thousand miles thick, that is, as far from here to Hell; but were they as thin as paper, the prisoners will be too weak to break through them to make their escape, "Binding him hand and foot, throw him into utter darkness."[6] What, then, will that sinner do, who was accustomed to command and have everything done his own way, even in despite of God himself, when he finds himself shut up in so deep an abode, under the feet of all creatures, even the devils themselves, never to recover, for a whole eternity, that liberty which was so dear to him? Oh, detestable liberty, which endeth thus in a slavery that has no end! How much better would it have been to have submitted one's self, for a short time, to the pleasant yoke of divine precepts than to live forever chained up in such dismal fetters!

II. Its Darkness

Consider that this prison will not only be extremely strait, but also extremely dark. It is true there will be fire, but deprived of light; yet so that the eyes shall suffer with the sight of most horrible appearances, and yet be debarred of the comfort which in the midst of all their terror, the lightnings themselves might cause in the frightfulest tempests, "The voice of the Lord descends like the flame of fire."[7] That will be true, because, as St. Thomas says, "There will be heat without brightness," by a contrary miracle to what was wrought in the Babylonian furnace, for there, by the command of God, the heat was taken from the fire, but not the light or brightness; but in Hell the fire will lose its light, but not its heat.[8] Moreover, this same fire burning with brimstone will have a searching flame, which being mingled with the rolling smoke of that infernal cave, will fill the whole place, and raise a storm of darkness according to what is written, "These are the persons to whom the storm of darkness is reserved forever."[9] Finally, the same mass of bodies heaped on one another will contribute to make up a part of that dreadful night, not a glimpse of transparent air being left to the eyes of the damned, thus darkened and almost put out. Ponder now the despair of a sinner buried in this manner, "He shall not see light forever."[10] Oh, poor wretch, who for a whole eternity shall not so much as behold one single ray of any friendly light! One night alone has sometimes made a poor prisoner turn quite gray. What effect then must that night, which shall never see day, cause in those unfortunate creatures? "There was a horrible darkness."[11] Among all the plagues of Egypt, if darkness alone was called horrible, what name shall we give to that darkness, which is not to last for three days only, but for all eternity!

III. Its Stench

Consider how much the misfortunes of this prison, so strait and obscure, must be heightened by the addition of the greatest stench. First, thither, as to a common sewer, all the filth of the earth shall run after the fire has purged it at the last day. Second, the brimstone itself continually burning in such prodigious quantity will cause a stench not to be bore. Third, the very bodies of the damned will exhale so pestilential a stink that if any one of them were to be placed here on earth, it would be enough, as St. Bonaventure observes, to cause a general infection.[12] "A stench shall arise from their carcasses," says the prophet, for so he calls them, though they are living bodies, and will continue so, as to the pain they shall suffer, but at the same time are worse than carcasses as to the stench that will come from them.[13] The devil appearing one day to St. Martin with purple robes and a crown on his head. "Adore me," said he, "because I am Christ, and deserve it." But the saint, assisted by a celestial light, answered him, saying, "My Lord is crowned with thorns and covered with blood. I know him not in this new dress."[14] The devil being discovered fled away, but left so great a stench behind him that this alone was sufficient for the saint to discover him. If then one single devil could raise such a stench, what will that pestiferous breath be that shall be exhaled in that dungeon, where all the whole crowd of tormenting devils and all the bodies of the tormented will be penned up together. Air itself, being for a time closely shut up, becomes insupportable: judge then what stink of such loathsome filth must be to those that are confined in it forever. This is the habitation which sinners voluntarily choose forever, provided they satisfy with a short dream the infamous desires of their corrupted flesh. These are the proud palaces, which they who despise the poor and turn them away as loathsome have built for themselves in their haughtiness. Heaven, bought with the blood of the Son of God and therefore never sufficiently to be valued, is exchanged for this prison. Oh, unfortunate exchange! Oh, change that will be lamented with a flood of tears, but that in vain forever, "The rich man died and was buried in Hell."[15]

THE SECOND CONSIDERATION FOR MONDAY: THE FIRE

I. Its Quality

Consider that the divine justice has chosen fire as the fittest instrument to punish those that rebel against God. Even among men there never was found a greater torment. It is, therefore, with reason called the greatest of all. Nevertheless, you must not think the fire of Hell is like ours. Happy, I say, would those unfortunate souls be, if they met with no other fires than what can be made on earth. The rich man mentioned in the Gospel does not barely say he was tormented by fire, but "I suffer in *these* flames," expressing in some kind the different quality of the infernal flames.[16] Our fire is created for the benefit of man, to serve him as a help in most arts, and for the maintaining of life, but the fire of Hell was only created for God to revenge himself of the wicked, "The punishment of ungodly flesh is fire."[17] Our fire is often applied to subjects not at all proportioned to its activity, but the fire of Hell is kindled by a sulfurous and bituminous matter, which will always burn with an unspeakable fury, as it happens in the thunder-bolt, which strikes with so much force, caused by the violence of that lighted exhalation: "Their part shall be in the burning lake with fire and brimstone."[18] Finally, our fire destroys what it burns; therefore, the more intense it is, the shorter it is; but that fire in which the damned shall forever be tormented shall burn without ever consuming

and is, therefore, by Christ compared unto salt, "For everyone shall be salted with fire," which torturing them with inconceivable heat in nature of fire will also hinder them from
being corrupted, as it is the nature of salt to do.[19] If a little
flame of our fire so much frightens us, if we cannot bear
never so little a while the flame of a candle, how shall we be
able to be buried forever in flames, whose violence exceeds all
imagination? O thou, who has not as yet repented for the sins
you committed last, thou knowest by faith that if thou were
to die at present, thou wouldst fall into that eternal furnace.
How canst thou then find in thy heart to lay down this book
before thou beggest pardon from thy heart for thy sins? How
canst thou have the courage to continue, I will not say months,
but even one moment, in the state of one condemned to Hell?
"How can you laugh? How can you sleep at rest?"[20]

II. Its Quantity.

Consider what strength this devouring fire will have on account of the great quantity thereof. This infernal prison being
to contain all the bodies of the damned, without being com-
penetrated one with another, it will be requisite it should be a
pit of many miles in circumference, depth, and height, considering the great number of its prisoners: "Hell has enlarged its
soul and opened its mouth without any limit."[21] Now all this
great pit will be full of fire, and if lighted straw, when there is
enough of it, will heat an oven, what will lighted brimstone do,
so violent as to quantity and so great as to quality? Besides, the
fire here will be shut up without any vent and, therefore, all its
flames will return by reverberation and, by consequence, be of
unspeakable activity. Who is there that can doubt that if a
whole mountain were thrown into this great furnace, but that
it would melt as soon as a piece of wax? This the devil was
forced to own, being asked by a soldier.[22] And without his testimony we have the irrefutable saying of the Holy Ghost that
assures us of it in the eighty-third Psalm, calling it, "A flame
burning mountains."[23] And yet, sinners, instead of being frightened, make a jest of these flames and are no more concerned at

them than if they were bonfires. "Though that flame burns and a river is set on fire, we still laugh and follow our delights," says St. John Chrysostom, full of astonishment.[24] Holy Job said, "His strength was not like that of stone, nor his flesh of brass," yet if thine were of stone and brass, it would in a moment be melted in that fire in which thou art to live forever, in case thou dost not detest and abandon thy wicked life.[25] I have said little, it is true, in saying thou went to live in that fire forever. I ought to have said that both thou and I, if we do not fear and love God, shall be like fire itself, because that flame is so fierce and so great it will not only afflict us without, as it happens with the fires in this world, but will penetrate our very bones, our marrow, and even the very principle of our life and being. "You will place them as a furnace of fire," says the prophet.[26] Everyone that is damned will be like a lighted furnace, which has its own flames in itself; all that filthy blood will boil in the veins, the brains in the skull, the heart in the breast, the bowels within that unfortunate body, surrounded with an abyss of fire, out of which it cannot escape. "Who of you will be able to live in a devouring fire," says the prophet Isaiah, "a fire that will turn you into itself and make of you a living flame?"[27] Let us answer, but let us first seriously think on it.

III. Its Intenseness.

Consider that whatever has been said either to the strength, the quality, or the quantity of this infernal fire, it is nothing in comparison to the intenseness it will have, as being the instrument of the divine justice, which will raise it above its natural force to produce most wonderful effects: "There came down fire from God out of heaven."[28] The infernal fire will be of that kind; it will have its rise from the foot of the throne of God, that is to say, it will receive an incredible vigor from the omnipotency of God, working, not with its own activity, but as an instrument with the activity of its agent, who will give to the flames such intenseness as he shall think convenient to revenge the outrages committed against him and to repair the injuries done to his glory. The creature serving you, the Creator, is lighted up into torment against the wicked.

If the fire, like the sword, falling with its own weight only, makes such havoc among us, what will it do in Hell, when assisted by an omnipotent arm? "If I shall whet my sword as lightning."[29] So that this fire, though corporeal, will not only burn the body, but the soul also. For, as God makes use of material water in baptism, not only to wash the body, but to cleanse and sanctify the soul, so in Hell he makes use of fire, though material, to punish her when sinful and unclean. The infernal fire, then, is an effect of the omnipotency of God injured by sinners; it is a visible sign of that infinite hatred which the divine goodness bears to sin, as also an invention of his wisdom to recover the honor taken from him by the wicked. Who, therefore, will be able to tell me to what degree those torments will amount, to be a blow proportionable to the arm of the Most High and an invention worthy of his mind? "Who knows the power of thy anger?"[30] Not being able to conceive this, as being above the capacity of our nature, how shall we be able to explicate it? Have mercy then of thy soul, and if thou hast no care of thy soul, have compassion, at least, of thy body, for which thou art at all times so solicitous. Consider how dear those forbidden pleasures are to cost, which thou grantest thy body in contempt of the law of God. Behold that eternal furnace is already lighted up and the breath of the anger of God is continually blowing it to increase, if possible, the violence of its flames. There are many there already for less faults than thine. We ought no longer then to add new matter to this fire by new sins, but by penance and tears to endeavor to put it out: "This is the time of crying. Woe be to you that laugh, for you shall cry and lament!"[31]

THE SEVENTH CONSIDERATION FOR SATURDAY: THE ETERNITY OF PAIN

I. It is Endless.

Consider that were the pains of Hell less racking, yet, being never to have an end, they would become infinite. What, then, will it be, they being both intolerable as to sharpness and endless as to duration! Who can conceive how much it adds to grief, its being never to have an end! The torment of one hour is a great pain, that of two must be twice as much; the torment of a hundred hours must be a hundred times as much, and so on, the pain still increasing in proportion of the time of its duration. What, then, must that be, which is to last infinite hours, infinite days, infinite ages? That pain certainly must be infinite, and surpass all our thoughts to conceive it. For, were it proposed to the damned to suffer either the sting of a bee in their eye for a whole eternity or to undergo all the torments of Hell for as many ages as there are stars in heaven, they would without doubt choose to be thus miserable for so many ages, and then to see an end of their misery, than to endure a pain so much less that was to have no end. Everything is short and may be despised that does not last forever, because it will always be nothing for an eternity. "For what," says St. Jerome, "can be called great that has an end?"[32] Whereas that which never ends can never be comprehended and therefore cannot but be feared by all, unless it be by such who have lost their senses. The worst of it is that the pain as well as the sin is devoured and not digested by sinners: "The mouth of the impious devours iniquity."[33] And if so, let us take a little time to measure this eternity, which surpasses all measure. Take an hour-glass into thy hand and say thus to thyself: If I were to be buried alive in the middle of a fire, for as many thousand years as there are grains in this little parcel of sand, which measure the fleeting hours, when should I see an end of my pain? The world has lasted so long and yet has not completed six thousand years, so that there would not as yet be above five grains taken away, which would not be more than some few atoms, in respect of the remaining quantity. And yet, if I die in mortal sin, I am obliged by faith to believe that after having suffered all these ages, none of my pain due to it will be passed and eternity will remain as entire as ever. Let us go on and imagine to ourselves a mountain of this small sand, so high as would reach from earth to heaven. Then let everyone say to himself: Were I to continue in flames so many thousand years as there are grains of sand in this vast mountain, when should I ever see an end of my torments? And yet, if I die in mortal sin, faith tells me that after all this none of my pains due to it will be diminished and that eternity will be as entire as ever. Let us then imagine this great mountain to be multiplied as often as there are sands in the sea, leaves on trees, feathers on birds, scales on fish, hairs on beasts, atoms in the air, drops of water that have rained, or will rain, to the Day of Judgment. What human understanding can ever comprehend so great a number, which can scarce be comprehended by an angel himself? And yet, if either you or I should die in mortal sin, we are assured by faith that we shall continue all this while in the fire and that all these years shall pass and, when over, none of our pain will be lessened nor so much as one instant taken from eternity. O eternity, then, O eternity! Either sinners have no faith or no senses! Canst thou deny that living in sin is not exposing thyself to the danger of falling into this abyss, from where there is no getting out forever? Thou canst deny it, if thou art a Christian. But, on the contrary, thou mayest say with truth that by living thus, thou art not above one step off the abyss or, rather, have already one foot in it: "By one degree only (as I may so say) I and death are divided."[34] Since, then, we may die at any moment, we may also any moment be lost forever. The exposing ourselves to such evident danger of burning for the space of a thousand years on account of some vile and transitory pleasure would undoubtedly be a very great madness. It would be a much greater madness to expose oneself to the danger of continuing ten thousand years. It would still be greater and greater to expose oneself to burn for a hundred thousand years. Will not, then, the exposing ourselves to burn forever, for so small a trifle, be an infinite madness? "After so small a pleasure, so great a misery!" says St. Bernard. "It is enough," says he, "to make one mad to think of eternity."[35] Whereas, it is quite otherwise, for to think attentively of it will make those that have lost their wits to find them again.

II. It is Unchangeable.

Consider that if this succession of ages without end could in Hell give any relief by variety, it would, on that score, be more tolerable, but how can it be tolerable, it being to be always the same in torments? Though the manna contained in itself all kinds of tastes, yet we find the people of Israel grew tired of it in the desert: "Our eyes," say they, "behold nothing else but manna."[36] And yet this, according to the interpreters, happened the second year only of their travels through the desert. What would they have said at the end of forty or one hundred years? Miserable sinners! If that eternity, which waits for thee, should expect thee at a continual feast, but still of the same kinds of meat, thou wouldst at last grow tired with it, that it was enough to cast thee into despair. What then will thy despair be, seeing that eternity expects thee in a place of torment, always the same with the same pains? You that cannot bear with a sermon unless it has some variety; nay, and what is more, you are even tired with a play that has not some interludes. How then will you be able to pass an eternity of misery, without ease, without change, without any comfort? Those who inhabit the torrid zone, though they are scorched with the burning sun-beams during the day, are at least refreshed in the night by cool breezes. A sick man may, after some fatigues, fall asleep for a little while and during that time forget all his pains. There is no wound in this world, either in soul or body, which does not receive some ease from time, but to the damned, all these hopes are vain. They shall not only experience the scorching rays of the divine justice, but shall lay under the weight of his thunder-bolts and shall never have either night, sleep, or time to soften their pains. If these unhappy wretches could at least deceive themselves by the persuasion that some time or other they should be eased, though it be never to happen, this might afford them some kind of comfort, but they cannot so much as do this, because God will have them constantly to bear before their eyes the sentence of their eternal damnation, written in characters never to be blotted out, and never to be able, so much as one moment, to turn their thoughts from it. If to those that undergo any torment every hour seems a day, how long will the misery of these poor souls appear that will never be interrupted for infinite ages? These unfortunate creatures will not only be tormented for an eternity, but will have eternity itself to torment them because, it being always in their sight, it will every moment oppress them with all its weight as an immense sphere of brass would press with all its weight the plain it lies on, though it actually touched it but at one point. Besides, the fear of a punishment to come afflicts oftentimes more than the punishment itself: "The fear of war is worse than the war itself."[37] So that we may say that eternity not only every moment tortures the damned, but that to the damned every moment is turned into many eternities. For, since evil is unavoidable, the expectation thereof is most certain, the fear of it perhaps more cruel than any executioner and the anticipation every moment redoubles the pain. You recoil to read these things and yet not to sin. If so, you fear a painted precipice, but fear not to cast yourself from a real one.

III. It is Just.

Consider that men reasoning always as men are astonished that God for so short a pleasure of a sinner should have decreed an everlasting punishment in the fire of Hell. Nor do they know how to reconcile in their thoughts this rigor, either with divine goodness, which is so compassionate, or with divine justice, which does not punish beyond reason. But ought not we rather to wonder at the astonishment of worldlings, grounded on the ignorance of spiritual things: "The sensual man does not perceive the things that are of the Spirit of God, for it is a folly to him and he cannot understand."[38] If sinners did but comprehend the malice of their sin, they would soon change their wonder into one far greater. They are, at present, amazed how God could for one only fault make Hell to be eternal, but when they come into the other world, they will wonder much more that he has not created a Hell and provided pains incomparably more cruel for every transgression. St. Augustine understood very well this truth, when he tells us, "The misery of the devils would never have been eternal, had not their malice been great."[39] For, otherwise, it would not have been proportionable. Consider, therefore, that every mortal sin is either a tacit or express contempt of the divine will and an injury to God. Now an injury is increased on two accounts, either by dignity of the person offended or the vileness of the offender. The majesty, therefore, of God being infinite, and our vileness in the lowest degree, it follows that the injury which we do him is in a manner infinite. It is an abyss of malice more destestable than all the injuries imaginable that can be done to creatures. The punishment, then, being to be proportioned to the sin, to reestablish the order which was violated by it, ought also to be infinite. But since it cannot be infinite in intenseness, because a creature is not capable of it, it must be infinite in extension and last forever. This same truth will be better known by considering that the malice of sin is so exorbitant as not to be atoned and satisfied for by the good works of all creatures and, therefore, to pay this debt, it was necessary the Son of God should take from his veins as a just price the treasures of his divine blood. That sin, then, which cannot be made amends for by any virtuous actions of creatures, though continued never so long, deserves a pain longer than any time and, therefore, deserves one that is everlasting. So that God can never be despised by any but fools. Whereas, if the pain due to the offenders of God were to end, both the judge and the sentence would be condemned. What is not eternal is nothing. For what will be nothing for a whole eternity may also be esteemed such at present. Thus they argue, who look upon the goodness of God, not as sinners do, as an indolent neglect of evil, but as a holiness infinitely opposite to sin, to which it bears an infinite hatred and is forced to demonstrate it to them and punish it with a pain corresponding to it, that is, without end. And thus he weighs things, who makes use of scales of the divine justice, which cannot be mistaken, and not of the false scales of the world, equally deceived and deceiving. Consider, then, how great an evil one mortal sin is, since it contains an eternal misery, as it were, in its bowels, so that if you can penetrate with the eye of the mind into that deep and wicked bottom, thou wouldest easily discover there in the seeds of an eternal fire, of eternal lamentation, of an eternal sorrow, of an eternal imprisonment, of an eternal stench, of an eternal despair, and of an eternal loss of all that is good. All this is contained in one sin, though the act be so short. Yet, like unto a basilisk's egg, it contains a poisonous progeny and more than one death. It may, therefore, be called Hell itself, or rather an evil which infinitely surpasses it, in as much as can be spoken or comprehended by us, and which is to be redoubled as many times in severity and pains as the soul will be found to have sins when she leaves this "land of misery and darkness, where the shadow of death is, and no order, but everlasting horror inhabits."[40] Have thou ever seriously thought on this truth? If thou hast thought of it, how is it possible that for so vile, so filthy, and so short a pleasure, thou throwest thyself by sinning so unconcernedly into an abyss of pain, which attends it? The precipice on thy side is unavoidable, if God, whom thou so frequently offendest, interposeth not his hand to keep thee from it. Ah, thou hast not seen these things; thou hast not understood them. If thou hast thought slightly of them, but not understood them, if thou hast not thought of them at all, what art thou doing? "Why art thou oppressed with sleep? Rise and call your God."[41] How canst thou rest in a state so near to being shipwrecked? If the evil were only probable and not certain from faith, ought it not to make thee tremble every moment? Beg, then, of God to free thee from it. Have recourse to confession, fly from that wicked company, avoid the danger of sin, frequent the sacraments, do penance, retire, if necessary from the world, to save thy soul. No care can be too great, where eternity is at stake.

A LIVING DEATH SHALL
FEED UPON THEM[1]

John Bunyan (1628–88) was a Puritan preacher and author. His best-known book was an immensely popular Christian allegory called The Pilgrim's Progress *(1678), but he wrote dozens of other religious pamphlets as well. Among his lesser-known works is a treatise on the Christian afterlife titled* The Resurrection of the Dead and Eternall Judgement, or, The Truth of the Resurrection of the Bodies Both of Good and Bad at the Last Day *(1665). This book repeated many of the tropes about the miseries of Hell well known from other seventeenth-century authors, but Bunyan made his mark on the history of the fate of the damned by imagining the resurrection of their bodies on the Day of Judgment. While every other account of the horrible fate awaiting wicked souls commenced with their sentence to an eternity in Hell, Bunyan dared to imagine the damned rising to the call of the angel's horn as rotting corpses even before the Last Judgment. According to his logic, the blessed and the damned are opposed in all things. If the blessed rose for the Judgment in spiritual bodies, it followed that the wicked rose up in bodies plagued with decay and corruption. He called this terrifying moment in salvation history "the resurrection of damnation." Thus, even before God issued his judgment, the wicked wore their sins for all to see on the wreckage of their reeking corpses, "having yet the chains of eternal death hanging on them."*

Having in the first place shewed you that the wicked must arise, I shall in the next place shew you the manner of their rising. And observe it, as the very title of the *just* and *unjust* are opposites, so they are in all other matters, and in their *Resurrections*.

First then, as the just in their *Resurrection* do come forth in incorruption, the unjust in their Resurrection shall come forth in their corruptions; for though the ungodly at their Resurrection shall forever after be incapable of having Body and Soul separate, or of their being annihilated into nothing, yet it shall be far from them to rise in incorruption, for if they arise in incorruption, they must arise to life, and also must have the Conquest over sin and death. But that they shall not, for it is the Righteous only that put on incorruption, that are swallowed up of life. The wicked's Resurrection, it is called the Resurrection of damnation. These in their very Resurrection shall be hurt of the second Death. They shall arise in death and shall be under it, under the gnawings and terrors of it, all the time of their Arraignment. As it were, a living death shall feed upon them; they shall never be spiritually alive, nor yet absolutely dead, but much after that manner, that natural death, and Hell, by reason of guilt, doth feed on him, that is going before the Judge to receive his Condemnation to the Gallows. You know, though a Felon go forth to the Gaol, when he is going to the Bar for his Arraignment, yet he is not out of prison or out of his Irons for that, his Fetters are still making a noise on his heels, and the thoughts of what he is to hear by and by from the Judge, is still frightening and afflicting his heart; Death, like some evil Spirit or Ghost, doth continually haunt him, and playeth the Butcher continually in his Soul and Conscience with frights and fears about the thoughts of the sudden and unsupportable after-clap by and by he is to meet withal.

Thus, I say, will the wicked come out of their Graves, having yet the Chains of eternal death hanging on them, and the talons of that dreadful Ghost fastened to their Souls. So that life will be far from them, even as far as Heaven is from Hell. This morning to them is even as the shadow of death . . . From Death to Eternity, it never shall be quenched; their bed is now among the flames. And when they rise, they will rise in flames. While they stand before the Judge, it will be in flames, even in the

flames of a guilty Conscience. They will in their coming before
the Judge be within the very Jaws of death and destruction.
Thus, I say, the ungodly shall be far from rising as the Saints,
for they will be even in the Region and shadow of Death. The
first moment of their rising, Death will be ever over them, ever
feeding on their Souls, and ever presenting to their hearts the
heights and depths of the misery that now must seize them, and
like a bottomless Gulf, must swallow them up . . .

The ungodly at their death are like the Thistle-seed, but at
their rising they will be like the Thistle grown: more noisome,
offensive, and provoking to rejection abundance. Then such
dishonor, shame, and contempt will appear in them that neither God nor Christ, Saints nor Angels, will so much as once
regard them or vouchsafe one to come near them . . . Their rising is called the *Resurrection* of the unjust, and so they at that
day will appear and will more stink in the nostrils of God and
all the Heavenly Hosts, than if they had the most irksome
Plague-sores in the World running on them. If a man at his
Birth be counted as one cast forth to the loathing of his person, how loathsome and irksome, dishonorable and contempt-
ible, will those be that shall arise Godless, Christless, Spiritless,
and Graceless, when the Trumpet sounds to their Judgment,
they coming out of their Graves far more loathsome and filthy
than if they should ascend out of the most filthy hole on
Earth . . .

As the Just shall arise as spiritual Bodies, so the unjust shall
arise only as mere and naked lumps of sinful nature, not having the least help from God to bear them up under this condition. Wherefore, so soon as ever they are risen out of their
Graves, they will feel a continual sinking under every remembrance of every sin and thoughts of Judgment; in their rising,
they fall, fall I say from thenceforth, and forever. And for this
Reason, the Dungeon into which they fall is called *bottomless*.
Because, as there will be no end of their misery, so there will
be no stay or prop to bare them up in it . . .

Now when the wicked are thus raised out of their Graves,
they shall together with all the Angels of darkness, their fellow
Prisoners, be brought up, being shackled in their sins, to the

place of Judgment, where there shall sit upon them *Jesus Christ*, the King of Kings, and Lord of Lords, the Lord chief Judge of things in Heaven, and things in Earth, and things under the Earth. On whose right hand and left shall sit all the Princes, and Heavenly Nobles, the Saints and the Prophets, the Apostles and Witnesses of Jesus, every one in his Kingly Attire upon the Throne of Glory . . . When every one is thus set in his proper place, the Judge on his Throne, with his Attendants, and the prisoners coming up to Judgment, forthwith there shall issue forth a mighty fire and tempest from before the Throne, which shall compass it round about. Which fire shall be as Bars and bounds to the wicked, to keep them at a certain distance from the Heavenly Majesty . . . This Preparation being made, to wit, the Judge with his Attendants on the Throne, the Bar for the Prisoners, and the Rebels all standing with ghastly Jaws, to look for what comes after. Presently the Books are brought forth, to wit, the Books both of Death and Life. And every one of them opened before the sinners, now to be judged and condemned.

THE DREAD OF HELL
PEOPLES HEAVEN:
THE NINETEENTH
CENTURY

Premodern traditions about eternal punishment in Hell slipped into decline in the nineteenth century as old certainties about the reality of infernal torments came under attack from two different fronts. Secular critiques of Christian doctrines multiplied. Armed with new information about the world gained from advances in the geological sciences and new theories like Darwinism, scholars and scientists called into question the divine authority of the Bible. At the same time, many Christians had a change of heart about Hell. Was God an immoral tyrant, they asked, to make human souls suffer such a cruel fate in the afterlife? The late nineteenth-century author Lionel A. Tollemache (1838–1919) thought so: "The wiser among us are seeking to drop Hell out of the Bible as quietly, and about as logically, as we already contrive to disregard the plain texts forbidding Christians to go to law, and Christian women to plait their hair." Catholic authors held firm, however, to their convictions about the meaning and character of the punitive afterlife. Throughout the nineteenth century, they produced innumerable treatises, sermons, and poems about the torments awaiting sinners there, confident that Hell was necessary as a moral sanction for an increasingly faithless human race. The dread of Hell, they argued, encouraged virtuous behavior that directed souls to Heaven.

HELL FOR CHILDREN[1]

The Catholic priest John Furniss (1809–65) stands alone in the history of Hell as the only author to have published a treatise on infernal punishment written specifically for "children and young persons." Furniss organized Christian camps for children in England and wrote religious tracts in simple language directed at young readers to motivate them to cultivate good behavior. His pamphlet The Sight of Hell *embraced the premodern Catholic tradition of depicting the sufferings of Hell in the most lurid and visceral terms. Though it was praised by William Meagher, the vicar general in Dublin, as a work boasting "a great deal to charm, instruct, and edify our youthful classes, for whose benefit it has been written," modern readers can draw their own conclusions about the merits of a religious tract for young people that depicts the souls of children trapped in burning ovens and forced to stand on red-hot floors.*

1. WHERE IS HELL?

Every little child knows that God will reward the good in Heaven and punish the wicked in Hell. Where, then, is Hell? Is Hell above or below? Is it on the earth, or in the earth, or below the earth?

It seems likely that Hell is in the middle of the earth. Almighty God has said that *"He will turn the wicked into the bowels of the earth."*[2]

3. HOW FAR IT IS TO HELL

We know how far it is to the middle of the Earth. It is just four thousand miles. So, if Hell is in the middle of the Earth, it is four thousand miles to the horrible prison of Hell.

It is time now to do what St. Augustine bids us. He says— "Let us go down to Hell while we live, that we may not have to go down to Hell when we die."[3] If we go and look at that Terrible Prison, where those who commit mortal sin are punished, we shall be afraid to commit mortal sin. If we do not commit mortal sin, we shall not go to Hell.

4. THE GATES OF HELL

St. Frances of Rome lived a very holy life.[4] Many times, she saw with her eyes her Angel Guardian at her side. It pleased the Almighty God to let her see many other wonderful things. One afternoon the Angel Gabriel came to take her to see Hell. She went with him and saw that terrible place. Let us follow in her footsteps, that we may see in spirit the wonderful things that she saw. Our journey is through the deep dark places under the earth. Now we will set off. We pass through hundreds and hundreds of miles of darkness. Now we are coming near the terrible place. See, there are the gates of Hell! When St. Frances came to the gates of Hell, she read on them these words written in letters of fire— "This is Hell, where there is neither rest, nor consolation, nor hope." Look, then, at those tremendous gates in front of you. How large they are. Measure, if you can, the length and breadth, the height and depth of the terrible gates. "Therefore hath Hell *opened her mouth without any bound.* Their strong ones, and their people, and their glorious ones go down into it."[5]

See also the vast thickness, the tremendous strength of those gates. In a prison on earth, there are not, perhaps, more than two or three hundred prisoners; still the gates of a prison are made most strong with iron and with bars and with bolts and with locks, for fear the prisoners should break down the gates and get away. Do not wonder, then, at the immense strength of the Gates of Hell. In Hell, there are not two or three hundred prisoners only. Millions upon millions are shut up there. They are tormented with the most frightful pains. These dreadful pains make them furious. Their fury gives them strength, such as we never saw. We read of a man who had the fury of Hell in him. He was so strong that he could easily break in pieces great chains of iron.[6] The vast multitudes in Hell, strong in their fury and despair, rush forward like the waves of the sea. They dash themselves up against the gates of Hell to break them into pieces. This is the reason why those gates are so strong. No hand of man could make such gates. Jesus Christ said that the Gates of Hell should not prevail against His Church, because in Hell there is nothing stronger than its gates.

Do you hear that growling thunder rolling from one end of Hell to the other? The Gates of Hell are opening.

5. THE FIRST LOOK INTO HELL

When the Gates of Hell had been opened, St. Frances with her angel went forward. She stood on the edge of the abyss. She saw a sight so terrible that it cannot be told. She saw that the size of Hell was immense. Neither in height, nor in depth, nor in length, could she see any end of it. *"None shall ever pass through it."*[7] She saw that Hell was divided into three immense places. These three places were at a great distance from one another. There was an upper Hell, and a middle Hell, and a lower Hell. *"Night came upon them from the lowest and deepest Hell."*[8] She saw that in the upper Hell the torments were very grievous. In the middle Hell, they were still more terrible. In the lowest Hell, the torments were above all understanding. When she had looked into this terrible place, her blood froze with fright!

6. FIRE

Now look into Hell and see what she saw. Look at the floor of Hell. It is red-hot like red-hot iron. Streams of burning pitch and sulfur run through it. The floor blazes up to the roof. Look at the walls, the enormous stones are red-hot; sparks of fire are always falling down from them. Lift up your eyes to the roof of Hell; it is like a sheet of blazing fire. Sometimes when you get up on a winter's morning, you see the country filled with a great thick fog. Hell is filled with a fog of fire. In some parts of the world, torrents of rain come down which sweep away trees and houses. In Hell torrents, not of rain, but of fire and brimstone, are rained down: *The Lord shall rain down on sinners fire and brimstone.*[9] Storms of hailstones come down on the earth and break the windows in pieces. But in Hell the hailstones are thunderbolts, red-hot balls of fire: *"God shall send thunderbolts against him."*[10] See that great whirlwind of fire sweeping across Hell: *"Storms of winds shall be the portion of their cup."*[11] Look how floods of fire roll themselves through Hell like the waves of the sea. The wicked are sunk down and buried in the fiery sea of destruction and perdition. You may have seen a house on fire. But you never saw a house made of fire. Hell is a house made of fire. The fire of Hell burns the devils who are spirits, for it was prepared for them. So it will burn the soul as well as the body. Take a spark out of the kitchen fire, throw it into the sea, and it will go out. Take a little spark out of Hell less than a pin-head, throw it into the ocean, it will not go out. In one moment, it would dry up all the waters of the ocean and set the whole world in a blaze: *"The fire, above its power, burned in the midst of the water."*[12] Set a house or town on fire. Perhaps the fire may burn for a week, or a month, but it will go out at last. But the fire of Hell will never go out; it will burn forever. It is *unquenchable fire.* St. Teresa says that the fire on the earth is only a *picture* of the fire of Hell.[13] Fire on earth gives light. But it is not so in hell. In Hell, the fire is dark.

7. DARKNESS

"Watchman, what of the night? The watchman said: The night comes."[14]

The watchman did not say that nights are coming, but only the night. He said so, because in Hell there is only one night, one eternal night, one everlasting night. The fire of Hell burns, but gives no light. No stray sunbeam, no wandering ray of starlight ever creeps into the darkness of Hell. All is darkness—thick, black, heavy, pitchy, aching darkness. It is not darkness like ours, which is only *an image of the darkness to come*. This darkness is thicker than the darkness of the land of Egypt, which could be touched with the hand. *"So, the wicked in Hell will never see light."*[15] This darkness is made worse by the smoke of Hell.

8. SMOKE

"The smoke of their torments shall go up forever and ever."[16]

Stop up that chimney where the fire is burning. In half an hour, the room will be full of smoke, so that you cannot stay there. The great fires of Hell have been smoking now for nearly six thousand years. They will go on smoking forever. There is no chimney to take this smoke off; there is no wind to blow it away. See those great, black, heavy sulfurous clouds rising up every moment from the dark fires. They rise up till the roof of Hell stops them. The roof drives them back again. Slowly they go down into the abyss of Hell. There they are joined by more dark clouds of smoke leaving the fires. So, Hell is filled with sulfur and smoke, in which no one on earth could breathe or live. How then do they live in Hell? In Hell they must live, but they are stifled and choked each moment, as if they were dying. Now listen!

9. TERRIFIC NOISE

"There shall be a great cry such as has not been heard before."[17]

You have heard, perhaps, a horrible scream in the dead of night. You may have heard the last shriek of a drowning man, before he went down to his watery grave. You may have been shocked in passing a madhouse, to hear the wild shout of a madman. Your heart may have trembled when you heard the roar of a lion in the desert or the hissing of a deadly serpent in the bushes.

But listen now—listen to the tremendous, the horrible uproar of millions and millions and millions of tormented creatures mad with the fury of Hell. Oh, the screams of fear, the groanings of horror, the yells of rage, the cries of pain, the shouts of agony, the shrieks of despair from millions on millions. There you hear them roaring like lions, hissing like serpents, howling like dogs, and wailing like dragons. There you hear the gnashing of teeth and the fearful blasphemies of the devils. Above all, you hear the roaring of the thunders of God's anger, which shakes Hell to its foundations. But there is another sound!

10. A RIVER

"It is the day of slaughter and of treading down, and of weeping to the Lord, the God of hosts."[18]

There is in Hell a sound like that of many waters. It is as if all the rivers and oceans of the world were pouring themselves with a great splash down on the floor of Hell. Is it really the sound of waters? It is. Are the rivers and oceans of the earth pouring themselves into Hell? No. What is it then? It is the sound of oceans of tears running down from countless millions of eyes. They cry night and day. They cry forever and ever. They cry because the sulfurous smoke torments their eyes. They cry because they are in darkness. They cry because they have lost the beautiful heaven. They cry because the sharp fire burns them.

Little child, it is better to cry one tear of repentance now than to cry millions of tears in Hell. But what is that dreadful sickening smell?

11. THE SMELL OF DEATH

"His stench shall ascend, and his rottenness shall go up."[19]
There are some diseases so bad, such as cancers and ulcers, that people cannot bear to breathe the air in the house where they are. There is something worse. It is the smell of death coming from a dead body lying in the grave. The dead body of Lazarus had been in the grave only four days. Yet Martha his sister could not bear that it should be taken out again.[20] But what is the smell of death in Hell? St. Bonaventure says that if one single body was taken out of Hell and laid on the earth, in that same moment every living creature on the earth would sicken and die.[21] Such is the smell of death from one body in Hell. What then will be the smell of death from countless millions and millions of bodies laid in Hell like sheep?—Ps. How will the horrible smell of all these bodies be, after it has been getting worse and worse every moment for ten thousand years? "They shall go out and see the carcasses of the men that have transgressed against Me. They shall be a loathsome sight to all flesh."[22]
Now let us enter into Hell and see the tremendous torments prepared for the wicked.

12. THE DEVIL

"An angel laid hold on the old serpent, which is the devil and Satan, and bound him, and cast him into the bottomless pit, and shut him up."[23]
Our journey lies across that great sea of fire. We must go on till we come to the middle of Hell. There we shall see the most horrible sight that ever was or will be—the great devil chained down in the middle of Hell. We will set off on our journey.

Now we are coming near the dwelling-place of Satan. The darkness gets thicker. You see a great number of devils moving about in the thick darkness. They come to get the orders of their great chief. Already you hear the rattling of the tremendous chains of the great monster! See! There he is: the most horrible and abominable of all monsters, the devil.

His size is immense! *"He shall fill the length of the land."*[24] St. Frances saw him. He was sitting on a long beam which passed through the middle of Hell. His feet went down into the lowest depths of Hell. They rested on the floor of Hell. They were fastened with great, heavy iron chains. These chains were fixed to an immense ring in the floor. His hands were chained up to the roof. One of his hands was turned up against Heaven to blaspheme God and the saints who dwell there. His other hand was stretched out, pointing to the lowest Hell! His tremendous and horrible head was raised up on high, and touched the roof. From his head came two immense horns. *"I saw another beast having two horns."*[25] From each horn smaller horns without number branched out, which like chimneys sent out fire and smoke. His enormous mouth was wide open. Out of it there was running a river of fire, which gave no light, but an abominable smell: *"Flame cometh out of his mouth."*[26] Round his neck was a collar of red-hot iron. A burning chain tied him round the middle. The ugliness of his face was such that no man or devil could bear it. It was the most deformed, horrible, frightful thing that ever was or will be. His great fierce eyes were filled with pride and anger and rage and spite and blood and fire and savage cruelty. There was something else in those eyes for which there is no name, but it made those on whom the devil's eyes were fixed tremble and shake as if they were dying. One of the Saints who saw the devil said she would rather be burned for a thousand years than look at the devil for one moment![27]

16. THE SOUL BEFORE SATAN

The devils carry away the soul which has just come into Hell. They bear it through the flames. Now they have set it down in front of the great chained monster, to be judged by him who has no mercy. Oh, that terrible face of the devil! Oh, the fright, the shivering, the freezing, the deadly horror of that soul at the first sight of the great devil. Now the devil opens his mouth. He gives out the tremendous sentence on the soul. All hear the sentence, and Hell rings with shouts of spiteful joy and mockeries at the unfortunate soul.

17. THE EVERLASTING DWELLING-PLACE OF THE SOUL

As soon as the sentence is given, the soul is snatched away and hurried to that place which is to be its home forever and ever! Crowds of hideous devils have met together. With cries of spiteful joy, they receive the soul. *"Demons and monsters shall meet. The hairy ones shall cry out to one another."*[28] See how these devils receive the soul in this time of destruction. *"In the time of destruction, they shall pour out their force. The teeth of serpents, and beasts, and scorpions, the sword taking vengeance on the ungodly unto destruction."*[29]

Immediately the soul is thrust by the devils into that prison which is to be its dwelling-place forever more. The prison of each soul is different according to its sins.

St. Teresa found herself squeezed into a hole or chest in the wall. Here the walls, which were most terrible, seemed to close upon her and strangle her. She found her soul burning in a most horrible fire. It seemed as if someone was always tearing her soul to pieces, or rather as if the soul was always tearing itself in pieces. It was impossible to sit or lie down, for there was no room. As soon as the soul is fixed in its place, it finds two devils, one on each side of it. There are spirits created for vengeance, and in their fury, they lay on grievous torments. St. Frances saw them. One of them is called the striking devil, the other the mocking devil.

18. THE STRIKING DEVIL

"Striking hammers are prepared for the bodies of sinners."[30]

If you want to know what sort of a stroke the devil can give, hear how he struck Job: "Satan went forth from the presence of the Lord, and *struck* Job with a grievous ulcer from the sole of his foot to the top of his head. Then Job took a tile and scraped off the corrupt matter, sitting on a dung-hill. Now when Job's friends heard all the evil that had come upon him, they came to him. For they had made an appointment to come together and visit and comfort him. And when they had lifted up their eyes afar off they did not know him. And crying, they wept and sprinkled dust on their heads. And they sat down with him on the ground for seven days and seven nights. And no one spoke a word to him, for they saw that his grief was very great."[31]

The devil gave Job one stroke, only one stroke. That one stroke was so terrible that it covered all his body with sores and ulcers. That one stroke made Job look so frightful that his friends did not know him again. That one stroke was so terrible that for seven days and seven nights his friends did not know him again. That one stroke was so terrible that for seven days and seven nights his friends did not speak a word, but sat crying, and wondering, and thinking what a terrible stroke the devil can give.

Little child, if you go to Hell, there will be a devil at your side to strike you. He will go on striking you every minute forever and ever, without ever stopping. The first stroke will make your body as bad as the body of Job, covered from head to foot with sores and ulcers. The second stroke will make your body twice as bad as the body of Job. The third stroke will make your body three times as bad as the body of Job. The fourth stroke will make your body four times as bad as the body of Job. How then will your body be, after the devil has been striking it every moment for a hundred million years without stopping?

But there was one good thing for Job. When the devil struck

Job, his friends came to visit and comfort him, and when they saw him, they cried. But when the devil is striking you in Hell, there will be no one to come and visit and comfort you and cry with you. Neither father, nor mother, nor brother, nor sister, nor friend will ever come to cry with you. "Weeping she has wept in the night, and the tears are on her cheeks, because there is none to comfort her amongst all them that were dear to her."[32] Little child, it is a bad bargain to make with the devil, to commit a mortal sin, and then to be beaten forever for it.

19. THE MOCKING DEVIL

"Shall they not take up a parable against him, a dark speech concerning him?"[33]

St. Frances saw that on the other side of the soul there was another devil to mock at and reproach it. Hear what mockeries he said to it: "Remember," he said, "remember where you are and where you will be forever; how short the sin was, how long the punishment. It is your own fault; when you committed that mortal sin, you knew how you would be punished. What a good bargain you made to take the pains of eternity in exchange for the sin of a day, an hour, a moment. You cry now for your sin, but your crying comes too late. You liked bad company; you will find bad company enough here. Your father was a drunkard and showed you the way to the public-house; he is still a drunkard. Look at him over there drinking red-hot fire! You were too idle to go to Mass on Sundays. Be as idle as you like now, for there is no Mass to go to. You disobeyed your father, but you dare not disobey him who is your father in Hell. Look at him, that great chained monster; disobey him if you dare!"

St. Frances saw that these mockeries put the soul into such dreadful despair that it burst out into the most frightful howlings and blasphemies.

But it is time for us now to see where the sinner has been put—his everlasting dwelling-place.

20. A BED OF FIRE

The sinner lies, chained down on a bed of red-hot blazing fire! When a man, sick of fever, is lying on even a soft bed, it is pleasant sometimes to turn round. If the sick man lies on the same side for a long time, the skin comes off, the flesh gets raw. How will it be when the body has been lying on the same side on the scorching, broiling fire for a hundred millions of years! Now look at that body, lying on the bed of fire. All the body is salted with fire. The fire burns through every bone and every muscle. Every nerve is trembling and quivering with the sharp fire. The fire rages inside the skull, it shoots out through the eyes, it drops out through the ears, it roars in the throat as it roars up a chimney. So will mortal sin be punished. Yet there are people in their senses who commit mortal sin!

21. WORMS

"The worm that dies not. He will give fire and worms into their flesh that they may burn and feel forever."[34] St. Basil says that in Hell there will be worms without number eating the flesh and their bites will be unbearable. St. Teresa says that she found the entrance into Hell filled with these venomous insects. If you cannot bear the sight of ugly vermin and creeping things on the earth, will you be content with the sight of venomous things in Hell, which are a million times worse? The bite or the pricking of one insect on the earth sometimes keeps you awake, and torments you for hours. How will you feel in Hell, when millions of them make their dwelling-place in your mouth and ears and eyes, and creep all over you, and sting you with their deadly stings through all eternity? You will not then be able to help yourself or send them away because you cannot stir hand or foot. One of the most painful things in the world is to be much frightened.

22. FRIGHT

"When they thought to lie hid in their obscure sins, they were horribly afraid and troubled. For neither did the den which held them keep them from fear. For noises coming down troubled them, and sad visions appearing to them, affrighted them."[35]

Do you know what is meant by being frightened out of one's senses? A boy wanted to frighten two other little boys. In the daytime, he took some phosphorus and marked with it the form of a skeleton on the wall of the room where the little boys always slept. In the daytime, the mark of phosphorus is not seen; in the dark, it shines like fire. The two little boys went to bed, knowing nothing about it. Next morning, they opened the door of the room where the two little boys had been sleeping. They found one boy sitting on his bed, staring at the wall, out of his senses. The other little boy was lying dead! This was fright.

You will be lying helpless in the lonesome darkness of Hell. The devils come in the most frightful shapes on purpose to frighten you. Serpents come and hiss at you. Wild beasts come and roar at you. Death comes and stares at you. How would you feel, if at the dark hour of midnight, one that was dead should come to your bedside and stand over you and mock at you? You hear the most horrible shrieks and dismal sounds which you cannot understand. The sinner, frightened out of his senses at those terrible sights in the darkness of Hell, roars out for help—but there is nobody to come and help him in his fright: *Being scared with the passing of beasts and the hissing of serpents, they died of fear.*[36]

———

Now look to those little doors all round the walls of Hell. They are little rooms or dungeons where sinners are shut up. We will go and look at some of them.

24. THE DUNGEONS OF HELL

(a) The First Dungeon: A Dress of Fire

"Are not your garments hot?"[37] Come into this room. You see it is very small. But see in the midst of it there is a girl, perhaps about eighteen years old. What a terrible dress she has on—her dress is made of fire. On her head, she wears a bonnet of fire. It is pressed down close all over her head; it burns her head; it burns into the skin; it scorches the bone of the skull and makes it smoke. The red-hot fiery heat burns into the brain and melts it: "I will burn you in the fire of my wrath, you shall be *melted* in the midst thereof as silver is melted in the fire."[38] You do not, perhaps, like a headache. Think what a headache that girl must have. But see more. She is wrapped up in flames, for her frock is fire. If she were on the earth she would be burned to a cinder in a moment. But she is in Hell, where fire burns everything, but burns nothing away. There she stands burning and scorched! She counts with her fingers the moments as they pass away slowly, for each moment seems to her like a hundred years. As she counts the moments, she remembers that she will have to count them forever and ever.

When that girl was alive she never thought about God or her soul. She cared only for one thing, and that was dress! Instead of going to Mass on Sundays, she went about the town and the parks to show off her dress. She disobeyed her father and mother by going to dancing houses and all kinds of bad places, to show off her dress. And now her dress is her punishment: *"For by what things a man sins, by the same also he is tormented."*[39]

(b) The Second Dungeon: The Deep Pit

"It came to pass that the rich man also died, and he was buried in the fire of Hell."[40] Think of a coffin not made of wood, but of fire, solid fire! And now come into this other room. You see a pit, a deep, almost bottomless, pit. Look down it and you will see something red-hot and burning. It is a coffin, a red-hot

coffin of fire. A certain man is lying fastened in the inside of that coffin of fire. You might burst open a coffin made of iron, but that coffin made of solid fire never can be burst open. There that man lies and will live forever in the fiery coffin. It burns him from beneath. The sides of it scorch him. The heavy burning lid on the top presses down close upon him. The horrible heat in the inside chokes him; he pants for breath; he cannot breathe; he cannot bear it; he gets furious. He gathers up his knees and pushes out his hands against the top of the coffin to burst it open. His knees and hands are fearfully burned by the red-hot lid. No matter, to be choked is worse. He tries with all his strength to burst open the coffin. He cannot do it. He has no strength remaining. He gives it up and sinks down again. Again, the horrible choking. Again, he tries; again, he sinks down; so he will go on forever and ever! This man was very rich. Instead of worshipping God, he worshipped his money. Morning, noon, and night, he thought about nothing but his money. He was clothed in purple and fine linen. He feasted sumptuously every day. He was hard-hearted to the poor. He let a poor man die at his door, and would not even give him the crumbs that fell from his table. When he came into Hell, the devil mocked him saying, "*What did pride profit you, or what advantage did the boasting of riches bring you? All those things have passed away like a shadow.*" Then the devil's sentence was that since he was so rich in the world, he should be very poor in Hell, and have nothing but a narrow, burning coffin.

(c) The Third Dungeon: The Red-Hot Floor

Look into this room. What a dreadful place it is! The roof is red-hot; the walls are red-hot; the floor is a thick sheet of red-hot iron. See, on the middle of that red-hot floor stands a girl. She looks about sixteen years old. Her feet are bare, she has neither shoes nor stockings on her feet; her bare feet stand on the red-hot burning floor. The door of this room has never been opened since she first set her foot on the red-hot floor. Now she sees that the door is opening. She rushes forward.

She has gone down on her knees on the red-hot floor. Listen! She speaks. She says, "I have been standing with my bare feet on this red-hot floor for years. Day and night my only standing-place has been this red-hot floor. Sleep never came on me for a moment, that I may forget this horrible burning floor. Look," she says, "at my burned and bleeding feet. Let me go off this burning floor for one moment, only for a single, short moment. Oh, that in this endless eternity of years, I might forget the pain only for a single moment." The devil answers her question, "Do you ask," he says, "for a moment, for one moment to forget your pain? No, not for one single moment during the never-ending eternity of years shall you ever leave this red-hot floor!" "Is it so?" the girl says with a sigh that seems to break her heart, "then at least, let somebody go to my little brothers and sisters who are alive, and tell them not to do the bad things which I did, so they will never have to come and stand on the red-hot floor." The devil answers her again, "Your little brothers and sisters have the priests tell them these things. If they will not listen to the priests, neither would they listen, even if somebody should go to them from the dead."

Oh, that you could hear the horrible, the fearful scream of that girl when she saw the door shutting, never to be opened anymore. The history of this girl is short. Her feet first led her into sin, so it is her feet which most of all are tormented. While yet a very little child, she began to go into bad company. The more she grew up, the more she went into bad company against the bidding of her parents. She used to walk about the streets at night and do very wicked things. She died early. Her death was brought on by the bad life she led.

(d) The Fourth Dungeon: The Boiling Kettle

"The days shall come when they shall lift you up on pikes and what remains of you in boiling pots."[41] Look into this little prison. In the middle of it there is a boy, a young man. He is silent; despair is on him. He stands straight up. His eyes are burning like two burning coals. Two long flames come out of his ears. His breathing is difficult. Sometimes he opens his

mouth, and breath of blazing fire rolls out of it. But listen! There is a sound just like that of a kettle boiling. Is it really a kettle that is boiling? No; then what is it? Hear what it is. The blood is boiling in the scalded veins of that boy. The brain is boiling and bubbling in his head. The marrow is boiling in his bones! Ask him, put the question to him, why is he thus tormented? His answer is, that when he was alive, his blood boiled to do very wicked things, and he did them, and it was for that he went to dancing-houses, public-houses, and theaters. Ask him, does he think the punishment greater than he deserves? "No," he says, "my punishment is not greater than I deserve; it is just. I knew it not so well on earth, but I know now that it is just. There is a just and a terrible God. He is terrible to sinners in Hell—but He is just!"

(e) The Fifth Dungeon: The Red-Hot Oven

"*You shalt make him as an oven of fire in the time of Thy anger.*"[42] You are going to see again the child about which you read in the *Terrible Judgment*, that it was condemned to Hell.[43] See! It is a pitiful sight. The little child is in this red-hot oven. Hear how it screams to come out. See how it turns and twists itself about in the fire. It beats its head against the roof of the oven. It stamps its little feet on the floor of the oven. You can see on the face of this little child what you see on the faces of all in Hell—despair, desperate and horrible!

The same law which is for others is also for children. If children knowingly and willingly break God's commandments, they also must be punished like others. This child committed very bad mortal sins, knowing well the harm of what it was doing and knowing that Hell would be the punishment. God was very good to this child. Very likely God saw that this child would get worse and worse, and would never repent, and so it would have to be punished much more in Hell. So, God in His mercy called it out of the world in its early childhood.

(f) The Sixth Dungeon: A Voice

Listen at this door. Hear that voice; how sad and sorrowful it sounds? It says, "Oh, I am lost, I am lost. I am lost when I might have been saved. I am in Hell, and I might have been in Heaven. How short my sin, how long the punishment! Besides, I might have repented; I might have told that sin, but I was ashamed to confess it. Oh, the day on which I was born, I wish it had never been. Accursed be that day; but I am lost—lost—lost forever—forever—forever." The voice dies away and you hear it no more!

30. NO PEACE

(b) A Picture of Hell

There was a glass that made things look three million times larger than they really are. A drop of dirty water was looked at through this glass. Millions of frightful little insects were seen in the water. These insects seemed to be always fighting and beating and trying to kill each other. They gave themselves no rest. It was always fighting, beating—beating, fighting. Sometimes thousands would throw themselves on other thousands and swallow them up alive. Sometimes they tore away pieces from each other's bodies, which still remained alive, only more frightful than before. Such is Hell!

31. ETERNITY

"These shall go into everlasting punishment."[44]

There is one thing which could change Hell into Heaven. An angel of God comes to the gates of Hell and says, "Listen to me, all ye people in Hell, for I bring you good news. You will still burn in Hell for almost countless millions of years. But a day will come, and on that day the pains of Hell will be no more! You will go out of Hell." If such a message came, Hell would no longer be Hell. Hell would no longer be a house of blasphemy, but a house of prayer and thanksgiving and joy. But such a message will never come to Hell, because God has said that the punishment of Hell shall be *everlasting*.

(a) The Question

You say what is meant by *everlasting*. It is both easy and difficult to answer this question. It is easy to say that the pains of Hell will last forever, and never have an end. It is difficult to answer the question, because our understandings are too little to understand what is meant by the word *ever*. We know ever well what is meant by a year, a million of years, a hundred million of years. But forever—Eternity—What is that?

(b) A Measure—A Bird

We can measure almost anything. We can measure a field or a road. We can measure the earth. We can measure how far it is from the earth to the sun. Only one thing there is which never has been and never will be measured, and that is Eternity—forever!

Think of a great solid iron ball, larger than the Heavens and the earth. A bird comes once in a hundred millions of years and just touches the great iron ball with a feather of its wing. Think that you have to burn in a fire till the bird has worn the great iron ball away with its feather. Is this Eternity? No.

(c) Tears—Sand—Dots

Think that a man in Hell cries only one single tear in ten hundred million years. Tell me how many millions of years must pass before he fills a little basin with his tears? How many millions of years must pass before he cries as many tears as there were drops of water at the deluge? How many years must pass before he has drowned the heavens and earth with his tears? Is this Eternity? No.

Turn all the earth into little grains of sand and fill all the skies and the heavens with little grains of sand. After each hundred millions of years, one grain of sand is taken away; oh, what a long, long time it would be before the last grain of sand was taken away. Is this Eternity? No.

Cover all the earth and all the skies with little dots like these: . . . Let every dot stand for a hundred thousand millions of years. Is this Eternity? No.

After such a long, long time, will God still punish sinners? Yes. *"After all this His anger is not turned away, His hand is still stretched out."*[45] How long, then, will the punishment of sinners go on? Forever, and ever, and ever!

33. WHAT ARE THEY DOING?

Perhaps at this moment, seven o'clock in the evening, a child is just going into Hell. Tomorrow evening at seven o'clock, go and knock at the gates of Hell and ask what the child is doing. The devils will go and look. Then they will come back again and say, *the child is burning!* Go in a week and ask what the child is doing; you will get the same answer—*it is burning!* Go in a year and ask; the same answer comes—*it is burning!* Go in a million of years and ask the same question; the answer is just the same—*it is burning*! So, if you go forever and ever, you will always get the same answer—*it is burning in the fire!*

What O'Clock—The Dismal Sound

Look at that deep pool of fire and brimstone. See, a man has just lifted his head up out of it. He wants to ask a question. He speaks to a devil who is standing near him. He says, "What a long, long time it seems since I first came into Hell; I have been sunk down in this deep pool of burning fire. Years and years have passed away. I kept no count of time. Tell me, then, what o'clock is it?" "You fool," the devil answers, "why do you ask what o'clock it is? There is no clock in Hell; a clock is to tell the time with. But in Hell, time is no more. It is Eternity!"

Perhaps on a dark, lonesome night, you may have seen something waving backward and forward in the air. The sound of it was sad and mournful. It frightened you, although it was but the branch of a tree.

Such a sound there is in Hell. It passes on without stopping from one end of Hell to the other. As it comes sweeping past, you hear it. What then is this dismal sound? It is the sound of Eternity—ever!—never!

A PLACE AT ODDS WITH MERCY[1]

For many critics, Furniss's depiction of Hell for children em-
bodied the least desirable aspects of the Christian tradition.
Shortly after the publication of The Sight of Hell, *G. Stan-*
dring condemned the pamphlet for promoting "the religion of
terror." Recognizing that "fear is the priest's best weapon, es-
pecially when applied to children," Standring dismissed with
disdain "the whole rigmarole of nonsense which makes up
this wretched little book." This review of Furniss's pamphlet
was a drop in the torrent of criticism against traditional views
of Hell that flooded the public in the later nineteenth century.
Typical of them was Austin Holyoake's Heaven & Hell: Where
Situated? A Search After the Objects of Man's Fervent Hope &
Abiding Terror, *in which the author deployed the ambiguity of*
biblical proof texts to poke fun at what he considered to be
the absurd deductions of Catholic thinkers about the location
and nature of the punitive afterlife.

Heaven is the hope of the Christian—Hell is his dread, his
fear, his abiding terror. What would Christianity be—that is,
the *modern* faith of Europe—without these two ideas, or sen-
timents, or beliefs, or whatever they may be called? Simply a
mild kind of superstition. The hope of an eternal reward for
doing right appeals with much force, there can be no doubt, to
the selfish; and the fear of eternal, never-ending torments, will
keep many a wretch in awe. But all who are swayed by such
motives must be inferior morally to those who do good because it is right to do so, and because it will benefit men

individually, and society generally, regardless of all consideration as to whether the doers of good will receive advantage themselves. Man's clear duty is to do right, to speak the truth, not only without reward, but even at his own cost if need be.

What shall we say about that other place of abode for departed spirits, the climate of which is so warm that the natives of central Africa will find it uncomfortable? Where is it situated? Oh, down below, of course; all Christians say so, and they alone know. Did not Christ descend into Hell? And yet it cannot be far from Heaven, for did not Dives and Lazarus hold a conversation together from their respective abodes? We are not quite sure that Hell is not in Heaven itself, for in Revelation xiv. 9 and 10, it says, "If any man worships the beast and his image, and receive his mark in his forehead, or in his hand, the same shall drink of the wine of the wrath of God, which is poured out without mixture into the cup of his indignation; and he shall be tormented with fire and brimstone in the presence of the holy angels and in the presence of the Lamb." We are not to suppose that a little Hell is kept among the holy angels for special use, or that they often go where Lucifer alone is King; and yet we cannot tell how men are to be tortured in their presence unless Hell *is* in Heaven. How ever that may be, we are assured that God himself is in Hell. If you doubt it, you need do no more than go to that royal prophet, that inspired writer, that man after God's own heart, who, in one of those sacred oracles which the Holy Spirit itself has dictated to him, acknowledges and owns it. "Whither shall I go," says David, "from thy spirit? Or whither shall I flee from thy presence? If I ascend up into Heaven, thou art there; if I make my bed in *Hell*, behold thou art *there*." We have Psalm 139 as our authority, and no one dare dispute *that*.

There seems to be no doubt in the minds of Christians, that the brimstone pit is somewhere within the interior of this planet, but that the Abode of Bliss is up in the clouds, or beyond them. Now if the other planetary bodies are inhabited by human beings—and scientific men are not aware of any reason why they should not be—if the Maker of all things punishes his children with burning torments who do not believe in Christ and Him crucified, where are the inhabitants of other planets to be sent when their hour comes? Are they sent here, or has each of the other vast worlds in space a nice little Hell of its own in which to put its erring subjects? If they come here, an enlargement of the premises must be constantly taking place. If Heaven is not upon this earth, and is never to be realised here—I prefer believing that Hell also is far up in the clouds, and a very long way too, so that the journey thither may take as much time as possible in its accomplishment.

The warm world beyond the grave is popularly known by many names. Hell is perhaps the most general term used by Christians; though it is sometimes designated by the appellations of Infernal Regions, Perdition, Abode of the Damned, and so on. Most orthodox Christians mean by the term Hell the everlasting lake of brimstone and fire; though there are still some in the Church, and we believe that they are of the best, who do not believe at all in a literal Hell of fire. The Catholics have a place which they call Purgatory, which is a sort of House of Detention, and not the penal settlement our Hell is supposed to be. There sinners can be released on tickets-of-leave after certain regulations have been complied with; our religious convicts are condemned for life (or death, whichever it may be) without the slightest hope of pardon. The Catholics themselves admit that once in Hell, you are in it forever. Michael Angelo, the celebrated painter, executed, by command of Pope Julius II, a splendid picture representing the Day of Judgment. Now Michael Angelo had placed among his other figures in the scene of Hell, several cardinals and prelates.[2] They had probably been guilty, like Bishop Colenso and some of the most intelligent men of our Church, of thinking for themselves, and, worst of all, of publishing the results of their thinkings. And this, we know, has been sufficient in all Christian ages to render any man quite unfit for the company of saints. However, some of the dignified and proper churchmen of Julius's time, who had probably never been guilty of an original thought in their lives, were extremely enraged at the picture, and made complaint of it to his Holiness, and entreated that he would lay his injunctions on the painter to efface them. To whom the Pope replied—"My dear brethren, Heaven has indeed given me the power of recovering as many souls from Purgatory as I think proper; but as to Hell, you know as well as I do, that my power does not extend so far, and those who once go thither, must remain there for ever!"

What is Hell? Where is it? Is it really the lake of fire some represent it to be? You will be eternally bewildered and completely confounded if you try to determine this question from the Bible itself. If Hell be below, it must be contained *within* the earth, for wherever you go on the surface of this globe, you will find the firmament still above and around you. If within, which is the way to it? Strange that no one has ever even by accident discovered it. The only entrance one can imagine to it, is the mouth of Vesuvius. But that cannot be the way, as it is not a brimstone pit, though sulfurous exhalations arise from it. No devil that we ever heard of, was seen to emerge from it—not even by the miracle-working monks who infest the country round about. We knew the right place has a door or grating, and that St. John saw the angel who kept the key. But it is *bottomless*, and therefore who knows but that Vesuvius is the other side—the front door in the rear, out of which the Devil pops when he wants to go roaring up and down the world? A bottomless pit full of liquid must be like a pot without a bottom filled with water, where all things are not only in a state of solution, but the solution itself is held in suspension!

We continually hear pious Christians say that the souls of unbelievers have gone, or are going, to *Perdition*. But there is a consolation in knowing that it is not Hell. Revelation xvii. 8, says that the beast which was so obliging as to carry the scarlet lady of Babylon, "shall ascend out of the bottomless pit and shall go into Perdition." Perhaps Perdition is the Catholic's Purgatory! Who knows? But then there is no mistake that Hell is Hell, and that the Freethinker will go there! Not quite so sure. Read Revelation xx. 14—"And Death and *Hell* were cast into the lake of fire." Where does this lead us? We have heard of a house being turned out of window, but we never heard of a pit being thrown into itself! This is one of those mysteries which "passeth all understanding." We still have the lake of fire, where human beings are to be burned for ever and ever, and yet never consumed. Now this is simply an impossibility. The human body, if thrown into a large fire, would be utterly destroyed in a very short time, and nothing could prevent it. Men cannot live in fire. It is the nature of fire to burn up, to destroy, to decompose any animal or vegetable substance that is cast into it. It would require properties of life to be altered before men could live in it for ever. Some will say, God can work a miracle. But we have no reason to suppose that he can. We know nothing of what God *can* do—we only know what *is*, and miracles do not take place. We must discard the idea of a burning Hell as a fiction conceived by a brutal and revengeful monster in human form, and afterward taken up and added to by fanatics, whose minds had been worked upon by superstition, till they believed as a reality, that which existed only in their own disordered imaginations.

———

Who, with human sympathies and affections, would like to go to a place where the nearest and dearest ties are broken? Where the husband is separated from the wife, the parent from the child, the brother from the sister? And not only separated, but where you will know that those you loved are writhing in agony unutterable. It is a doctrine which requires a fiend or a saint to believe in it. We are told that a certain king of the Frisons, named Redbord, when on the very point of being baptized, took it into his head to ask the Bishop, who was preparing him in consequence of his changing his religion, where he should find his ancestors and predecessors.[3] The Bishop having told him, that as they had all died Pagans, they could enjoy no portion of the heavenly inheritance, but were all in Hell, "Nay, then," replied the King, lifting his foot out of the font into which he had already dipped it, "if that be the case, take back again your baptism and your paradise; I had much rather go to Hell, and be there among a good and numerous company, with my illustrious ancestors, and other persons of my own rank, than to your Paradise, from which you have shut

out all these brave peoples, and filled it up with none but pau-
pers, miscreants, and people of no note."

————

The Bible, or any other book, which teaches the doctrine of
Hell torments, is not, cannot be, a revelation from a God of
love and mercy. It is the crude production of an ignorant, a su-
perstitious, a priest-ridden, and brutal people. The Bible alone,
of all books in the world, first promulgated the monstrous, the
fiendish doctrine of eternal, never-ending torments prepared
for all men, not one-millionth part of whom ever saw or heard
of it. This doctrine, so far from keeping men good, makes
good men bad, and brutalizes all who believe in it. It distracts
men's minds from the duties of this life, and deludes them into
the belief of another which, when looked at calmly and with
reason, will be seen to contain no element worthy of their ac-
ceptance, or capable of promoting permanent happiness.

HELL OF OUR OWN MAKING: THE TWENTIETH CENTURY AND BEYOND

By the late nineteenth century, belief in the reality of Hell was in rapid retreat in the wake of secular and rationalist critiques of age-old Christian doctrines about the horrors contained therein. But the idea of Hell has survived in the modern age in the most insidious ways. For two millennia, Western Christians believed in the notion that Hell was a place apart from the world of the living, a subterranean realm where divine justice meted out unimaginable punishments to sinners for all eternity. But in the decades around 1900, Hell found a safe haven in Western culture as an enduring metaphor for conditions of suffering and squalor in this life. During the industrial transformation of England, Friedrich Engels described the filth and debris of urban Manchester as "this Hell upon Earth." In the American South, A. S. Leitch condemned "the moral hideousness of child labor" that profited the "aristocratic stockholders of Hell's mills of the South," while abolitionists decried the cruelty of "the hell-concocted system of American slavery."

In the twentieth century, Hell has made great advances despite the appearance of its retreat. The Western tradition may have repudiated the idea of an otherworldly place of eternal punishment, but it was ready to internalize Hell as a state of mind, as a human condition, and as a guiding principle for interacting with other people. In Jean-Paul Sartre's play No Exit (1944), three Hell-bound characters unexpectedly find themselves trapped together in a plain drawing room. In the closing lines of the play, the realization hits home: "So this is hell. I'd *never have believed it. You remember all we were told about torture-chambers, the fire and brimstone, the burning marl. Old wives' tales! There's no need for red-hot pokers. HELL IS—OTHER PEOPLE!"*

With the rise of killing technologies that have enabled mass murder and destruction on an unprecedented scale, Hell transformed from a passive metaphor to an active inspiration in the devastating wars of the twentieth century. From the extermination camps of eastern Europe to the irradiated ruins of Japanese cities, Christian soldiers—Axis and Allied— actualized with merciless detachment many of the hellish scenes of suffering and carnage that had been nurtured in the Western imagination for centuries. By creating Hell for other people on earth, they unwittingly became the tormenting demons their ancestors had feared.

Theaters of war were not the only cradles of Hell in the twentieth century. The conditions of incarceration in modern American prisons, both for criminals and for political detainees, have maximized the suffering of those individuals in an effort to make their lives a living Hell. Abandoning God's justice in the world to come, prison administrators have devised methods of torment as ingenious and cruel as the imagination of any medieval prelate, with one significant difference. In premodern thought, God in his infinite wisdom dispensed divine justice on sinners in the afterlife. In the modern economy of justice, despite their manifest fallibilities, human beings have assumed the roles of divine judge and hellish tormentor, God and demon, to inflict torment on their fellow human beings.

THE DEATH FACTORIES[1]

During World War II (1939–45), Nazi Germany constructed extermination camps to kill millions of people, primarily Jews. Among the most notorious of these camps was Treblinka, located in a forest near Warsaw in occupied Poland. Treblinka was in operation for fifteen months (July 1942–October 1943). In this short time, the Nazis murdered between 700,000 and 900,000 Jews in its gas chambers, making it the deadliest extermination camp after Auschwitz. The camp closed in the fall of 1943 after a revolt by Jewish slave-laborers, and the Nazis dismantled the buildings and plowed over the grounds to hide evidence of genocide in the wake of the Soviet advance. Traveling with the Red Army as a war correspondent, Vasily Grossman, a Jewish Russian journalist, was the first author to write an eyewitness account of the extermination camp at Treblinka. He also interviewed former prisoners who had escaped during the revolt. His only point of reference for describing the atrocities of the camp was Dante's Inferno (see pp. 139–65), but the horrors of literature paled before the reality of such cruelty and suffering: "Not even Dante, in his Hell, saw scenes like this."

First people were robbed of their freedom, their home, and their Motherland; they were transported to a nameless wilderness in the forest. Then, on the square by the station, they were robbed of their belongings, of their personal letters, and of photographs of their loved ones. After going through the fence, a man was robbed of his mother, his wife, and his child.

After he had been stripped naked, his papers were thrown into a fire; he had been robbed of his name. He was driven into a corridor with a low stone ceiling; now he had been robbed of the sky, the stars, the wind, and the sun.

Then came the last act of the human tragedy—a human being was now in the last circle of the Hell that was Treblinka.

The door of the concrete chamber slammed shut. The door was secured by every possible kind of fastening: by locks, by hooks, by a massive bolt. It was not a door that could be broken down.

Can we find within us the strength to imagine what the people in these chambers felt, what they experienced during their last minutes of life? All we know is that they cannot speak now . . . Covered by a last clammy mortal sweat, packed so tight that their bones cracked and their crushed rib cages were barely able to breathe, they stood pressed against one another; they stood as if they were a single human being. Someone, perhaps some wise old man, makes an effort to say, "Patience now—this is the end." Someone shouts out some terrible curse. A holy curse—surely this curse must be fulfilled? With a superhuman effort a mother tries to make a little more space for her child: may her child's dying breaths be eased, however infinitesimally, by a last act of maternal care. A young woman, her tongue going numb, asks, "Why am I being suffocated? Why can't I love and have children?" Heads spin. Throats choke. What are the pictures now passing before people's glassy dying eyes? Pictures of childhood? Of the happy days of peace? Of the last terrible journey? Of the mocking face of the SS man in that first square by the station, "Ah, so that's why he was laughing . . ." Consciousness dims. It is the moment of the last agony . . . No, what happened in that chamber cannot be imagined. The dead bodies stand there, gradually turning cold.

———

At first there was real difficulty with the process of cremation; the corpses would not burn. There was, admittedly, an attempt to use the women's bodies, which burned better, to help burn the men's bodies. And the Germans tried dousing the bodies with gasoline and fuel oil, but this was expensive and turned out to make only a slight difference. There seemed to be no way around this problem, but then a thickset man of about fifty arrived from Germany, a member of the SS and a master of his trade. Hitler's regime, after all, had the capacity to produce experts of all kinds: experts in the use of a hammer to murder small children, expert stranglers, expert designers of gas chambers, experts in the scientifically planned destruction of large cities in the course of a single day. The regime was also able to find an expert in the exhumation and cremation of millions of human corpses.

And so, under this man's direction, furnaces were constructed. Furnaces of a special kind, since neither the furnaces of Majdanek nor those of any of the largest crematoria in the world would have been able to burn so vast a number of corpses in so short a time.

The excavator dug a pit 250 to 300 meters long, 20 to 25 meters wide, and 6 meters deep. Three rows of evenly spaced reinforced-concrete pillars, 100 to 120 centimeters in height, served as a support for giant steel beams that ran the entire length of the pit. Rails about five to seven centimeters apart were then laid across these beams. All this constituted a gigantic grill. A new narrow-gauge track was laid from the burial pits to the grill pit. Two more grill pits of the same dimenions were constructed soon afterward; each took 3,500 to 4,000 corpses at once.

Another giant excavator arrived, followed soon by a third. The work continued day and night. People who took part in the work of burning the corpses say that these grill pits were like giant volcanoes. The heat seared the workers' faces. Flames erupted eight or ten feet into the air. Pillars of thick greasy smoke reached up into the sky and stood there, heavy and motionless. At night, people from villages thirty or forty kilometers away could see these flames curling above the pine forest that surrounded the camp. The smell of burned flesh filled the whole area. If there was a wind, and if it blew in the direction of the labor camp three kilometers away, the people there almost suffocated from the stench. More than eight hundred prisoners—more than the number of workers employed in the furnaces of even the largest steel and iron plants—were engaged in the work of burning the bodies. This monstrous workshop operated day and night for eight months, without interruption, yet it still could not cope with the millions of human bodies. Trains were, of course, delivering new contingents to the gas chambers all the time, which added to the work of the grill pits.

––––––––

The SS singled out for particular torment those who had participated in the uprising in the Warsaw ghetto. The women and children were taken not to the gas chambers, but to where the corpses were being burned. Mothers crazed with horror were forced to lead their children onto the red-hot grid where thousands of dead bodies were writhing in the flames and smoke, where corpses tossed and turned as if they had come back to life again, where the bellies of women who had been pregnant burst from the heat and babies killed before birth were burning in open wombs. Such a spectacle was enough to rob the most hardened man of his reason, but its effect—as the Germans well knew—was a hundred times greater on a mother struggling to keep her children from seeing it. The children clung to their mothers and shrieked, "Mama, what are they going to do to us? Are they going to burn us?" Not even Dante, in *his* Hell, saw scenes like this.

After amusing themselves for a while with this spectacle, the Germans burned the children.

––––––––

The summer of 1943 was exceptionally hot. For weeks on end there was no rain, no clouds, and no wind. The work of burning the corpses was in full swing. Day and night for six months the grill pits had been blazing, but only a little more than half of the corpses had been burned.

The moral and physical torment began to tell on the prisoners charged with this task; every day fifteen to twenty prisoners committed suicide. Many sought death by deliberately infringing the regulations.

"To get a bullet was a luxury," I heard from a baker by the

name of Kosow, who had escaped from the camp. In Treblinka, evidently, it was far more terrible to be doomed to live than to be doomed to die.

Cinders and ashes were taken outside the campgrounds. Peasants from the village of Wólka were ordered to load them on their carts and scatter them along the road leading from the death camp to the labor camp. Child prisoners with spades then spread the ashes more evenly. Sometimes these children found melted gold coins or dental crowns. The ashes made the road black, like a mourning ribbon, and so the children were known as "the children of the black road." Car wheels make a peculiar swishing sound on this road, and, when I was taken along it, I kept hearing a sad whisper from beneath the wheels, like a timid complaint.

Toward the end of June it turned suffocatingly hot. When graves were open, steam billowed up from them as if from gigantic boilers. The heat of the grills—together with the monstrous stench—was killing even the workers who were moving the corpses; they were dropping dead onto the bars of the grills. Billions of overfed flies were crawling along the ground and buzzing about in the air. The last hundred thousand corpses were now being burned.

After August 2, Treblinka ceased to exist. The Germans burned the remaining corpses, dismantled the stone buildings, removed the barb wire, and torched the wooden barracks not already burned down by the rebels. Part of the equipment of the house of death was blown up; part was taken away by train. The grills were destroyed, the excavators taken away, the vast pits filled in with earth. The station building was razed; last of all, the track was dismantled and the crossties removed. Lupines were sown on the site of the camp, and a settler by the name of Streben built himself a little house there. Now this house has gone; it too was burned down. What were the Germans trying to do? To hide the traces of the murder of millions in the Hell that was Treblinka? Did they really imagine this to be possible? Can silence be imposed on thousands of people who have witnessed transports bringing the condemned from every corner of Europe to a place of conveyor-belt execution? Did the Germans really think that they could hide the dead, the heavy flames, and the smoke that hung in the sky for eight months, visible day and night to the inhabitants of dozens of villages and hamlets? Did they really think that they could force the peasants of Wólka to forget the screams of the women and children—those terrible screams that continued for thirteen months and that ring in their ears to this day? Can the memory of such screams be torn from the heart?

We arrived at Treblinka in early September 1944, thirteen months after the day of the uprising. For thirteen months from July 1942 the executioners block had been at work—and for thirteen months from August 1943, the Germans had been trying to obliterate every trace of this work.

It is quiet. The tops of the pine trees on either side of the railway line are barely stirring. It is these pines, this sand, this old tree stump that millions of human eyes saw as their freight wagons came slowly up to the platform. With true German neatness, white-washed stones have been laid along the borders of the black road. The ashes and crushed cinders swish softly. We enter the camp. We tread the earth of Treblinka. The lupine pods split open at the least touch; they split with a faint ping and millions of tiny peas scatter over the earth. The sounds of the falling peas and the bursting pods come together to form a single soft, sad melody. It is as if a funeral knell—a barely audible, sad, broad, peaceful tolling—is being carried to us from the very depths of the earth. And, rich and swollen as if saturated with flax oil, the earth sways beneath our feet—earth of Treblinka, bottomless earth, earth as unsteady as the sea. This wilderness behind a barbed-wire fence has swallowed more human lives than all the earth's oceans and seas have swallowed since the birth of mankind.

The earth is casting up fragments of bone, teeth, sheets of paper, clothes, things of all kinds. The earth does not want to keep secrets.

And from the earth's unhealing wounds, from this earth that is splitting apart, things are escaping of their own accord. Here they are: the half-rotted shirts of those who were murdered, their trousers and shoes, their cigarette cases that have turned green, along with little cogwheels from watches, penknives, shaving brushes, candlesticks, a child's shoes with red pompoms, embroidered towels from the Ukraine, lace underwear, scissors, thimbles, corsets, and bandages. Out of another fissure in the earth have escaped heaps of utensils: frying pans, aluminum mugs, cups, pots and pans of all sizes, jars, little dishes, children's plastic mugs. In yet another place—as if all that the Germans had buried was being pushed up out of the swollen, bottomless earth, as if somone's hand were pushing it all out into the light of day: half-rotted Soviet passports, notebooks with Bulgarian writing, photographs of children from Warsaw and Vienna, letters penciled in a childish scrawl, a small volume of poetry, ration cards from Germany . . . And everywhere there are hundreds of perfume bottles of all shapes and sizes—green, pink, blue . . . And over all this reigns a terrible smell of decay, a smell that neither fire, nor sun, nor rain, nor snow, nor wind have been able to overcome. And thousands of little forest flies are crawling about over all these half-rotted bits and pieces, over all these papers and photographs.

We walk on over the swaying, bottomless earth of Treblinka and suddenly come to a stop. Thick wavy hair, gleaming like burnished copper, the delicate lovely hair of a young woman, trampled into the ground; and beside it, some equally fine blond hair; and then some heavy black plaits on the bright sand; and then more and more . . . Evidently these are the contents of a sack, just a single sack that somehow got left behind. Yes, it is all true. The last hope, the last wild hope that it was all just a terrible dream, has gone. And the lupine pods keep popping open, and the tiny peas keep pattering down—and this really does all sound like a funeral knell rung by countless little bells from under the earth. And it feels as if your heart must come to a stop now, gripped by more sorrow, more grief, more anguish than any human being can endure . . .

FIRE IN THE SKY[1]

The atomic age began on the morning of July 16, 1945, with the detonation of the world's first nuclear weapon in the Jornada del Muerto desert in New Mexico. As the mushroom cloud bloomed in the desert sky, J. Robert Oppenheimer (1904–67), the director of the Los Alamos Laboratory that designed the weapon, remembered a haunting utterance attributed to the god Vishnu in the Hindu scripture the Bhagavad Gita: "Now I am become Death, the destroyer of worlds." Oppenheimer and his team of physicists had unlocked a new, unprecedented destructive power. Three weeks later, on August 6 and 9, 1945, American forces unleashed this power by detonating weapons of similar design over Hiroshima and Nagasaki, Japan, incinerating tens of thousands of people instantly, mostly civilians, and killing many tens of thousands more in the months thereafter due to burns, radiation sickness, and other injuries.

No country has ever employed atomic weapons in warfare after the bombing of Hiroshima and Nagasaki, but the specter of the fear that nuclear fire could rain from the sky has haunted every nation on earth ever since. The creation of this killing technology is one of the most frightening ways that modern human beings have enabled themselves to render whole cities into the burning hellscapes imagined by Christian authors throughout history. The infernal analogy was not lost on critics of nuclear weapons. In a lecture presented after winning the Nobel Peace Prize in 1964, Martin Luther King Jr. (1929–68) identified war as one of the great evils confronting the world: "A world war— God forbid!—will leave only smoldering ashes as a mute

*testimony of a human race whose folly led inexorably to ulti-
mate death. So if modern man continues to flirt unhesitatingly
with war, he will transform his earthly habitat into an inferno
such as even the mind of Dante could not imagine."*

*Japanese survivors experienced firsthand the reality of a nu-
clear holocaust that Western authors could only shudder to
contemplate. Among them was Yoshitaka Kawamoto, who
was thirteen years old when the atomic bomb detonated a ki-
lometer away from his school in the Zakoba-cho district of
Hiroshima. His escape from the concussive force of the initial
explosion and the collapse of his school is nothing short of mi-
raculous. Kawamoto's firsthand account of the human carnage and personal suffering caused by a nuclear blast is far
more harrowing to read than historical accounts of the torments awaiting sinners in Hell because it actually happened.
Marking the seventy-second anniversary of the bombing in
August 2017, Hiroshima mayor Kazumi Matsui warned his
audience: "This hell is not a thing of the past. As long as nuclear weapons exist and policymakers threaten their use, their
horror could leap into our present at any moment. You could
find yourself suffering their cruelty."*

One of my classmates, I think his name is Fujimoto, he mut-
tered something and pointed outside the window, saying, "A
B-29 is coming." He pointed outside with his finger. So I began
to get up from my chair and asked him, "Where is it?" Looking
in the direction that he was pointing toward, I got up on my
feet, but I was not yet in an upright position when it happened.
All I can remember was a pale lightning flash for two or three
seconds. Then, I collapsed. I don't know much time passed before
I came to. It was awful, awful. The smoke was coming in from
somewhere above the debris. Sandy dust was flying around. I was
trapped under the debris and I was in terrible pain and that's
probably why I came to. I couldn't move, not even an inch. Then,
I heard about ten of my surviving classmates singing our school

song. I remember that. I could hear sobs. Someone was calling his mother. But those who were still alive were singing the school song for as long as they could. I think I joined the chorus. We thought that someone would come and help us out. That's why we were singing a school song so loud. But nobody came to help, and we stopped singing one by one. In the end, I was singing alone. Then I started to feel fear creeping in. I started to feel my way out pushing the debris away little by little, using all my strength. Finally, I cleared the things around my head. And with my head sticking out of the debris, I realized the scale of the damage. The sky over Hiroshima was dark. Something like a tornado or a big fireball was storming throughout the city. I was only injured around my mouth and around my arms. But I lost a good deal of blood from my mouth, otherwise I was OK. I thought I could make my way out. But I was afraid at the thought of escaping alone. We had been going through military drills every day, and they had told us that running away by oneself is an act of cowardice, so I thought I must take somebody along with me. I crawled over the debris, trying to find someone who was still alive. Then, I found one of my classmates lying alive. I held him up in my arms. It is hard to tell, his skull was cracked open, his flesh was dangling out from his head. He had only one eye left, and it was looking right at me. First, he was mumbling something, but I couldn't understand him. He started to bite off his finger nail. I took his finger out from his mouth. And then, I held his hand. Then he started to reach for his notebook in his chest pocket, so I asked him, I said, "You want me to take this along to hand it over to your mother?" He nodded. He was going to faint. But still I could hear him crying out, saying "Mother, Mother." I thought I could take him along. I guess that his body below the waist was crushed. The lower part of his body was trapped, buried inside of the debris. He just refused to go; he told me to go away. And by that time, another wing of the school building, or what used to be the school building, had caught on fire. I tried to get to the playground. Smoke was filling in the air, but I could see the white sandy earth beneath. I thought this must be the playground, then I started to run in that direction. I turned back and I saw my classmate Wada looking at me. I still remember the situation and it still appears in my dreams. I felt sorry for him, but it was the last time I ever saw him. As I was running, hands were trying to grab my ankles. They were asking me to take them along. I was only a child then. And I was horrified at so many hands trying to grab me. I was in pain, too. So all I could do was to get rid of them— it's terrible to say—but I kicked their hands away. I still feel bad about that. I went to Miyuki Bridge to get some water. At the riverbank, I saw so many people collapsed there. And the small steps to the river were jammed, filled with people pushing their way to the water. I was small, so I pushed on to the river along the small steps. The water was full of dead people. I had to push the bodies aside to drink the muddy water. We didn't know anything about radioactivity at that time. I stood up in the water and so many bodies were floating away along the stream. I can't find the words to describe it. It was horrible. I felt fear. Instead of going into the water, I climbed up the riverbank. I couldn't move. I couldn't find my shadow. I looked up. I saw the cloud, the mushroom cloud growing in the sky. It was very bright. It had so much heat inside. It caught the light and it showed every color of the rainbow. Reflecting on the past, it's strange, but I could say that it was beautiful. Looking at the cloud, I thought I would never be able to see my mother again. I wouldn't be able to see my younger brother again. And then, I lost consciousness. When I came to, it was about seven in the evening. I was in the transportation bureau at Ujina. I found myself lying on the floor of the warehouse and an old soldier was looking in my face. He gave me a light slap on the cheek and he said, "You are a lucky boy." He told me that he had gone with one of the few trucks left to collect the dead bodies at Miyuki Bridge. They were loading bodies, treating them like sacks. They picked me up from the riverbank and then threw me on top of the pile. My body slid off and when they grabbed me by the arm to put me back onto the truck, they felt that my pulse was still beating, so they reloaded me onto the truck carrying the survivors. I was really lucky.

THE SUM OF SUFFERING[1]

Incarceration is one of the main forms of punishment in the modern United States. A staggering number of people currently inhabit American prisons. In 2013, more than two million adults were being held in federal and state prisons and county jails, totaling almost 1 percent of the resident population (1 in 110). Prisoners often endure violent discipline and repressive conditions with very little administrative oversight. This is especially the case with solitary confinement, a form of imprisonment that isolates an inmate from human contact for twenty-two to twenty-four hours a day, both as a cruel form of punishment and as a way to protect inmates from one another. About eighty thousand inmates (5 percent of the national prison population) currently endure solitary confinement in American penal institutions. For many critics, this kind of extreme physical and social isolation is nothing less than torture. For the inmates themselves, it feels like an inescapable Hell.

In his essay "A Sentence Worse Than Death" (2013), William Blake has depicted the realities of solitary confinement from the inside. In 1987, while in court on a drug charge, Blake attempted to escape. He wrestled a gun from a guard and murdered a deputy before he was apprehended. He is now serving a sentence of seventy-seven years to life for his crimes. But because Blake is considered an especially dangerous offender, he is living out his sentence, and very likely the rest of his life, in permanent solitary confinement. Blake's account of his twenty-five years in near constant social isolation recalls the suffering of premodern sinners consigned to Hell, but for him the dread and despair of endless imprisonment is a crushing reality. Moreover, the term "solitary" is inaccurate. In his confinement, Blake is surrounded by other inmates enduring the same cruel punishment, whose furious screams and pitiful wailing create an incessant and maddening cacophony. Add to these terrifying sounds the inescapable stench of human excrement, the chronic fatigue caused by lack of sleep, and the severe mental anguish of never-ending loneliness, Blake's life sentence has become a living Hell. Given the sum of this inhumane treatment, it is little wonder that incidents of self-harm and suicide abound among inmates in solitary confinement.

"You deserve an eternity in Hell," Onondaga County Supreme Court judge Kevin Mulroy told me from his bench as I stood before him for sentencing on July 10, 1987. Apparently he had the idea that God was not the only one qualified to make such judgment calls.

———

What nobody knew or suspected back then, not even I, is that when the prison gate slammed shut behind me, on that very day I would begin suffering a punishment that I am convinced beyond all doubt is far worse than any death sentence could possibly have been. On July 10, 2012, I finished my twenty-fifth consecutive year in solitary confinement, where at the time of this writing I remain. Although it is true that I've never died and so don't know exactly what the experience would entail, for the life of me I cannot fathom how dying any death could be harder or more terrible than living through all that I have been forced to endure for the past quarter century.

Prisoners call it the box. Prison authorities have euphemistically dubbed it the Special Housing Unit, or SHU (pronounced "shoe") for short. In society it is known as solitary confinement. It is twenty-three-hour-a-day lockdown in a cell smaller than some closets I've seen, with one hour allotted to "recreation" consisting of placement by oneself in a concrete-enclosed yard or, in some prisons, a cage made of steel bars. There is nothing in a SHU yard but air; no TV, no balls to bounce, no games to play, no other inmates, nothing. There is also very little allowed in a SHU cell: three sets of plain white underwear, one pair of green pants, one green short-sleeved button-up shirt, one green sweatshirt, one pair of laceless footwear that I'll call sneakers for lack of a better word, ten books or magazines total, twenty pictures of the people you love, writing supplies, a bar of soap, toothbrush and toothpaste, one deodorant stick, but no shampoo.

Life in the box is about an austere sameness that makes it difficult to tell one day from a thousand others. Nothing much and nothing new ever happens to tell you if it's a Monday or a Friday, March or September, 1987 or 2012. The world turns, technology advances, and things in the streets change and keep changing all the time. Not so in a solitary confinement unit, however. I've never seen a cell phone except in pictures in magazines. I've never touched a computer in my life, never been on the Internet and wouldn't know how to get there if you sat me in front of a computer, turned it on for me, and gave me directions. SHU is a timeless place, and I can honestly say that there is not a single thing I'd see looking around right now that is different from what I saw in Shawangunk Correctional Facility's box when I first arrived there from Syracuse's county jail in 1987. Indeed, there is probably nothing different in SHU now than in SHU a hundred years ago, save the headphones. Then and now there were a few books, a few prison-made clothing articles, walls and bars and human beings locked in cages. And misery.

There is always the misery. If you manage to escape it yourself for a time, there will ever be plenty around in others for you to sense; and although you'll be unable to look into their eyes and see it, you might hear it in the nighttime when tough guys cry not-so-tough tears that are forced out of them by the unrelenting stress and strain that life in SHU is an exercise in.

I've read of the studies done regarding the effects of long-term isolation in solitary confinement on inmates, seen how researchers say it can ruin a man's mind, and I've watched with my own eyes the slow descent of sane men into madness—sometimes not so slow. What I've never seen the experts write about, though, is what year after year of abject isolation can do to that immaterial part of our middle where hopes survive or die and the spirit resides. So please allow me to speak to you of what I've seen and felt during some of the harder times of my twenty-five-year SHU odyssey.

I've experienced times so difficult and felt boredom and loneliness to such a degree that it seemed to be a physical thing inside so thick it felt like it was choking me, trying to squeeze the sanity from my mind, the spirit from my soul, and the life from my body. I've seen and felt hope becoming like a foggy, ephemeral thing, hard to get ahold of, even harder to keep ahold of as the years and then decades disappeared while I stayed stuck in the emptiness of the SHU world. I've seen minds slipping down the slope of sanity, descending into insanity, and I've been terrified that I would end up like the guys around me who have cracked and become nuts. It's a sad thing to watch a human being go insane before your eyes because he can't handle the pressure that the box exerts on the mind, but it is sadder still to see the spirit shaken from a soul. And it is more disastrous. Sometimes the prison guards find them hanging and blue; sometimes their necks get broken when they jump from their beds, the sheet tied around the neck that's also wrapped around the grate covering the light in the ceiling snapping taut with a pop. I've seen the spirit leaving men in SHU, and I have witnessed the results.

The box is a place like no other place on planet Earth. It's a place where men full of rage can stand at their cell gates fulminating on their neighbor or neighbors, yelling and screaming and speaking some of the filthiest words that could ever come from a human mouth, do it for hours on end, and despite it all never suffer the loss of a single tooth, never get their heads knocked clean off their shoulders. You will never hear words more despicable or see mouth wars more insane than what occurs all the time in SHU, not anywhere else in the world, because there would be serious violence before any person could speak so much foulness for so long. In the box the heavy steel bars allow mouths to run with impunity when they could not

otherwise do so, while the ambiance is one that is sorely con-
ducive to an exceedingly hot sort of anger that seems to press
the lips on to ridiculous extremes. Day and night I have been
awakened by the sound of rage being loosed loudly on SHU
gates, and I'd be a liar if I said that I haven't at times been one
of the madmen doing the yelling.

I have lived for months where the first thing I became aware
of upon waking in the morning is the malodorous funk of
human feces, tinged with the acrid stench of days-old urine,
where I ate my breakfast, lunch, and dinner with that same
stink assaulting my senses, and where the last thought I had
before falling into unconscious sleep was: "Damn, it smells
like shit in here." I have felt like I was on an island surrounded
by vicious sharks, flanked on both sides by mentally ill inmates who would splash their excrement all over their cells, all
over the company outside of their cells, and even all over themselves. I have seen days turn into weeks that seemed like they'd
never end without being able to sleep more than short snatches
before I was shocked out of my dreams, and thrown back into
a living nightmare, by the screams of sick men who had lost all
ability to control themselves, or by the banging of the cell bars
and walls being done by these same madmen. I have been so
tired when sleep inside was impossible that I went outside into
a snowstorm to get some rest.

The wind blew hard and snowflakes swirled around and
around in the small SHU yard at Shawangunk, and I had on but
one cheap prison-produced coat and a single set of state clothes
beneath. To escape the biting cold I dug into the seven- or
eight-foot-high mountain of snow that was piled in the center
of the yard, the accumulation from inmates shoveling a narrow path to walk along the perimeter. With bare hands gone
numb, I dug out a small room in that pile of snow, making myself a sort of igloo. When it was done I crawled inside, rolled
onto my back on the snow-covered concrete ground, and almost instantly fell asleep, my bare head pillowed in the snow. I
didn't even have a hat to wear.

An hour or so later I was awakened by the guards come to
take me back to the stink and insanity inside: "Blake, rec's

over . . ." I had gotten an hour's straight sleep, minus the few minutes it had taken me to dig my igloo. That was more than I had gotten in weeks without being shocked awake by the *ca-rack!* of a sneaker being slapped into a Plexiglas shield covering the cell of an inmate who had thrown things nasty; or the *thud-thud-thud!* of an inmate pounding his cell wall; or bars being banged and gates being kicked and rattled; or men screaming like they're dying and maybe wishing that they were; or to the tirade of an inmate letting loose his pent-up rage on a guard or fellow inmate, sounding every bit the lunatic that too long a time in the mind-breaking confines of the box had caused him to be.

I have been so exhausted physically, my mental strength tested to limits that can cause strong folks to snap, that I have begged God, tough guy I fancy myself, "Please, Lord, make them stop. Please let me get some peace." As the prayers went ungranted and the insanity around me persisted, I felt my own rage rising above the exhaustion and misery—no longer now in a begging mood: "Lord, kill those motherfuckers, why don't you!" I yelled at the Almighty, my own sanity so close to being gone that it seemed as if I were teetering along the edge of a precipice and could see down to where I'd be dropping, seeing myself shot, sanity a dead thing killed by the fall. I'd be afraid later on, terrified, when I reflected back on how close I had seemed to come to losing my mind, but at that moment all I could do was feel anger of a fiery kind: anger at the maniacs creating the noise and the stink and the madness; anger at my keepers, the real creators of this hell; anger at society for turning a blind eye to the torment and torture going on here that its tax dollars are financing; and, perhaps most of all, anger at myself for doing all that I did that never should have been done that put me into the clutches of this beastly prison system to begin with. I would be angry at the world; enraged, actually, so burning hot was what I would be feeling.

I had wet toilet paper stuffed hard into both ears, socks folded and pressed into my ears, a pillow wrapped around the sides and back of my head covering my ears, and a blanket tied around all that to hold everything else in place, lying in bed praying for sleep. But still the noise was incredible, a thunderous cacophony of insanity, sleep impossible. Inmates lost in the throes of lava-like rage firing philippics at one another for reasons even they didn't know, threatening to kill one another's mommas, daddies, even the children, too. Nothing is sacred in SHU. It is an environment that is so grossly abnormal, so antithetical to normal human interactions, that it twists the innards of men all around who for too long dwell there. Their minds, their morals, and their mannerisms get bent badly, ending far off center. Right becomes whatever and wrong no longer exists. Restraint becomes a burden and is unnecessary with concrete and steel separating everyone, so inmates let it go. Day after day, perhaps year after year, the anger grows, fueled by the pain caused by the conditions till rage is born and burning so hot that it too hurts.

Trying to put into words what is so unlike anything else I know or have ever experienced seems an impossible endeavor because there is nothing even remotely like it any place else to compare to, and nothing that will do to you on the inside what so many years in SHU has done to me. All that I am able to articulate about the world of a Special Housing Unit and what it is and what it does may seem terrible to you indeed, but the reality of living in this place for a full quarter of a century is even more terrible still. You would have to live it, experience it in all its aspects with the fullness of its days and struggles added up, to really appreciate and understand just how truly terrible this plight of mine has been, and how truly ugly life in the box can be at times, even for just a single day.

I spent nine years in Shawangunk's box, six years in Sullivan's, six years in Great Meadow's, and I've been here in Elmira's SHU for four years now, and through all of this time I have never spent a single day in a Mental Health Unit cell because I attempted or threatened suicide, or for any other reason. I have thought about suicide in times past when the days had become exceedingly difficult to handle, but I'm still here. I've had some of my SHU neighbors succumb to the suicidal thoughts, though, choosing death over another day of life in the box. I have never bugged out myself, but I've known times that I came too close. I've had neighbors who came to SHU normal men, and I've seen them leave broken and not anything resembling normal anymore. I've seen guys give up on their dreams and lose all hope in the box, but my own hopes and dreams are still alive and well inside me. The insidious workings of the SHU program have yet to get me stuck on that meandering path to internal destruction that I have seen so many of my neighbors end up on, and perhaps this is a miracle. So thanks be to God for the miracle; I'd rather be dead than lose control of my mind.

Had I known in 1987 that I would spend the next quarter century in solitary confinement, I would certainly have killed myself. If I took a month to die and spent every minute of it in severe pain, it seems to me that on balance that fate would still be far easier to endure than the past twenty-five years have been. If I try to imagine what kind of death, even a slow one, would be worse than twenty-five years in the box— and I have tried to imagine it—I can come up with nothing. Set me afire, pummel and bludgeon me, cut me to bits, stab me, shoot me, do what you will in the worst of ways, but none of it could come close to making me feel things as cumulatively horrifying as what I've experienced through my years in solitary. Dying couldn't take but a short time if you or the state were to kill me; in SHU I have died a thousand internal deaths. The sum of my quarter century's worth of suffering has been that bad.

To some judges sitting on high who've never done a day in the box, maybe twenty-five years of this isn't cruel and unusual. To folks who have an insatiable appetite for vengeance against prisoners who have committed terrible crimes, perhaps it doesn't even matter how cruel or unusual my plight is or isn't. For people who cannot let go of hate and know not how to forgive, no amount of remorse would matter, no level of contrition would be quite enough, only endless retribution would be right in their eyes. Like with Judge Mulroy, only an eternity in hell would suffice. But then, given even that, the unforgiving haters would not be satisfied that hell was hot enough; they'd want the heat turned up higher. Thankfully these folks are the few; in the minds of the many, at a point, enough is enough.

No matter what the world would think about things that they cannot imagine in even their worst nightmares, I know that twenty-five years in solitary confinement is utterly and certainly cruel, more so than death by an electric chair, gas chamber, lethal injection, bullet in the head, or even immolation could possibly be. The sum of the suffering caused by any of these quick deaths would be a small thing next to the sum of the suffering that this quarter century in SHU has brought to bear on me. Solitary confinement for the length of time that I have endured it, even apart from the inhuman conditions that I have too often been made to endure it in, is torture of a terrible kind. And anyone who doesn't think so surely knows not what they are thinking.

I have served a sentence worse than death.

GUANTÁNAMO MIXTAPE

Advocates for prison reform have lobbied actively for the elimination of solitary confinement lasting more than fifteen days in American prisons. Political detainees have far fewer advocates and little recourse to justice. In January 2002, the Bush administration founded the Guantánamo Bay detention camp in Cuba to detain and interrogate enemy combatants captured during the War on Terror. Since then, hundreds of detainees have been held in indefinite detention without trial for the war crimes that they had allegedly committed. While in detention, they have been subjected to cruel and degrading treatment. Red Cross inspectors and detainees who have been released have reported abuses that constitute torture, such as sleep deprivation, physical mistreatment, and cruel confinement.

One of the more unusual methods employed by US interrogators to break the will of detainees during harsh interrogation at Abu Ghraib, Bagram, Mosul, and elsewhere is the use of loud music. The 2006 edition of the US Army's field manual for interrogation advocated the use of abusive sound as a method of interrogation, a practice corroborated by former detainees who were subject to this abuse. At Guantánamo, inmates reported being held in chains without food or water in total darkness "with loud rap or heavy metal blaring for weeks at a time." This music played several roles during interrogation. It provoked fear, distress, and disorientation, crowding out the thoughts of the detainee and bending their will to the interrogators'. Even when played at excruciatingly high volume (often as loud as 100 decibels during harsh interrogation, the equivalent of a jackhammer), music leaves no marks on detainees and sheds no blood; it inflicts severe physicial and psychological pain without betraying any evidence of its source.

Music carried cultural content as well, which interrogators employed to intimidate and humiliate detainees. The lyrics of rap and heavy metal songs were threatening to hear, but the purring and panting of female singers like Christina Aguilera seem to have been chosen specifically to offend the religious sensibilities of Islamist prisoners. The ironic, cloying sentiment and maddening repetition of songs for children, like the "I Love You Song" by Barney and Friends, and commercial jingles, like the "Meow Mix" theme, made these tunes especially effective instruments of torture. Lastly, loud music also had an influence on US interrogators themselves, who digested the violent lyrics of heavy metal and rap songs to strip themselves of any empathy for their captives.

Here follows a sample of the songs played again and again at maximum volume to break the will of enemy combatants at Guantánamo Bay and other US detention centers around the world. In the context of harsh interrogation with no legal recourse or hope of freedom, these songs and others like them became the soundtrack of Hell for those subjected to them.

Christina Aguilera, "Dirrty"
Barney and Friends, "I Love You Song"
Deicide, "Fuck Your God"
Drowning Pool, "Bodies"
Eminem, "Kim"
Marilyn Manson, "The Beautiful People"
The "Meow Mix" Theme
Nine Inch Nails, "Somewhat Damaged"
Queen, "We Are the Champions"
Britney Spears, ". . . Baby One More Time"

Notes

TARTARUS, PRISON OF THE TITANS

1. Hesiod, *Theogony*, trans. Dorothea Wender (New York: Penguin Books, 1973), pp. 45–48.
2. ALALE! was a battle cry.

NETHERWORLD MEGAFAUNA

1. Translated by Scott G. Bruce from Seneca, *Hercules Furens*, lines 782–829, ed. Margarethe Billerbeck, in *Seneca, Hercules Furens: Einleitung, Text, Übersetzung und Kommentar* (Leiden, the Netherlands: Brill, 1999), pp. 144 and 146.

ODYSSEUS AT DEATH'S DOOR

1. Homer, *The Odyssey* 11.617–28 and 11.643–731, trans. Robert Fagles (New York: Viking Penguin, 1996), pp. 267–70.

SOCRATES PONDERS
THE PUNISHMENT OF SOULS

1. Plato, *Phaedo* 113d–14c, trans. Christopher Rowe, in *Plato, The Last Days of Socrates: Euhyphro, Apology, Crito, Phaedo* (New York: Penguin Books, 2010), pp. 163–65.

INTO THE REALM OF SHADOWS

1. Virgil, *The Aeneid* 6.273–377, 6.439–553, 6.628–32, and 6.637–727, trans. Robert Fagles (New York: Viking, 2006), pp. 190–93, 195–98, and 200–203.

2. Duplicitous relationships sealed the fate of these women: Phaedra was the wife of Theseus, and she fell in love with Hippolytus, his son by another woman. When Hippolytus rejected her, Phaedra told Theseus that he had raped her. In revenge, Theseus killed his son, and the guilt-ridden Phaedra commited suicide. Procris was a woman who suspected her husband of cheating on her. When she surprised him on a hunt, he inadvertently killed her with an arrow. In exchange for the gift of the Necklace of Harmonia, Eriphyle persuaded her husband to undertake a doomed raid on Thebes and was slain in vengeance by their son Alcmaeon.

3. A second group of ill-fated women: Evadne's husband died at the siege of Thebes; she threw herself on his funeral pyre in grief. Pasiphaë was the queen of Crete who commited adultery with a bull, producing the Minotaur. Laodamia was the wife of Protesilaus and commited suicide when he died during the Trojan War. Caeneus was a woman named Caenis who had been raped by Poseidon. When he offered her a wish, she chose to become a man.

THE FIRE AND THE WORM

1. Translated by Scott G. Bruce from the Latin *Visio Pauli*, ed. M. R. James, in *Apocrypha Anecdota: A Collection of Thirteen Apocryphal Books and Fragments* (Cambridge: The University Press, 1893), pp. 28–34.

2. A cubit was a unit of measurement based on the distance between a grown man's fingertips and elbow (about eighteen inches).

THE RICH MAN AND LAZARUS

1. Translated by Scott G. Bruce from the Latin Vulgate version of Luke 16.19–31.

DEATH'S DEFEAT:
THE HARROWING OF HELL

1. Translated by Scott G. Bruce from the Latin *Euangelium Nichodemi*, ed. H. C. Kim, in *The Gospel of Nicodemus: Gesta Salvatoris, edited from the Codex Einsidlensis, Einsiedeln Stifts-*

bibliothek, MS 326 (Toronto: Pontifical Institute of Mediaeval Studies, 1973), pp. 35–46.

2. Isaiah 9.1–2.
3. Luke 2.30–32.
4. John 1.29.
5. Luke 3.22.
6. Matthew 26.38.
7. Psalms 106.15–17.
8. Compare Isaiah 26.19.
9. Compare Hosea 13.14.
10. Compare Psalms 23.8–10.
11. Psalms 29.2–6.
12. Psalms 97.1–2.
13. Compare Psalms 149.9.
14. Compare Habakkuk 3.13.
15. Psalms 47.15.

BEYOND THE BLACK RIVER

1. Translated by Scott G. Bruce from Gregory the Great, *Dialogorum libri quattuor* 4.37.3–14, ed. Adalbert de Vogüé, in *Grégoire le Grand, Dialogues, Tome III (Livre IV)*, Sources chrétiennes 265 (Paris: Edition du Cerf, 1980), pp. 126, 128, 130, 132, and 134.

BEHOLD, THE FIRE DRAWS NEAR ME

1. Translated by Scott G. Bruce from *Bede's Ecclesiastical History of the English People* 3.19, eds. Bertram Colgrave and R. A. B. Mynors (Oxford: Clarendon Press, 1969), pp. 272 and 274.
2. Isaiah 43.2.
3. Here Bede is summarizing his source for this story: a short, anonymous Latin account of the life of Fursa composed in the late seventh century.

DRYHTHELM RETURNS FROM THE DEAD

1. Translated by Scott G. Bruce in *The Penguin Book of the Undead: Fifteen Hundred Years of Supernatural Encounters* (New York: Penguin Classics, 2016), pp. 81–87.

THE ISLAND OF THE FIRE GIANTS

1. Translated by Scott G. Bruce from *Navigatio sancti Brendani abbatis* 23–25, ed. Carl Selmer, in *Navigatio Sancti Brendani Abbatis from Early Latin Manuscripts* (Notre Dame, IN: University of Notre Dame Press, 1959), pp. 61–70.
2. A Roman *stade* was a distance of 125 paces, approximately 606 feet.

WELCOME TO HELL

1. Translated by Scott G. Bruce from *Visio Tnugdali* 2–3, ed. Albrecht Wagner, in *Visio Tnugdali: Lateinisch und Altdeutsch* (Erlangen, Germany: Verlag von Andreas Deichert, 1882), pp. 9–12.
2. Compare 2 Samuel 22.4–6 and Psalms 17.2–3.

THE PUNISHMENT FITS THE CRIME

1. Translated by Scott G. Bruce from *Visio Tnugdali* 4–11, ed. Albrecht Wagner, in *Visio Tnugdali: Lateinisch und Altdeutsch* (Erlangen, Germany: Verlag von Andreas Deichert, 1882), pp. 12–25 and 27–32.
2. For the length of a cubit, see p. 256, n. 2, above.
3. Job 40.23.
4. Fergusius and Conallus are the Latin names for Fergus mac Roich and Conall Cearnach, two pagan characters of Irish mythology in the Ulster Cycle and members of the cohort of the mythological hero Cú Chulainn.
5. Psalms 125.6 and Luke 6.25.
6. Compare Matthew 7.13.

THE GREAT BELOW

1. Translated by Scott G. Bruce from *Visio Tnugdali* 12–14, ed. Albrecht Wagner, in *Visio Tnugdali: Lateinisch und Altdeutsch* (Erlangen, Germany: Verlag von Andreas Deichert, 1882), pp. 32–39.
2. Ec. 9.10.
3. See p. 256, above
4. In medieval Europe, the palm was a unit of measurement equal to one quarter of a Roman foot (approximately three inches).

5. The source of this quotation is the book of Wisdom 6.7. This apocryphal Jewish text was composed in Greek in the first century CE and later translated into Latin as part of the Vulgate Bible.

LESSONS IN HORROR

1. Translated by Scott G. Bruce from Honorius Augustodunensis, *Elucidarium* 3.13–14, ed. Yves Lefèvre, in *L'Elucidarium et Les Lucidaires: Contribution, par l'histoire d'un texte, à l'histoire des croyances religieuses en France au moyen âge* (Paris: E. de Boccard, 1954), pp. 447–48.
2. Psalms 141.8.
3. Psalms 85.13.
4. Luke 16.22.
5. Compare Revelation 8.8.
6. Matthew 8.12.
7. Job 10.22.

PREACHING PAIN

1. Translated by Scott G. Bruce from *Instructio sacerdotis seu tractatus de praecipuis mysteriis nostrae religionis* 14, ed. J. P. Migne, in *Patrologiae Cursus Completus: Series Latina* 184 (Paris: Garnier Fratres, 1879), cols. 791–92.
2. The author's authoritative source seems to have been an early medieval account of the martyrdom of Saint Sebastian (died c. 288 CE), in which the saint provided a catalogue of the horrors of Hell and the pleasures of Heaven in an effort to convert his household to Christianity: *Ex gesta S. Sebastiani desumpta* 3, in *Acta sanctorum quotquot toto orbe coluntur*, Junii 4, eds. Jean Bolland et al. (Paris and Rome: Apud Victorem Palme, 1867), vol. 24, p. 469.
3. Matthew 8.12.
4. Compare Job 24.19.
5. Wisdom 11.17.
6. Isaiah 66.24.
7. Isaiah 3.24.
8. Psalms 10.7.
9. Proverbs 19.29.
10. Psalms 34.21.

THREE TALES OF TORMENT

1. Translated by Scott G. Bruce from Caesarius of Heisterbach, *Dialogus miraculorum* 1.32–34, ed. Horst Schneider, in *Caesarius von Heisterback, Dialog über die Wunder*, 5 vols. (Turnhout, Belgium: Brepols, 2009), vol. 1, pp. 290, 292, 294, 296, 298, 300, 302, 304, and 306.
2. Compare Matthew 16.23.
3. The practice in question was necromancy, which derives from the Greek root *necro-* ("dead") and *manteia* ("divination").
4. Caesarius is referring to a late twelfth-century collection of Cistercian miracle stories known as the *Book of the Visions and Miracles of Clairvaux*. See *Liber visionum et miraculorum Clarevallensium*, eds. G. Zichi, G. Fois, and S. Mula (Turnhout, Belgium: Brepols, 2017).
5. Deuteronomy 19.15.
6. Ludwig II, Landgrave of Thuringia (1128–72), nicknamed "Ludwig the Iron."

WARNINGS FROM BEYOND THE GRAVE

1. Translated by Scott G. Bruce from Caesarius of Heisterbach, *Dialogus miraculorum* 12.2, 12.6, 12.18–19, 12.21, and 12.41, ed. Horst Schneider, in *Caesarius von Heisterback, Dialog über die Wunder*, 5 vols. (Turnhout, Belgium: Brepols, 2009), vol. 5, pp. 2178, 2180, 2196, 2214, 2216, 2218, 2222, 2278, and 2280. Translations of three of these stories have previously appeared in *The Penguin Book of the Undead: Fifteen Hundred Years of Supernatural Encounters*, ed. Scott G. Bruce (New York: Penguin Books, 2016), pp. 109–10 and 114.
2. See pp. 122–24, above.
3. See pp. 122–24, above.
4. Wisdom 6.7.

THE ABOMINABLE FANCY

1. Translated by Scott G. Bruce from Thomas Aquinas, *Summa Theologica*, tertia pars, quaestio 94, articuli 1–3, in idem, *Opera Omnia*, 16 vols. (Rome: Romae Typographia Polyglotta, 1882), vol. 12, pp. 226–27.

2. Aquinas used the term "wayfarer" (*viator*) to describe human beings on their journey through this world toward the heavenly kingdom.

3. Here and elsewhere, the gloss refers to the *Glossa Ordinaria*, a collection of patristic and early medieval commentaries on the Bible compiled in the twelfth century.

4. The unnamed philosopher is Aristotle (384–22 BCE), the tutor of Alexander the Great and one of the most influential philosophers of the ancient world. There was a revival of interest in his treatises in the twelfth and thirteenth centuries, when Christian scholars began to translate them into Latin from Arabic translations and Greek originals.

5. Isaiah 66.24.

6. Gregory, *Moralia* 12, commenting on Gregory, *Moralia in Job* 12.26, ed. Aristide Bocognano, in *Grégoire le Grand, Morales sur Job: Troisième partie (Livres XI-XVI)* (Paris: Editions du Cerf, 1974), pp. 186, 188.

7. Aquinas used the term "comprehensor" (*comprehensor*) to describe an individual who has attained a full knowledge of the Christian truth. The term is generally reserved for the blessed in Heaven and stands in contrast to the "wayfarer" (*viator*), whose goal in life's journey is to become a comprehensor.

8. Psalms 57.11.

9. Isaiah 56.24.

10. James 1.2.

THROUGH THE GATES OF HELL

1. Adapted and rendered into idiomatic English by Scott G. Bruce from *The Divine Comedy of Dante Alighieri*, trans. Henry Wadsworth Longfellow, 3 vols. (London: George Routledge and Sons, 1867), vol. 1, pp. 14–19 (*Inferno*, Canto 3, lines 1–136).

THE FILTHY FEN

1. Adapted and rendered into idiomatic English by Scott G. Bruce from *The Divine Comedy of Dante Alighieri*, trans. Henry Wadsworth Longfellow, 3 vols. (London: George Routledge and Sons, 1867), vol. 1, pp. 43–44 (*Inferno*, Canto 7, lines 97–130).

2. This tower marks the boundary of the infernal city of Dis, which housed the souls of heretics imprisoned in burning tombs for their denial of immortality.

THE BOILING BLOOD

1. Adapted and rendered into idiomatic English by Scott G. Bruce from *The Divine Comedy of Dante Alighieri*, trans. Henry Wadsworth Longfellow, 3 vols. (London: George Routledge and Sons, 1867), vol. 1, pp. 68–73 (*Inferno*, Canto 12, lines 1–139).

2. The "infamy of Crete" is the monstrous Minotaur, the mythological bull-headed man who lived in a labyrinth in the palace of King Minos of Crete.

3. Virgil mocks the monster by evoking the memory of the "king of Athens," Theseus, who killed the Minotaur with the help of Minos's daughter Ariadne.

4. The earthquake that occurred during the crucifixion of Christ was also felt in Hell. See Matthew 27.51.

5. All three of these centaurs (half-men, half-horses) were well known in ancient literature: Nessus was killed by Heracles for abducting his wife Deianeira, and his poisoned blood later killed Heracles in turn; Chiron was known for his wisdom and became a tutor of the hero Achilles; and Pholus also featured in stories about Heracles.

6. Alexander the Great (356–323 BCE) and Dionysius I of Syracuse (c. 432–367 BCE) were both remembered as conquerors and despots.

7. Azzolin was Ezzelino III da Romano, tyrant of Padua (1194–1259). Obizzo II d'Este (c. 1247–93) was Marquis of Ferrara, who was smothered by his son.

8. This is the shade of Guy de Montfort (1244–91), who in 1271 murdered his cousin Prince Henry of Almain at the altar in the church of San Silvestro in Viterbo. Henry's heart was later kept on a bridge in London.

9. A litany of violent generals, conquerors, and villains: Attila the Hun (c. 406–53), whose armies ravaged the borders of the Roman Empire; the Greek general Pyrrhus (c. 319–272 BCE), who won victories but at the cost of heavy losses ("Pyrrhic victories"); Sextus (67–35 BCE) was the son of Pompey the Great, who fought tenaciously against Marc Antony at the end of the Roman Republic; Rinier da Corneto and Rinier Pazzo were famous brigands in early fourteenth-century Italy.

THE FOREST OF THE SUICIDES

1. Adapted and rendered into idiomatic English by Scott G. Bruce from *The Divine Comedy of Dante Alighieri*, trans. Henry Wadsworth Longfellow, 3 vols. (London: George Routledge and Sons, 1867), vol. 1, pp. 74–80 (*Inferno*, Canto 13, lines 1–151).
2. As recounted in Book 3 of Virgil's *Aeneid*.
3. This is the soul of Pietro della Vigna (c. 1190–1249), who was the chancellor and secretary of Emperor Frederick II in Palermo. Dante's depiction of suicides as bleeding, talking trees takes its inspiration from Virgil's portrayal of Polydorus, son of Priam, in Book 3 of the *Aeneid*.
4. The "harlot" is a metaphor for jealousy, which led to accusations of court intrigue, which unraveled the king's confidence in his trusted adviser, who committed suicide as a result.
5. Arcolano of Siena and his companion Jacomo da Sant'Andrea were notorious squanderers of money. Both of them lived in the early thirteenth century.
6. This anonymous suicide hailed from Florence, a city originally dedicated to Mars and thus destined to suffer the violence of warfare.

TRAPPED UNDER ICE

1. Adapted and rendered into idiomatic English by Scott G. Bruce from *The Divine Comedy of Dante Alighieri*, trans. Henry Wadsworth Longfellow, 3 vols. (London: George Routledge and Sons, 1867), vol. 1, pp. 211–16 (*Inferno*, Canto 34, lines 1–99 and 133–39).
2. Judas Iscariot was the disciple of Christ who betrayed him with a kiss and later hanged himself in remorse (Matthew 27.3–10).
3. Cassius and Brutus were two of the conspirators who murdered Julius Caesar on the Ides of March (March 15) in 44 BCE.

THE SHARP PANGS OF
A WOUNDED CONSCIENCE

1. William Dawes, "Sermon IV on Matthew 25.41," in *Sermons Preached upon Several Occasions Before King William and Queen Anne* (London: H. Hills, 1709), pp. 53–61.
2. Luke 16.19–31.
3. Luke 16.19–31.

4. Isaiah 66.24; and Mark 9.46–47.
5. Revelation 14.11 and 20.10.

INTO THAT ETERNAL FURNACE

1. Giovanni Pietro Pinamonti, *Hell Opened to Christians to Caution Them from Entering into It* (London: Thomas Richardson and Son, 1845), pp. 15–21, 23–31, and 88–101.
2. Jeremiah 2.20.
3. Psalms 11.6.
4. Job 24.21.
5. Pinamonti is paraphrasing an anonymous late medieval devotion text (*De Similitudinibus*), which he has mistakenly attributed to Anselm of Canterbury (c. 1033–1109).
6. Matthew 22.13.
7. Psalms 29.7.
8. Thomas Aquinas commented on the quality of hellfire in *Summa Theologica*, tertia pars, quaestio 97, articulus 5. On the miracle of the Babylonian furnace, see Daniel 3.19–25.
9. 2 Peter 2.17.
10. Psalms 49.19.
11. Exodus 10.22.
12. Many authors have repeated the attribution of this sentiment to the Franciscan Saint Bonaventure (1221–74), but it cannot be verified.
13. Isaiah 34.3.
14. Sulpicius Severus, *Life of Saint Martin* 24, trans. Thomas Head and Thomas F. X. Noble, in *Soldiers of Christ: Saints and Saints' Lives from Late Antiquity and the Early Middle Ages* (University Park: The Pennsylvania State University Press, 1995), p. 26.
15. Luke 16.22.
16. Luke 16.24.
17. Compare Jude 1.7.
18. Revelation 21.8.
19. Mark 9.49.
20. Virgil, *The Aeneid*, 4.560.
21. Isaiah 5.14.
22. The source of this anecdote, which is attributed to the Cistercian author Caesarius of Heisterbach (c. 1180–1240), is unknown.
23. Psalms 83.14.

24. This statement is attributed to the renowned preacher John Chrysostom (c. 349–407 CE). He preached often in the city of Antioch before becoming the archbishop of Constantinople in 397. Hundreds of his sermons are extant.

25. Job 6.12.

26. Psalms 20.10.

27. Isaiah 33.14.

28. Revelation 20.9.

29. Deuteronomy 32.41.

30. Compare Psalms 90.11.

31. Luke 6.25.

32. Jerome, "Homily 19 on Psalm 89 (90)," trans. Sister Marie Liguori Ewald, in *The Homilies of Saint Jerome, Volume 1* (Washington, D.C.: The Catholic University of America Press, 1964), p. 148.

33. Proverbs 19.28.

34. 1 Kings 20.3.

35. Pinamonti falsely attributes this quotation to St. Bernard's letter to the monks of La Grande Chartreuse. Compare Bernard of Clairvaux, Letter 12, in *St. Bernard of Clairvaux Seen Through His Selected Letters*, trans. Bruno Scott James (Chicago: Henry Regnery Company, 1953), pp. 46–56.

36. Numbers 11.6.

37. Seneca, *Thyestes*, line 572.

38. 1 Corinthians 2.14.

39. Augustine, *On the City of God Against the Pagans* 2.13.

40. Job 10.22.

41. Jonah 1.6.

A LIVING DEATH SHALL
FEED UPON THEM

1. John Bunyan, *The Resurrection of the Dead and Eternall Judgement, or, The Truth of the Resurrection of the Bodies Both of Good and Bad at the Last Day* (London: Francis Smith, 1665), pp. 94–102.

HELL FOR CHILDREN

1. J. Furniss, *The Sight of Hell*, Books for Children and Young Persons 10 (Dublin: James Duffy & Co., 1874), pp. 3–10, 12–21, and 23–25.

2. Compare Psalms 63.9.
3. The source of this quotation, which Furniss attributes to Augustine, is unknown.
4. Saint Frances or Francesca of Rome (1384–1440). Her feast day is March 9.
5. Isaiah 5.14.
6. See Mark 5.2–5.
7. Isaiah 34.10.
8. Wisdom 17.13.
9. Psalms 11.6.
10. Compare Job 20.23.
11. Psalms 11.6.
12. Wisdom 16.19.
13. The widely read account of the life of Saint Teresa of Ávila (1515–82) recounted a vision of Hell experienced by the saint, from which this reference is taken.
14. Isaiah 21.6.
15. Psalms 49.19.
16. Revelation 14.11.
17. Exodus 11.6.
18. Compare Isaiah 22.12–13.
19. Joel 2.20.
20. See John 11.38–44.
21. See p. 264, n. 12, above.
22. Isaiah 66.24.
23. Revelation 20.2–3.
24. Isaiah 8.8.
25. Revelation 13.11.
26. Job 41.19.
27. Teresa of Ávila. See, n. 13, above.
28. Isaiah 34.14.
29. Ecclesiasticus 39.34–36.
30. Proverbs 19.29.
31. Job 2.7–13.
32. Lamentations 1.2.
33. Habakkuk 2.6.
34. Compare Isaiah 66.24.
35. Wisdom 17.3.
36. Wisdom 17.19.
37. Job 37.17.
38. Compare Ezekiel 22.20–22.
39. Wisdom 11.17.

40. See Luke 16.22–24.
41. Amos 4.2.
42. Psalms 21.9.
43. This is another book authored by Furniss, titled *The Terrible Judgment, and the Bad Child* (1864).
44. Compare Matthew 25.41.
45. Isaiah 9.12.

A PLACE AT ODDS WITH MERCY

1. Austin Holyoake, *Heaven & Hell: Where Situated? A Search After the Objects of Man's Fervent Hope & Abiding Terror* (London: Austin & Co., 1873), pp. 1, 4–8.
2. Michelangelo (1475–1564), the celebrated Renaissance artist from Florence, Italy.
3. Radbod was the last king of Frisia (c. 680–719 CE). This anecdote about his refusal to be baptized appeared in Harduin's *Life of Wulframm of Sens*, composed around 800 CE.

THE DEATH FACTORIES

1. Vasily Grossman, "The Hell of Treblinka," trans. Robert and Elizabeth Chandler with Olga Mukovnikova, in *The Road: Stories, Journalism, and Essays* (New York: New York Review of Books, 2010), pp. 144–45, 147–50, 153, and 156–60.

FIRE IN THE SKY

1. Yoshitaka Kawamoto, "Testimony of Yoshitaka Kawamoto," *Voices of Hibashuka*, Hiroshima Peace Cultural Center and NHK, www.inicom.com/hibakusha/yoshitaka.html.

THE SUM OF SUFFERING

1. William Blake, "A Sentence Worse Than Death," in *Hell Is a Very Small Place: Voices from Solitary Confinement*, eds. Jean Casella, James Ridgeway, and Sarah Shourd (New York and London: The New Press, 2016), pp. 26–33.

Index

dots, 219–20
dragons, 114, 116
dress of fire, 214
dungeons of Hell, 213–18
  boiling kettle, 216–17
  deep pit, 214–15
  dress of fire, 214
  red-hot floor, 215–16
  red-hot oven, 217
  sad voice, 218
Dryhthelm, 68–74

Ecclesiastical History of the
    English People (Bede), 65–67
Echidna, 8
Egypt, xiii, 3–4, 182, 205
Elucidarium (Honorius),
    113–14, 115
Engels, Friedrich, 231
Enquiry into the Nature and Place
    of Hell, An (Swinden), 170
envy, 175
Epic of Gilgamesh, The, 3
Erebus, 15, 16
Eriphyle, 28
eternity, 172, 177–78,
    187–92, 194
  Furniss on, 209, 218–20, 227
  sound of, 220–21
Eurydice, 12
Eurystheus, 12
Evadne, 28
extermination camps, xv,
    232, 233
  Treblinka, 233–39
Ezzelino III da Romano
    (Azzolin), 153

Farrar, Frederic William, 131
fear, 175
  death from, 213
  Furniss on, 213

of Hell, as persuasion, xvi,
    111–12, 115, 171, 199,
    222, 227
of punishment, vs. punishment
    itself, 190
Federigo, 157
Fergusius (Fergus mac Roich), 91
fire, 4, 29, 36, 114, 115–16, 171,
    172, 177, 180, 181,
    188–89, 192
  in *Apocalypse of Paul,* 37–44
  bed of, 212
  Bunyan on, 194–95
  coffin of, 214–15
  dress of, 214
  Dryhthelm and, 68–72
  fiery chains, 114, 116
  fire giants, 75–76
  Furniss on, 202, 204, 205,
    208, 209, 212, 214–15, 220
  Fursa and, 65–67
  at gates of Hell, 202
  God and, 185–86
  Holyoake on, 224–26
  intensity of, 185–86
  quality of, 183–84
  quantity of, 184–85
  Tundale and, 88, 89, 92, 93,
    96, 100, 103
First Council of Lyon, 111
floor, red-hot, 215–16
Florence, 263*n*
fornicators, 38–41, 96–97
Fourth Lateran Council, 111
Frances of Rome, Saint, 202–4,
    208, 209, 211
Frederick I (Frederick
    Barbarossa), Holy Roman
    Emperor, 122
Frederick II, Holy Roman
    Emperor, 263*n*
Furies, 23, 24, 30, 31

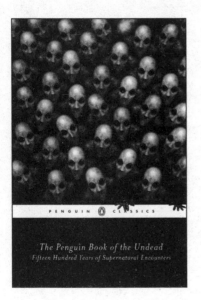